ARABS IN AMERICAN CINEMA (1894-1930):

FLAPPERS MEET SHEIKS IN NEW MOVIE GENRE

Abdelmajid Hajji

First printing: June, 2013

Printed in the United States of America

ISBN-13: 978-1490507354
ISBN-10: 1490507353

CONTENTS

Chapter One

INTRODUCTION

This book identifies, presents and critically evaluates a corpus of films dealing with Arabs and Arabic themes produced in the United States during the silent era, or the period 1894-1930. Underlying and guiding this work is the premise that American (and indeed, all Western) films dealing with Arabs took shape, functioned, and are ultimately better understood by reference to the encompassing and pervasive cultural system of Orientalism. Responding to the conditions and demands of Orientalism and reflecting a historically entrenched and confrontational attitude towards Arabs and their environment, these films share sufficient common themes, types, plotlines, motifs and a recognizable iconography to be considered as forming a distinct film genre. This genre, which I label the "Oriental genre," constitutes the most appropriate critical framework to present and explore a hitherto unassembled yet extremely rich corpus of films on the traditional Orient (now roughly the region corresponding to North Africa and the Middle East).

The book reposes on a two-part structure; the first of which furnishes the historical and theoretical background, extensively invoking the system of Orientalism and how it has (and to a large degree still does) managed to shape all kinds of discourse geared toward the traditional Orient. That this system was devised to deal with the Orient –to understand it, to contain it, and to keep it under control– is elucidated through a survey of the history of peaceful and non-peaceful contacts between the West and the Islamic Orient.

The second part introduces the films, and undertakes the analysis of various samples with particular emphasis on the portrayal of Arabs in their perceived physical, social and cultural environment. With documented and telling exceptions, this portrayal is found to be generally insensitive, nearly always fantastic, and at times downright racist. The study concludes with a look at the development of the Oriental genre after 1930, briefly suggesting points of continuity and differences between the silent cinema's portrayal of Arabs and their more recent appearances in modern cinema and television.

In an article entitled "Our Sensational Films Libel West," published in *The New York Times* on October 31, 1926, Indian poet-laureate Rabingdranath Tagore described the depiction of night life, sex relations, crime and other undignified scenes in the American films released throughout Asia and Africa as constituting a "libel on Western civilization". The presentation of these undignified scenes, Tagore stressed, were just as pernicious as the exaggerated filmic treatment of Asiatic life offered to the West. While the "libelous" representations of Western life were having a mischievous influence on the average Indian film-goer, "the exaggerations of Oriental life were misleading Western audiences and keeping East and West apart." In the same report, the colonial Bengal Board of Censors in India similarly expressed their fear that filmic "misrepresentations of Western life lead to a political as well as to a social depreciation of the white man in the eyes of the Orientals." Their argument was that, since the bazaars of the Orient were equipped with cinema theaters, and the Oriental spectator "cannot discriminate between the general and the particular," then Western civilization would appear to them to be composed exclusively of "cheerful, triumphant crooks, of women whose morals and manners would not be tolerated in the East behind the veil –much less in public life." Worse, the portrayal of Western luxury and extravagance in film would lead the impoverished Oriental audiences to wrongly conclude that "the East is being exploited by the West in order to indulge [its] extravagance."

The New York Times article allows a number of insights into Hollywood's filmic representation of the "Other". While Tagore deplored the fact that *both* the Oriental and the "white man" were inappropriately and derogatorily represented in film; the British-

2

controlled Bengal Board of Censors discerned only one misrepresentation: the white man's. Perhaps unknowingly, the white man was slowly undermining his "prestige" in Asia and Africa through self-misrepresentation to an Oriental audience that is morally and racially his unquestionable inferior. An interesting view was allowed by the writer of the report, who consistently used the term "misrepresentation" with regard to the portrayal of Westerners in film, but invariably employed the term "exaggeration" to designate a similar representation of Oriental life and peoples. As such, while a white man could be misrepresented, the image of an Oriental, whatever the distance or the degree of slant, could only be exaggerated; that is, magnified at the contours but essentially remaining "true" to its source and referent. Expectedly, the East/West dichotomy, the very justification of the colonial enterprise, is supported in the article by a grid of oppositions: civilized versus peasant, all-knowing versus undiscriminating, a West that is enjoying the "triumphs of commerce and science," versus an Orient which is very much a "stranger to these benefits". Long established by early anthropology, morality, religion, and "common sense"; these oppositions provided the parameters at the center of the system of Orientalism; along which the films of this study operated and were ultimately construed by Western audiences.

Additionally, the warning by the Bengal Censors that American films were responsible for "undermining the prestige of the white man" allows for some observations which the present study takes into account. First, American films are not always synonymous with white men's films, much less with colonial films. The point will frequently be made here that early American filmmakers, while subscribing to the essentially Western system of Orientalism, did not invariably and wholly adopt the European colonial thesis: at times they even permitted the contradictions of colonialism to surface in their films and a number of contemporary film reviewers even rebuked some colonial practices shown in, for example, the Foreign Legion films (the French, by contrast, did not allow filmic irreverence to the colonial ethos). This is possible because the film medium ordinarily allows for intentional and unintended disruptions of the preferred order through the interplay of visual and verbal elements, often unbeknownst to or beyond the control of the filmmakers themselves. Through the visual sculpting of shadows and light, the intricate relationship between the star system and the audience, and particularly, one might add, a proclivity for doing business in the twilight zone of "moral" ambivalence, American silent films often allowed ethnic types to transcend their trivial existence and swarthy looks to become highly resourceful individuals, debonair Sheiks, and cultivated lovers. Rather than viewing these "positive" characterizations as Freudian slips, the present study dwells on them as highly significant deviations, not only within their specific filmic contexts but also as pointers to larger ideological manifestations.

If Tagore was among the first Orientals to articulate what was a widely shared feeling regarding the misrepresentation of Orientals and non-whites in general, reactions against misrepresentations of ethnic and national minorities in the United States were not then uncommon; and when they occurred they were acrimonious and sometimes tragically violent, as demonstrated by the protests occasioned by D. W. Griffith's film, *The Birth of a Nation* (1915). The practice of casting the "Other" in demeaning roles has motivated sociologists and critics to study stereotyping in media, doubtless in an effort to understand and to perhaps suggest a way out of the negative phenomenon. The present work, although in many ways breaking away from the majority of film "image studies", has nonetheless benefited from the valuable insight of previous research on types.

The representation in cinema of national and ethnic types, as well as women, received only scant attention from film critics and reviewers during the silent period. Surprisingly also, the "slighted" communities themselves (excluding the African-American well-documented anger at the Griffith offending film) did not voice any coordinated rejection of the practice. One explanation for the lack of sustained critical questioning by ethnic minorities, in particular the Arabs living in the United States, of their screen representations was perhaps their desire to be assimilated into American society, and for some into a particular socio-economic stratum. The lack of seriousness accorded to film's cultural significance was also another factor.

Sociologist Walter Lippmann's pioneering work on stereotypes, *Public Opinion* (1922), was exceptional both for its timing and insightful conclusions. In it, Lippmann charted the pervasiveness of stereotypes, both positive and negative, in modern society; noting

4

that while they serve as an economical means of transmitting information, an aid to the "bewildering effect of trying to see the world steadily and as a whole;" they also have limiting aspects, which function as veritable blinkers on our view of reality. (96) Underlining the pervasiveness and the strength of stereotypes, Lippmann stressed: "We are told about the world before we see it. We imagine most things before we experience them. And these perceptions, unless education has made us acutely aware, govern deeply the whole process of perception. For the most part we do not first see, and then define; we define first and then see. In the great blooming, buzzing confusion of the outer world we pick out what our culture has already defined for us, and we tend to perceive that which we have picked out in the form stereotyped for us in our culture." (81)

Applied to the medium of film, Lippmann's ideas resurfaced in the work of German-born film critic, Siegfried Kracauer, who was entrusted by UNESCO after World War II with investigating "the conceptions which the people of one nation entertain of their own and of other nations." The resulting study, "National Types as Hollywood Presents Them," looked at Hollywood's depiction of the British and the Russians, tracing their respective images before, during, and after World War II. Several conclusions were reached: first, certain types (e.g., the British snob, the mad Russian) persisted throughout the period; second, the images of the British were more fully delineated than those of the Russians; and third, groups appeared and disappeared on the screen according to changes in national priorities." (Krakauer 1949, 88-122) In his other and most famous work, *From Caligari to Hitler*, Kracauer likewise demonstrated that the films of a nation reflect its "mentality." In his view, film is best suited for reflecting "mass desires," not only because the individual biases of filmmakers are usually discouraged by the group nature of filmmaking, but also because sundry commercial and audience considerations combine to ensure an accurate reflection of a nation's "mental climate".

After the seminal work of Kracauer, types and their portrayal in cinema in the United States were rarely examined. It was not until the rise in the 1960s of the Civil Rights Movement and the Women's Movement, which coincided with the appropriation of film as a legitimate academic discipline that a series of studies on stereotypes began to be undertaken, involving a number of ethnic groups as well as women. For example, there appeared, under the rubric of Black studies, Donald Bogle's *Toms, Coons, Mulattos, Mammies and Bucks* (1973), Daniel Leab's From *Sambo to Superstar: The Black Experience in Motion Pictures* (1974), and Thomas Cripps' *Slow Fade to Black: The Negro in American Film 1900-1942* (1977). The Jewish experience was treated in Lester Friedman's Hollywood's Image of the Jew (1982) and Patricia Erens' *The Jew in American Cinema* (1984). In the field of women's studies, Marjorie Rosen's *Popcorn Venus: Women, Movies and the American Dream* (1973) and Molly Haskell's *From Reverence to Rape: The Treatment of Women in the Movies* (1973) were pioneering works. Other studies and dissertations have examined Hollywood's treatment of American Indians, the Japanese, the Chinese, the Irish, the Latinos, and other groups constituting the ethnic mosaic of the United States. *The Kaleidoscopic Lens: How Hollywood Views Ethnic Groups* (1980) contains studies on several minorities, as does *Ethnic Images in the American Film and Television* (1978), a collection of articles on the subject of ethnic representation in media.

However, despite the wealth of studies on ethnic and national groups since then, no specialized book-length study of the Arab in Hollywood has been published. After the present study had been finished, American film scholar Jack Shaheen published such a book, an impassioned *cri de coeur* titled *Reel Bad Arabs: How Hollywood Vilified a People*. It was gratifying to discover that he had quoted from my work, and most importantly, leaned closely on my filmography of early American films on Arabs; painstakingly established for the first time in any book of film history or criticism. Jack Shaheen's previous book, The *T.V. Arab,* looks at the treatment of Arabs in the important medium of television. In it, Shaheen is throughout sensitive to the negative portrayal of Arabs in television, and is therefore desirous of a quick and positive change to which he thinks television executives –high in his scale of blame– may be amenable. There have been some articles dealing with Arab representation in mass media, with particular concentration on news, textbooks, and television. It was not until the mid-eighties that articles on filmic portrayal of the Arab began to reach film magazines. The impassioned article, "The Arab in American Cinema: A Century of Otherness," by Laurence Michalek appearing in *Cinéaste* in 1986, is an example. The nineties brought a host of feminist and post-colonialist perspectives on the Hollywood Arab, with for the first time some seriousness of intent, as in Gaylyn Studlar and Mathew Berstein, *Visions of the East: Orientalism in Film,* although the work suffers from some patchiness caused in large measure by the absence of a comprehensive filmography on Arabs.

Although not specifically dealing with film, Edward Said's seminal book, *Orientalism,* provides a rich base for studying the representation of Arabs in American cinema. An essential argument of Edward Said is that the system of Orientalism spans and explains all the disciplines directed towards managing the Orient. The system is so "authoritative," Said asserts, "that no one writing, thinking, or acting on the Orient could do so without taking account of the limitations on thoughts and action imposed by Orientalism" (3). Like other disciplines, Western cinema dealing with Oriental themes has been greatly influenced and was in part shaped by Orientalism. More significant, Oriental films of the silent era not only replenished their store of images, themes, and types from the Western cultural system of Orientalism, but in exploiting Oriental themes and rehashing old imperialist positions (whipped up by the Foreign Legion films, for example), they in turn helped to strengthen and perpetuate the colonial disposition of Orientalism. However, it should be noted, in no way did the latter completely smother the values of creativity, individuality, or difference: important markers of art and a mainstay for the social relevance of the film medium. Hence, in concurrence with Said, this study will frequently seek to establish the important presence of "the determining imprint of individual writers upon the otherwise anonymous collective body of a discursive formation like Orientalism" (23). Instilling in their texts their personal philosophies and signatures, individual filmmakers and other creative talent, such as director Rex Ingram and super-star Rudolph Valentino, succeeded in expressing themselves with a large measure of freedom from the limitations of Hollywood, generic constraints, or ideological blinkers; challenging thus the bounds of the Orientalist cultural system (though one might argue, without ever managing to totally break free from it).

The present study will carefully shun the realist position seeking to correlate a representation to its referent in "reality". Said considered representations *"as representations"* not as "natural" depictions of the

Orient (3). If such correlation is attempted, difficulties are bound to be legion; not least of them the delimitation of the geographical and sociological entity referred to here as the Orient. The term "Orient" and "Oriental" have always been vague to define. In the usage of many European intellectuals at the end of the nineteenth century, the terms covered India to the East, places like Turkey, Palestine, Egypt, in the middle and Morocco to the far west. In common American usage, "Oriental" refers to things and peoples from East Asia countries; and to add to the vagueness, the SOED notes that in America, "Orient" has been occasionally used to mean Europe. For this study, the Oriental, used often interchangeably with the Arab, is a combination of a physical being and a mental picture of the races that inhabit what I occasionally refer to as the traditional Orient, comprising the non-Arab but Muslim lands of Iran and Turkey, in addition to the Arab territories. The modern political entities of the present Middle-East, being for the most part the consequence of post-war era configurations, hinder more than help useful identification. For example, the term "Syrian" found in some film titles in the silent period was at the time almost interchangeable with "Arab", referring to, in addition to the people of present Syria, immigrants from Lebanon, Palestine, Jordan, and even Iraq.

Many film historians and critics rightfully downplay and altogether avoid the frustrating path linking representation to some "reality". In her study of the Jew in American cinema, Patricia Erens dismisses this temptation, stating that "I am less interested in the discrepancy between authentic Jews and their screen manifestations. Rather I have attempted to establish a typology of screen types, and to analyze the ways these types function in individual films as expressions of latent attitudes in society (28). Similarly, critic Christine Gledhill argues, in her article "A Contemporary Film Noir and Feminist Criticism," that the issue in the representation of women (and by analogy, that of minorities and types) is not one of degree of faithfulness to a putative reality. As a result, she cautions that an individual's notion of "the realistic" leads to disagreement and the "elimination of the chance to examine the power of recognition which certain structures or stereotypes may invoke." (12)

The present study aims as well to explore and chart similar thought structures sustaining Oriental films. It attempts to go beyond the panoply of stereotypes; beyond the graffiti as it were, to the mind-set of those responsible for splattering it walls. American city officials will recognize that summarily whitewashing the graffiti off the walls will only invite more layers of the same; they will agree however that through understanding and painstaking engagement, sparkle may be re-introduced into a gutted inner city.

Importantly, the present book stakes out a claim for difference from other image studies as it sets out to argue and lay the foundations for a distinct film genre, which I call "the Oriental genre". I believe and hope to demonstrate that films on Arabs produced during the silent era do indeed fit the conventional demands and conditions of a mature genre as defined by film critics such as Thomas Schatz and Steve Neale, among others.

Motivated by Allan Williams' call for more "genre studies with real historical integrity, Steve Neale proposes that this could be done through, "1) starting with a genre's 'pre-history,' its roots in other media; 2) studying all films, regardless of perceived quality; and 3) going beyond film content to study advertising, the star system, studio policy, and so on in relation to the production of films" (Neale, "Questions of Genre," 66). A possible route through these propositions, in the view of Neale, is the argument that genres come about as a result of integrating two regimes of verisimilitude: "Genres do not consist only of films: they consist also, and equally, of specific systems of expectations and hypotheses which spectators bring with them to the cinema, and which interact with films themselves during the course of the viewing process" (46) With regard to representations in general, Tzvetan Todorov had already pointed out in his article, "Typology of Detective Film," two types of verisimilitude: generic verisimilitude, and a wider social and cultural verisimilitude. Although states that "verisimilitude, taken in this [the generic] sense, designates the work's relation to literary discourse: more exactly, to certain of the latter's subdivisions, which form a genre." In the other verisimilitude, the relation is established "between the work and a scattered discourse that in part belongs to each of the individuals of a society but of which none may claim ownership; in other words to *public opinion*" (47).

The first part of this book will be devoted almost exclusively to what is implied by Todorov's second type of verisimilitude; that is, to the social and cultural contexts responsible for the creation and consumption of the Oriental genre. The "scattered discourse," which belongs to all yet "none may claim sole ownership" of, is what has been referred to here as the system of Orientalism. As Neale states, "genres do not consist only of films: they consist also, and equally, of specific systems of expectations and hypothesis which spectators bring with them to the cinema, and which interact with films themselves during the course of the viewing process (46). As noted above, films on Arabs drew from a reservoir of images, ideas, and themes already established by the cultural system of Orientalism. Western audiences during the silent era (and afterwards) subscribed to the same system that nourished the scores of films on the Arabs and Orient. Both the films and the audiences shared a set of expectations in relation to what constitutes an Oriental object and experience; such expectations were instrumental in the making, the consumption, and the development of the Oriental film genre.

Adopting a genre approach for this study is not without its risks. To say that the system of Orientalism shaped the Oriental genre is essentially relating internal and formal elements of the films to external, social and cultural phenomena. Genre criticism has traditionally done just that; linking, for instance, the western film to the frontier ethic, the gangster film to outlaw capitalism, and the horror film to specific psychological patterns in the wake of great wars and other catastrophes of a lingering impact. In the present case, however, positioning the system of Orientalism as a determining factor in the formation and understanding of Oriental films will not be done at the expense of other elements, such as aesthetics, the star system, and the contribution of individual filmmakers. These elements will be incorporated into the genre perspective as meaningful facets of the multiple interacting relationships, rather than as conflicting demands.

At the end of this introduction, some precision and clarifications are in order. The most pressing one concerns the notion of the Arab as referred to by the films and therefore this study. Did the silent films on Arabs refer to and somehow reflect the early Arab-Americans in the United States, as other films did with regard to other ethnic groups such as the African-American, the Chinese, or the Irish? The answer necessitates a brief historical detour.

Ever since its foundation, the United States of America has

enjoyed great ethnic diversity, but it was not until the second half of the nineteenth-century that recognizable ethnic formations began to emerge. Arabs, however, did not begin to arrive in meaningful numbers to the United States until the very end of the nineteenth century, and thereafter only gradually. A number of factors combined to create the right condition for a steady flow of Arab immigrants to the United States, including Ottoman misrule in the Levant, which had led to sectarian strife in Syria and Lebanon; European powers' encroachment on the greater Middle East; a demographic increase which limited land resources coupled to frequent droughts could not sustain; and the irresistible appeal of economic opportunities represented by the vast resources of North America. The first generation of Arab settlers became farmers, peddlers, or small merchants, and with increased capital and the acquisition and command of the English language (speeded up by the interpersonal nature of peddling) Arab immigrants became shop owners, and their children white-collar workers and professionals. Although intensely proud of their Arab roots, most early Arab immigrants adopted strategies of assimilation through social mobility, self-improvement, inter-racial marriage, and/or through the force of acculturation. After the first rounds of immigration (preponderantly Christian), the increasingly larger numbers of incoming Arabs (mostly Muslim) found rapid and total assimilation more and more difficult.

Unlike other ethnic groups, the early Arab community in the United States did not find itself reflected in the early motion pictures. Of a filmography of more than two hundred listings, only one documentary, *The Syrian Immigrant* (1920), deals entirely with Arab immigrants in the United States; and the very few fiction films that point out to these immigrants straddle both American and Oriental environments. One of the earliest references to the Arab immigrant occurs in a Pathé one-reeler, *Arabian Dagger* (1908), where interestingly less interest was shown in the Arab peddler than in his dagger, the weapon in a murder. (That an Arabian dagger should be particularly deadly or involved in a murder mystery is not without precedent, as will be seen later).

One might argue that Arab immigrants received an attention commensurate with their modest numerical status. However, there exists another explanation: the dearth of American silent films reflecting the Arab immigrants' experience in America is largely due

11

to the fact that the Arab in these films is mostly a concept, a trope, a fabrication of the imagination of Westerners. That the Arabs in America were not perceived to be good or bad neighbors, in fact were not perceived at all in the films of the early period is a testimony to the grip of the all-encompassing traditional view of Arabs as had been developed and fanned out by the system of Orientalism. Even studies dealing with the present media representation of Arabs –a representation that is more and more conscious of the realities of Arab-Americans and Middle Easterners– cannot afford to be oblivious to the overwhelming nature of the inherited views about them.

Finally, unlike much of the current work on image studies benefiting from an already established and a more or less definitive corpus of films, this study had to piece-by-piece erect a filmography of films on Arabs covering the period 1894-1930. It transpired that about two-thirds of entries are fiction films and the remainder is composed of scenics, travelogues, or documentaries. The non-fiction titles, especially the scenic views and travelogues of the early period (1894-1910), are extremely short: from less than a minute in the first years to five minutes and more as films developed in length and technique. Most of the entries range in length from three to eight and ten reels, and only a few of the fiction films are one- or two-reelers. On the other hand, the decision to cap the silent era with the year 1930 and not with the more iconic date of 1927 (the birth year of the talkies) is dictated by the fact that silent films on Arabs (as on other subjects) continued to be made well after 1927. This was consistent with the fact that the conversion to sound of movie theaters in the United States was not as rapid as first believed, while overseas it actually took many more years for it to happen on a large scale.
Compiling the present filmography was complicated by the fact that the catalogues spanning the period 1894-1930 are not as complete or as exhaustive as a researcher might wish. The very important volumes of *The American Film Institute Catalog of Motion Pictures Produced in the United States: Feature Films* do not cover the formative period 1894-1910. Unfortunately also, they do not include films of less than three reels, an omission that not only affects a large number of very important fiction films but also nearly all documentaries and travelogues. Moreover, even when they include

listings by subject, some other catalogues lack comprehensive generic groupings to designate films featuring Arabic types and themes. Some of the difficulties encountered by these compilers are perhaps understandable, as for instance when a movie is more about adventure, war, exotism, etc., than it is about the Arab. However, to characterize a movie showing Sudanese natives being mowed down by British artillery in Sudan as a film about war –and exclusively classifying it as such– is not unlike saying that the killing of Indians in Hollywood's Westerns is about marksmanship. Furthermore, the compilers were not geographically and historically attuned; consequently, there was some confusion surrounding such labels as 'Turk,' 'Mohammedan,' 'Moslem,' 'Arab,' and 'Syrian,' often used and construed interchangeably at the time by the audience and the critics alike (and also by the Immigration Services of the United States, according to existing records).

Certainly, the greatest limitation this study had to face was the inability to view even half the films contained in the filmography; although a similar limitation haunts nearly all studies which have to deal with film texts from the silent period. Since most early films have been lost to deterioration and neglect, our view of the silent era, to a great extent, is a function of the surviving texts. This should not forever be the case. While film restoration may someday fill some gaps, it is perhaps indispensable that other techniques of knowing about the films that are irrevocably lost or simply difficult to access may be tried, and to some extent, relied upon. The bulk of information about the films in this study was extracted from the synopses included in the American Film Institute Catalogs, the biographies of stars and directors, the articles and the books on the history of the silent cinema, and most important, from the trade papers, the fan magazines, and the newspapers of the period. Fan and trade publications, as well as contemporary newspapers, offer not only large amounts of information on individual films, directors, stars, audiences, exhibition practices, and publicity, but also a wealth of essential opinion and criticism from critics and reviewers of the time. The latter's work usually included important facts about audience attendance, performances, the kind of advertisement accompanying the films, and even some valuable 'tips' for the exhibitors on how to better manage a movie theater to attract patrons.

Needless to say, caution had to be observed, as trade publications and fan magazines are by definition self-serving vehicles that survive on advertisements of the films they present; yet, this does not mean that their sometimes "tainted" evidence should be ignored. Film historians Allen and Gomery have rightly pointed out that "in any branch of historical research, what we have are not 'good' data and 'bad' data, but sources of varying degrees of mediation and complexity" (39). Sustained vigilance, comparing reviews, and mostly, a familiarity of the general style and approach of the publication (*Variety*, for example, was more measured in its praise than the *Moving Picture World*) are indispensable strategies for this type of research.

Importantly, the publications of the period were valuable sources for determining the extra-filmic information essential to firmly establish the films within their relevant social, economic, psychological, and generic contexts. The discourse of the industry and the press accompanying the Oriental genre is often as important as the internal elements constituting the film texts themselves. François Truffaut once remarked: "when a film achieves a certain success, it becomes a sociological event" (Truffaut 100). The accounts of the press and trade publications are indispensable for tracking and measuring the impact on the audience and the reverberation within society of some phenomenal film successes, such for example, the hit "Sheik films" of the mid-1920s. At times, reviewers and journalists helped people understand and spell out what was sometimes only suggested in the silent movies; at others, they played the role of cultural mediators and popularizers of the Orientalist tradition, reinforcing such imagery as the mystery, violence, and fabulous wealth of the East. They applauded films when they fit the mythical views of the Orient, and chided others when, for one instance, the actor playing the Oriental was not sufficiently darkened to fit the Moor type. One reviewer even reproached a film for allowing its Sheik to weep; Sheiks, he reminded all, were tough desert creatures always above such a lowly emotion.

Chapter Two

THE RISE OF ORIENTALISM AND THE AMERICAN ORIENTAL EXPERIENCE

Orientalism and the Shaping of the Oriental Image

The intense European interest in the Near-East, in reality, predated by many centuries the post-renaissance drive for colonies, going back at least to the rise of Islam in the early seventh century. Partly out of curiosity, mostly to subdue and maintain Eastern peoples under watch and control, knowledge about their culture was needed; giving rise to the system of Orientalism.

The function of Orientalism is "to understand, in some cases to control, manipulate, and even incorporate, what is a manifestly different world" (Said 12). Nineteenth-century Western scholars with a deep interest in the Muslim East, like Sylvester de Sacy, Ernest Renan, Edward William Lane, are said to have "made Orientalism effective and congruent with the interests and political concerns of imperialist rulers" (Shaar 69). It is ironic that the system of Orientalism, projecting a lopsided relationship between Europe and the Islamic Orient, developed during the first part of the nineteenth century, a time when Europe itself had just emerged from the painful and arbitrary political terror of the previous centuries. Seemingly, the consolidation of knowledge and the widespread emancipation of the Western individual in the nineteenth century did not extend to non-Europeans. In fact, gains in the area of individual freedoms in Europe signaled, if not caused, a gradual erosion of freedom and self-determination among non-Westerners.

Edward Said and Foucault on Power and Representation

The view which regards power as antithetical to knowledge has been challenged by Michel Foucault, with direct implications for the discourse of Orientalism and the relationship between East and West. Foucault argued that discourse is the result of power relationships, and that "there is no power relation without the correlative constitution of a field of knowledge, nor any knowledge that does not presuppose and constitute at the same time power relations." Power-driven discourse, Foucault affirmed, creates difference through the processes of classification, tabulation and comparison; as the exercise of power in society "presupposes new forms of scientific discourse through which deviant groups are defined and controlled" (Turner 23-24). For example, the categories of 'criminal,' 'insane,' and 'deviant' as developed in the post-Enlightenment disciplines of criminology and penology are "the manifestations of a scientific discourse by which the normal and sane exercise power along a systematic dividing line of sameness" (Turner 24).

The correlation between knowledge and power in the work of Foucault forms the central structural grid around which Edward Said developed his influential presentation, analysis, and critique of Orientalism. For Said, the apparently neutral opposition, Occident/Orient, bespeaks definite power relationships. He stressed, "to believe that the Orient was created simply as a necessity of the imagination is to be disingenuous." Indeed, the relationship between Occident and Orient stands as one "of power, of domination, of varying degrees of a complex hegemony .... The Orient was Orientalized not only because it was discovered to be "Oriental" in all those ways considered commonplace by an average nineteenth-century European, but also because it *could be* —that is submitted to being— made Oriental" (Said's emphasis, 5-6).

According to Said, Orientalism means a number of things. There is first the academic designation, which considers that "anyone who teaches, writes about, or researches the Orient ... either in its specific or its general aspects, is an Orientalist, and what he or she does is Orientalism." Then there is the second designation, which treats Orientalism as "a style of thought," based on a clear-cut distinction between the Occident and the Orient. In its third manifestation, Orientalism refers to "the corporate institution for dealing with the Orient;" and as such, it is a "Western style for dominating, restructuring, and having authority over the Orient." Said went on to affirm that the interchange between the three designations is quite constant (2-3).

Taking his cue from Foucault's analysis of discourse, especially the suggestion that "the same rules governing the distribution of statements within a discourse may be common to a wide variety of apparently separate disciplines," (Turner 26) Edward Said observed that Orientalism spans and explains all the disciplines directed towards managing the Orient. Accordingly, an unambiguous epistemological division between West and East guided the artists, philosophers, administrators, and others whose subject was the peoples and culture of Orient. Said maintained that all artists dealing with the Orient from their varied perspectives should locate themselves vis-à-vis the Orient. For a writer, and by extension a filmmaker, this location will include, when translated into his text, "the kind of narrative voice he adopts, the type of structure he builds, the kind of images, themes, motifs that circulate in his text –all of which add up to deliberate ways of addressing the reader, containing the Orient, and finally representing or speaking in its behalf (20).

America and the Oriental Experience

Said observed early in his book that Orientalism is "a dynamic exchange between individual authors and the large political concerns shaped by the three great empires –British, French, and American in whose intellectual but imaginative territory the writing was produced" (14). Though not exactly a world empire in the nineteenth century, the fledgling nation of the United States would soon become "concerned with the Orient in ways that prepared for its later, overtly imperial concern" (293). At a time when the Orient was a testing ground for imperialists and budding artists alike, America began to show a sustained interest in the East; an interest that would soon become institutionalized by the foundation in 1842 of the American Oriental Society. America began imitating and contributing to the Orientalist ethos, predisposed for that by a homegrown rigorous Puritanism and the identification with the ancestral Europe. A more immediate reason for the interest in the Near East was provided by America's desire for self-preservation and survival as a nation, which early American political thinkers had predicated on commerce and expansion.

The contribution of America to the Orientalist discourse –the result of its own experience with the Orient– is of great significance to this study, as it helps to explain and account for the diversity of issues, themes, locales, and styles of treatment in films about Arabs. The attention of the United States towards the Islamic Orient in the nineteenth century was geographically two-pronged: the Barbary States and the Holy Land. After its independence, the United States' survival depended to a large degree on its performance as a trader with the outside world. However, as Historian Robert Stookey explains, many great obstacles stood in front of this ambition: "The exclusivist policies of the European monarchies closed off access to their West Indies colonies, and, across the Atlantic a hostile Britain had either to be bypassed to the north through the Baltic or to the south into the Mediterranean. In the latter case, American trade with southern Europe, North Africa, the Levant, and Turkey depended on the sufferance of the Barbary States (Stookey 2).

Before the War of Independence, American trading ships in the Mediterranean were guaranteed safe passage because of the fee traditionally paid to the Barbary States by Great Britain. Once British passes were withdrawn from American traders, the United States was left to deal single-handedly with the privateering policy of the North African states. According to historian Paul Zingg, both "diplomatic negotiation and military force" were used to reach satisfactory treaties of peace and commerce (96-97). It was during the early nineteenth-century that a few American ethnocentric assumptions about Arabs began to take shape, nearly all stemming from the repeated and exasperating grounding of American commercial ships. The Americans considered the Barbary sea raiders as 'pirates' and the policies of the Sultan of Morocco and the Dey and Bey of Algeria and Tunisia strictly piratical. Such uncompromising characterization, Zingg argues, went against the view of the North African states, for which these actions were perfectly legitimate in view of the continuing state of war between Christian Europe and the Muslim states. This "semantic misunderstanding" (97) between Americans and the Barbary States must have rendered treaty negotiations more complicated.

The United States policy toward the Barbary States generally respected the non-interventionist policy contained in the Monroe Doctrine, but European imperialism's take-over of Algeria and

Tunisia caused American policy to assume a more visible role, in particular with regard to Morocco. The Algeciras Conference (1905) and the famous "Perdicaris affair" (on which the 1973 film, *The Wind and the Lion*, is loosely based) about the kidnapping of a presumably American national by a Riffian chieftain, provided Theodore Roosevelt with the opportunity to become more assertive, in particular with the Morocco issue. As a result of its exasperating trade experiences with the Barbary States in the Western Mediterranean and with the Ottomans in the East, America soon found itself adopting the discourse of the powerful traditional West: barbarian versus civilized, West versus East. Such discourse reached strident notes in Theodore Roosevelt's declaration about Muslim Turkey: "Spain and Turkey are the two powers I would rather smash in the world" (DeNovo 5).

President Roosevelt's later views concerning the partitioning of the Middle East and Africa were in perfect agreement with the traditional European imperial philosophy. At the Algeciras Conference, Roosevelt was reported to have told the French ambassador: "As for the Moorish business, I wish to heaven, not in your interest but in the interest of all civilized mankind, that France could take all Morocco under its exclusive charge" (ibid 27). Likewise, when Roosevelt landed in Cairo after his much-heralded visit to the African jungles (widely relayed by some documentaries, see filmography), he not only commended British rule in Egypt as a service to civilization, but went on to argue against the aspirations of the Egyptian Nationalist Movement on the ground that the Egyptian people were far from ready to stand on their feet (ibid 49).

For Americans then, Arabs were viewed at best passively as "targets for American initiatives" (Heggoy, et al 100). North Africans were particularly vulnerable, in the words of Zingg, as "volunteer American airmen bombed them in [the] 1925 campaign against the Riff, American missionaries berated their heathen ways in a widespread effort at Christian recruitment, and American business anticipated lucrative efforts from sales to them" (102-103). For many American readers of *Reader's Digest*, the *Christian Science Monitor*, *Cosmopolitan* and other publications of the early twentieth-century, North Africa was a land where "white Fathers" experienced the joy of selling Bibles to the natives. Likewise, contemporary travel accounts frequently depicted the region as a "land of religious mystery, ill-omen, and sensual pleasure," (95) heightening the existing fascination with exotic places such as harems and oases.

To the east in the Levant, American traders were joined by traditional fellow travelers: the Protestant missionary. Missionaries have long sought to take the gospel to the millions of what they believed to be heathens, pagans, and even to Eastern Christians whose "sterile" ritual stood in the way of the Scriptures. However, despite the large number of missions dispatched to the region, little progress was generally registered; as a report by the Western Turkey Mission bemoaned in 1900: "no large spiritual results can be reported, and there is no general spirit of inquiry and not many accessions to the Protestant community…. The missionaries feel that this condition of things is a temporary phase and that the power of the gospel is working in ways, many of which are unseen" (DeNovo 11).

Interestingly, some of these 'unseen' ways would take the path of wish fulfillment and fantasy about conversion, seen in some films of the silent period. In one of these, *The Sheik*, (George Melford, 1921), viewers were offered the sudden and final discovery that the charismatic Arab lead had actually been a Christian all along.

Likewise, Napoleon's Egyptian adventure not only shook the entire East, but made the region safe and attractive for the archaeologist, the scholar, and the intrepid tourist of both sexes. The much-publicized exploits of archaeologists would supply an enduring theme to Hollywood: the reincarnation of the mummy. Similarly, the American tourist, either as a distraught maid, a captured addition to the Sheik's or sultan's harem, or a *blasé* American lady seeking to be bewitched by the beauty of the moon-washed desert, would become recurring features in many films.

Chapter Three

THE EMERGENCE AND CONSOLIDATION OF THE ARAB STEREOTYPE

Arabs have almost always been presented as negative entities in American (and European) cinema. As leads or as secondary characters, Arabs were assigned limited and stereotypical roles as a result of the stereotypical delimitation imposed by the system of Orientalism and in accordance with their perception by Westerners.

Stereotypes are not always negative, nor are they exclusively aimed at debasing other national, ethnic or gender groups. Walter Lippmann believed that they also provide an economical means of transmitting information. Although stereotypes limit our view of reality, they may serve as practical and economical shortcuts to complex phenomena that may appear overwhelming to the perceiver. For filmmakers especially, using stereotypes saves time, money and effort. In genre films in particular, stereotypes constitute an essential component of the 'idiolect' shared by the films, the filmmakers, and the viewers. On the debit side, stereotypes constitute serious obstacles to clear perception: "we pick out what our culture has already defined for us, and we tend to perceive that which we have picked out in the form stereotyped for us by our culture" (Lippman 81). The system of Orientalism has been the supplier of a formidable array of images, themes, perceptions; hallowed by time and therefore indispensable to anyone who comes in contact with the Orient. Stereotypes about the Orient were multiplied and magnified before they were fanned to every corner of the world by the Hollywood image factory.

From an early time, Western culture slowly and methodically proceeded to manage and stereotype the Orient for its own people. When Europe broke free from the despotism of European monarchies –which interestingly eighteenth-century critics and writers have repeatedly likened to Eastern tyrannies– many Western writers and thinkers began to portray Islam based on the new argument that the land of Islam is critically lacking in the autonomous institutions of bourgeois society. Islamic societies, according to this view, did not have "independent cities, an autonomous bourgeois class, rational bureaucracy, legal reliability, personal property," and the rights embodied and guaranteed by bourgeois culture (Turner 26). From a sociological point of view, the Orient was found to be "characterized by the absence of a civil society," as it was governed by Oriental despots who controlled the large masses directly and single-handedly, without the benefits of the institutions that should link the ruled to the ruler (Turner 26). Such a belief was so strong and 'self-evident' that it was subsequently transposed into Oriental films (in particular the films of the Orientalist sub-category; see next chapter). So, unlike the classic Western film genre's portrayal of society, where lawyers, sheriffs, banks, and community elders mediate between the community and the larger society, in films about the Orient one rarely sees the police, a serious court, or any other viable civil agency standing between the ruler and the ruled. One may wonder whether these conclusions about Oriental societies were invariably supported by the facts on the ground, or whether they represented a projection onto the Oriental arena of one of the most European nagging concerns; namely, the possible a re-emergence of despotic rule. What is a fact is that the Western society making comparisons and issuing judgments enjoyed the privilege of initiating the discourse, appropriating for itself such positive features as rationality, progress, democratic institutions, and economic development. Indeed, part of the function of Orientalism was to explain "the progressive features of the Occident and the social stationariness of the Orient" (Turner 26).

As a theme, the stagnation of the East was invoked repeatedly by colonialists and apologists for European expansion. The British imperialist Balfour, for example, advocated a complete Western take-over of the East to rescue it from its lethargy. He insisted: "First of all, look at the fact of the case. Western nations as soon as they emerge into history show the beginnings of those capacities of self-government…. You may look through the whole history of the Orientals in what is called, broadly speaking, the East, and you never find traces of self-government. All their centuries –and they have been great– have been passed under despotisms, under absolute government" (Said 33).

The Arab Type in Western Art and Literature

A survey of the Western portrayal of the Arab in Western literature and popular culture is best done if made to cover two periods. The first one begins with the rise of Islam and ends in the beginning of the nineteenth-century, either with the 1799 Napoleonic Campaign in Egypt, or with the Romantic revolution of the 1820s. The second period begins with the end of the first, and ends with the period corresponding to the concern of this study.

Although largely the construct of religious polemicists, the image of the Arab as a threatening 'Other' may be better surveyed in Western secular literature in general and that of the medieval age in particular, as Critic Rana Kabbani has done successfully in her book, *Europe's Myths of Orient.* Capitalizing on the adversarial and emotional aspects of a ubiquitous anti-Islamic discourse, medieval secular literature used the West/East conflict as background as well as a concern for its romances. Thus, Arabs (Arabs and Muslims were nearly always interchangeable in the Medieval perspective) appear as villains in the *Chanson de geste*, and as evil Saracens in the *Song of Roland* to be killed by Christian knights. In *Piers Plowman*, Prophet Mohammed is presented as a religious transgressor with infernal powers; before that, Dante's most famous work, *la Commedia Divina*, had assigned him to the lowest circle in hell, where the disseminators of heresy are gathered, to be forever cleft in two for their heresy.

Middle English romances unfailingly depicted the triumph of Christianity over Islam. According to Dorothee Metlitzki's *The Matter of Araby in Medieval England*, these romances often contained wish-fulfilling embodiments, such as "the Saracen giant killed by a Christian hero, the defeated emir, the converted Saracen, and most importantly, the Saracen princess in love with the Christian knight" (15). The theme of conversion, from Islam to Christianity, was also popular in Western literature. There were a number of accounts of Christian knights overpowering Saracen kings with the help of the latter's wives or daughters. In the romance of The *King of Tars*, for example, a Christian princess agrees to marry a black and heathenish Saracen king in order to save her people from destruction. The child from their union is born deformed, but baptism turned him into a handsome and whole infant. Pleased, the Saracen king requested to undergo the same operation. He too was transformed by baptism and turned white (Kabbani 16). Another romance, *Floris and Blaucheflur*, offered one of the earliest descriptions of a harem, complete with eunuchs as ferocious guards, standing by as a sultan is receiving beautiful female slaves from merchants.

On stage, the Elizabethan renaissance made frequent use of the stock of conventional Eastern characters. The Saracen, the Turk, the Moor and the Blackamoor were, like the Jew, essential villains in the dramas of the period. From classical sources (Cicero and Horace, for example), the London stage borrowed the image of the fabulous East, (Kabbani 17). Shakespeare was one of the first artists to blend classical sources with contemporary anti-Islamic feelings, producing an ambiguous, albeit less crude or dismissive view of the Orient. Yet, even for Shakespeare, the Orient meant lust and spelt danger. Othello, despite being a killer of Turks and a noble savage, "was not allowed to 'tup' the 'white yew' uncurbed." Mark Antony's voyage to the East signaled the beginning of his loss of power and eventual downfall. This East, in the words of Rana Kabbani, "arrived in Cleopatra's barge. It was a mixture of new delights: the pomp of pageant, the smell of perfume and incense, the luxurious brocades that shimmered in the sun, and most notably, the woman herself– queen, love-object, mistress and despot–was the East, the Orient created for the Western gaze"(22).

Although most continued to treat the Orient and its people with extreme mistrust, in the mind of some imaginative writers of the nineteenth-century the region became an indispensable site of exoticism and a literary frontier of untold possibilities. In fact, long before "the Oriental Renaissance" of the nineteenth century, Western feelings towards the Orient were not always unambiguous or totally condemning. For example, when Dante committed Mohammed to the lowest sphere of hell in his *Commedia Divina*, he significantly placed Saladin (the famous Muslim general of the Crusades) and Averroes (a Muslim philosopher) in a higher sphere as essentially redeemable; with Aristotle, Plato, and other pagan luminaries of antiquity. The contrasting treatment of these Oriental figures is symptomatic of an undercurrent of genuine fascination with the Orient, cutting across all arts and channels of discourse, including cinema (as the Sheik films' analyses in this study will illustrate).

The fascination with the Orient coincided and grew with the emergence of a number of factors, among which are the dwindling threat posed by the Ottoman empire, the increased contact with the Orient, the translation of Oriental literature into European languages, and the gradual surrender of control of the Orient to the Western powers. Indeed, as Kabbani wrote, "the more fully the Orient fell under the sway of European powers, the deeper it became sublimated in the imagination, in literature, painting, music, and fashion" of the West (138). The translation of the *Arabian Nights* in the late eighteenth century was an especially significant event, after which the East was never the same. So fired up was the imagination of Europeans by this literary collection that many a traveler into the Orient held the region up to its mirror, often to one's surprise or disappointment.

By the late 1820s, Hugo confirmed, in the preface to "Les Orientales," the enormous attraction exercised by the East over the romantics in particular and the general public at large: "Au siècle de Louis XIV," he wrote, "on a été Helleniste, maintenant on est Orientaliste" (403). The romantics mostly emphasized the exotic, the grotesque, and the unfamiliar in the Orient. Muslims appear in their writings as polygamists, violent, and politically irresponsible; ironically, not entirely reprehensible traits in the view of many romantics. The Orient also became an inexhaustible quarry for exotic hues and a huge bazaar for props and trinkets. The *couleur locale* was for the Romantics as important as the study of social manners was for the neoclassical writers and painters; therefore, minarets, domes, sand, palm trees, exotic gardens, crescents, light and shadows, swords and daggers, constituted a romantic repertoire *par excellence*. Oriental cities, such as Cairo and Istanbul, were treated as symbols of sensuality, while their meandering architecture confirmed views of Oriental sophistication and intrigue. In the labyrinthine Oriental cities, the Sultan and Pasha were portrayed as holding absolute power, which they exercised to satisfy cruel and sadistic drives. Non-urban Oriental spaces, such as the deserts and oases, stood for simplicity, or primitiveness, and always for mystery.

The Oriental woman was constantly invoked in the romantic literature of the nineteenth-century. As a harem favorite, scheming and silently disposing of the bodies of female competitors; or as an incarcerated victim, forgotten and consumed by her humiliation, the Oriental woman represented both a sensual menace to be heeded and an attractive Orient to be possessed. William Lane, the famous nineteenth-century Arabist and scholar of Egyptian manners, associated the Orient, like Flaubert, with the escapism of sexual fantasy. He described his first sighting of Egypt in these amorous terms: "As I approached the shore, I felt like an Eastern bridegroom, about to lift the veil of his bride, and to see, for the first time, the features that were to charm, or disappoint, or disgust him" (qtd. in Kabbani 67).

Romantic painters were also impressed by, and labored to express, the sexual charms and exoticism of the East. Their attention to detail was such that Théophile Gautier claimed that, for the descendants of Orientals, his and his contemporaries' paintings would become the sole documents of how their fathers dressed and looked: "les Turcs qui voudront savoir quels costumes portaient leurs pères ne les retrouverons que dans les tableaux de Decamps" (qtd. in Kabbani 74. Translation: *"For the people of the Orient who may want to know what costumes their forebears wore there may be no better source than Decamps's paintings"*). In their studios, romantic painters amassed various Oriental trinkets, such as daggers, swords, knives and pistols; props that represented, remarked Kabbani, "an explosive and dangerous place where murder was a simple occurrence, where barbaric cruelty and opulence displayed themselves openly." (75) The paintings themselves reflected and heightened the view of the Orient as a land of gore and gems (see later the analyses of *The Lady of the Harem, Kismet,* and *The Thief of Bagdad,* for examples of the cinematic transplantation of this idea). Eugène Delacoix's painting, *"La Mort de Sardanapalé"* (1928) ("The Death of Sardanapale") finished before his actual visit to the Orient, borrows the violent images of the Orient from the Byron poem of the same name. In this painting, an Oriental despot sits on his luxurious bed, watching with indifference his naked concubines being stabbed to death by three dark villains. Violence and eroticism are mixed as the bodies of the concubine assume positions of sexual abandon, while the gems (the victims are heavily bejeweled) and the naked bodies exude an air of opulence. Violence also constituted the theme of another painting, Henri Renault's *"Exécution sans jugement sous les rois maures"* ('Execution without Judgment under Moorish Kings' 1870), where a guard who has just executed a man wipes the blood-tainted blade on his sleeve, completely unmoved. The dripping blood forms shapes that parody the arabesque design of the background. Another recurring image in the paintings of the time, connoting both the violence and the impenetrability of the East, is that of the guard. Guards, most often black men, were usually presented as blocking the entrance to a harem, a mosque, or a palace. The *"Garde du Sérail"* ('The Guard of the Seraglio' 1859) by Jean-Léon Gérôme, shows a towering and cruel guard, armed with dagger, pistol, and ax, ferociously guarding the passageway to a seraglio.

In Orientalist paintings the villain is almost always dark or black, and almost always portrayed in aggressive and threatening roles. *"The Prisoner"* (1883) of Filippo Baratti shows a bound white man being humiliated by two dark men (Douglas Fairbanks in the film, *Bound in Morocco*, finds himself in the same situation). Such villainy is often accentuated by casting Oriental males in the ignoble role of traders in female bodies (a trope not used in silent films on Arabs but curiously overused in modern Hollywood productions). In addition to eroticism, violence and villainy also furnish the world of Edwin Long's painting, *"The Babylonian Slave Market"* (1875) and John Faed's *"Bedouin Exchanging a Slave for Armour"* (1857). A well-known slave-market scene is to be found in Gérôme's *"Le Marché d'Esclaves,"* where nudity and other details of the sex slave trade are exposed. Here, the teeth of a naked female are being inspected to determine her age, her nudity paraded in front of a group of male would-be buyers; while other female victims await their turn with resignation (similar scenes of intrusive inspection are familiar to viewers of films and television programs dealing with the history slavery in America).

The images of captive beauty as purveyed by these paintings were immensely appealing to Western males. Kabbani explained the fascination thus, "since the Victorian imagination could not conceive of female eroticism divorced from female servitude; since in the core of the nineteenth-century sexuality there lurked all the conflicts of power and powerlessness, wealth and poverty, mastery and slavehood, the spectacle of subject women (and boys) could not be but exciting" (80-81). Interestingly, the desirable women in these paintings were hardly ever "foreign looking;" instead, they conformed more to "conventional standards of European beauty" (81). In fact, a most desirable type, made famous by the accounts of Gerard de Nerval, was the fair-skinned Circassian, who was exotic enough to the Westerner without being too dark for his taste.

To a certain degree, the romantic painters offered Europe what it wished to see. Perhaps also, in electing to describe the violence and sexual anarchy of the East, they were indirectly portraying the repressive character of Western bourgeois morality. Certainly, the serious painters of landscape and peoples never attained the popularity of their counterparts who specialized in the harem, bath scenes, and slave-markets. Inspired more by an imaginary Orient, the Orient of the mind, than by what they actually saw or experienced during their travels in the East, European painters portrayed an already heavily Orientalized Orient. This state of affairs was not dissimilar to the atmosphere reigning in Hollywood as it decided to bring the Arab region and Arabic themes to its studio lots.

Chapter Four

THE BIRTH OF THE ORIENTAL FILM GENRE

Towards a Definition of the Oriental Genre

Definitions of genres sound all but tautological: a detective film is one that deals with the investigation of a crime; a Western is a film set in the American Western frontier; etc. One definition of the Western genre, provided by Jean Mitry, rises above the others for being a little more elaborate: a Western is "a film whose action, situated in the American West, is consistent with the atmosphere, the values and the conditions of existence of the Far West between 1840 and 1900" (276). At the risk of mimicking Mitry's definition, I offer my own definition of the Oriental genre: "an Oriental genre film is one in which the action, situated wholly or partly in the Arab and Muslim lands, is consistent with the Western perception of the atmosphere, the behavior, the values, and conditions of existence of the inhabitants of the traditional Orient." Like all definitions, this one may survive only if buttressed by a host of additions and exceptions.

The Oriental Genre Meets its Audience

The foregoing sections, covering the rise of the system of Orientalism in the West and the positions occupied by the Arab type in the Orientalist-driven discourses up to the advent of cinema, concur with film scholar Thomas Schatz's reminder that movies "are not produced in creative or cultural isolation, nor are they consumed that way" (vii). As soon as movies began to tell stories, films dealing with Oriental subjects began to hit the screens and were immediately perceived as belonging to a specific film category drawing from that imaginary realm attached to the traditional Orient. Arguably, few genres had enjoyed a higher or quicker degree of recognition from early audiences than this Oriental genre. One of the earliest feature films, *Tragedy of the Desert* (1912), was introduced to the audience in a manner reflecting and purposefully invoking an existing and fairly replenished Oriental frame of reference. When the trade paper *The Moving Picture World* advertized the film using such stock expressions as, "Egypt: realm of mystery," and "the Unchanging East" (29 June 1912), it no doubt anticipated from the audience some prior exposure to Oriental lore.

Familiarity with popular concepts and images about the Orient was definitely assumed and called for, even at an early stage in the Oriental genre's development. Thus, in his review of the *Princess of Baghdad* (Charles Gaskill, 1913), Hanford C. Judson assumed that a section of the audience, the literate patrons for sure, would recognize in the picture the popular *Arabian Nights* theme: "The spectator who would enjoy looking at fine etchings illustrating the *Arabian Nights* would find a great deal of interest here" (*Moving Picture World*, Sept. 1913: 991). Similarly, when Fox released its film, *Ali Baba and the Forty Thieves* (S. A. Franklin and C. M. Franklin, 1917), reviewer Walter K. Hill assumed a general knowledge of the story, therefore electing to focus the attention on the technical possibilities created by the new cinematic medium: "William Fox has brought the 'open Sesame' of fiction to the screen to swing wide open the faculty of the photo-play enjoyment; to gladden the observer of this pretty fantasy with every detail" (*The Moving Picture World* 7 Dec. 1918). There is no doubt that stories from the Arabian collection (see Chapter 7, for a survey of reception in Europe) were fairly known, as is further demonstrated by this press presentation of Fairbanks' popular vehicle, *The Thief of Baghdad* (Raoul Walsh, 1924): "Imagine a clever satire on the *Arabian Nights* with marvelous photography and you have an inkling of Douglas Fairbanks's new picture" (*The New York Times* 19 Mar. 1924).

The audience's familiarity with Oriental lore was assuredly a bonus for film exhibitors and poster artists, always in search of publicity tricks to draw more patrons to the movie theaters. Like the films they intended to advertise, posters of Oriental films found a ready stock of presumed folk wisdom, stereotypes and attitudes in the wealth of material on the Orient. One piece of presumed Orientalist 'wisdom' emblazoned across a poster for the popular film, *The Sheik* (George

Melford, 1921), proclaimed: "'when an Arab sees a woman he wants he takes her,' ancient Proverb of Arabia" Ascribing this hedonistic aphorism to the Arabs not only plays to the audience's fantasies but also anchors the film in the Orientalist tradition, in particular to the sub-theme of the Orient as a site of untrammeled sexuality. Similarly, for an early Fairbanks' film, *Bound in Morocco* (Allan Dwan, 1917), a trade magazine advised film exhibitors to use the following angles of advertisement in the posters: "Fairbanks Hopping Through Morocco While the Wild Tribes Battle" and, "Fairbanks Acrobatics From the Harem to the Hot Sands" (*The Moving Picture World* 10 Aug. 1918). Another battery of pre-conceived images filled the poster accompanying the release of *One Arabian Night* (Ernst Lubitsch, 1921). Here, the pencil sketches of the film's characters, heavily Orientalized themselves, bore the following descriptive captions: "Sheik: master of the palace magnificent–lord of a hundred wives– swift to wrath;" "The Chief Eunuch: Tough is his lot –verily his is a dog's life– keeper of the hundred jealous wives in the mighty Sheik's harem;" and, "The Gates of the Harem: Strange secrets they guard, veiled lives, beautiful wives. Of living men, none but the mighty Sheik may pass their frowning portal. Intrigues, a low whistle in the night, murderings, the kiss of sword and scimitars... (*The Moving Picture World* 8 Oct. 1921)." The description reads like the paraphrase of Eugène Delacroix's painting, "*La Mort de Sardanapale*," Henri Renault's "*Exécution sans jugement sous les rois maures*," and Jean-Léon Gérôme's the "*Garde du Sérail*".

In the tradition of Western painters who fanned out throughout the Orient ransacking bazaars for props to augment their inspiration, the movies and their support services and industries went on to appropriate the Orient, offering it to the audience as packaged olfactory, gustatory, and sensual experiences. For the opening of *The Thief of Baghdad* (Raoul Walsh, 1924), the owner of Liberty Theatre, Morris Gest, saw fit to give his movie theater "a thoroughly Oriental atmosphere, with drums, ululating vocal offerings, odoriferous incense, perfume from Baghdad, magic carpets and ushers in Arabian attire, who during the intermission made a brave effort to bear cups of Turkish coffee to the women in the audience" (*The New York Times* 19 Mar. 1924).

Turkish coffee being offered to women by male ushers in immaculate uniforms was an interestingly appropriate gesture in view of the popularity of the Oriental genre with women in general and the flapper elements in particular. Some theaters went to extreme lengths in their search for ways to evoke the Orient to their audiences. For *An Arabian Knight* (Charles Swickard, 1920), the exhortation to exploit traditional imagery was not hampered by the fact that the film's male lead does not look like an Arab; indeed he was a famous Japanese actor, Sessue Hayakawa. Adept in turning a disadvantage into salable commodity, Hollywood deliberately packaged the exotism of this actor as relevant to the Arabic atmosphere. The advertisement in *The Moving Picture World* urged exhibitors: "Play up Hayakawa, and dwell on the richness of this Arabic environment. If you can build a balcony in the Arabic fashion over the entrance, you can use a muezzin to give the call to prayer and spiel for the picture. Hinge most of the sales talk on the new locale of the picture, advertising Hayakawa as an Arab (*The Moving Picture World* 25 Sept. 1920)."

The press and the industry's discourse about the Oriental genre demonstrate that the cultural verisimilitude as represented by the system of Orientalism not only supplied the films with their subject matter, but went further to help shape the content and style of the disparate discourses connecting the films to their audiences. The system of Orientalism was embracing enough to serve as a common reference to all; the audience, the film industry and the films themselves. Film reviewers in the press and particularly in the trade and fan magazines, together with the film makers and exhibitors of Oriental films, succeeded in focusing and promoting the new film genre as an offering distinct from the largely nondescript mass of films churned out by dozens of studios for the thousands of nickelodeons and picture palaces.

Genre is by definition a perceptual concept, and the silent era audiences who consumed and called for more Oriental films seemed to possess the appropriate generic framework. The fact that the label, 'Oriental genre,' was not used is wholly immaterial to the functioning of a genre. In general, during the silent period and even well afterwards, film critics and viewers were not in the habit of referring to films as belonging to clearly defined genres. Notwithstanding the absence of appellations, audiences often reacted to and entertained specific expectations with regards to specific clusters of films. The Oriental genre was no exception.

While the general contours of the Oriental genre were recognized in the late teens, it was only after the release of the popular film *The Sheik* (George Melford, 1921) that the public began to demand more of what was then called "Oriental subjects". The film industry promptly moved to meet the audiences' expectations, as evidenced by producer and studio boss, Jesse L. Lasky, who after the preview of *The Sheik* acknowledged: "I don't think I have ever made a production in which we were more constantly confronted with the realization that we simply had to satisfy the public's expectations" (*The Moving Picture World* 1 Oct. 1921: 534). Pointing to similar audience tastes a year later, *The Moving Picture World* remarked: "The public is devoting considerable of its moments for diversion to things Arabian, in reading, hearing and seeing. The Arab has attained sudden prominence and Sheiks are all over the place" (15 April. 1922). Clearly, a minor cinematic and cinema-driven "Oriental renaissance' was on the march.

As early as 1923, film critics and reviewers began to communicate with the audiences using somewhat generic references. The film, *One Stolen Night* (Robert Ensminger, 1923), was presented by one reviewer as belonging to a group of films called "the Sheik class": "Atmospherically, the story belongs to the Sheik class. The locale is Arabia and most of the scenes are on the desert with outlaw raids to furnish the melodrama" (*The Moving Picture World* 10 Feb. 1923). In the same year, there was an interesting attempt to distinguish between a genre film and a film genre, when *The Moving Picture World* remarked that *The Tents of Allah* (Charles Logue, 1923) is "an exceptionally good Sheik picture. The story is so entertaining, and the atmosphere so intriguing that it should please even where there has been a reaction against this type of attraction" (*The Moving Picture World* 10 Feb. 1923). The designation, "this type of attraction," or "Sheik picture" became "desert stuff" for another publication, *Variety*, which commented on the same film as follows: "at this late date desert stuff has had its vogue and the features with the Arabian steeds and grains of sand no longer have the appeal" (*Variety* 5 April 1923). This view, however, was not shared by many; in fact, film reviewers first began concluding that this "desert stuff" was losing its appeal as early as 1921, the year *The Sheik* was released, and kept reiterating the belief as late as 1930. Yet, these were also often forced to acknowledge the potency of the Oriental formula. For example, when in 1926 *The Son of the Sheik* (George Fitzmaurice) brought back Valentino in "a 100 per cent Sheik picture, in theme treatment and locale" (*The Moving Picture World* 7 Aug. 1926). *The New York Times* acknowledged that "when one has an excellent recipe as that of a box office attraction what use is there in violating the tradition?" (2 Aug. 1926)

The Structure of the Oriental Genre

The Oriental genre is demonstrably a rich and expansive genre. The numerous variations at the levels of plot animation and intensification, directorial emphasis, esthetics, sources, technical and commercial considerations, have all contributed to appreciable deviations and diversity within the Oriental formula. To illustrate, both *The Thief of Baghdad* (George Fitzmaurice, 1926) and *Under Two Flags* (Tod Browning, 1923) belong to the Oriental genre, perfectly fitting the definition given above; still, it is clear that the styles, characters, and plot directions of these two films are palpably dissimilar, as indeed might be expected from a fantasy and a war film. In view of such immense variations I propose to divide the Oriental genre into three categories or groups: the 'Realist-Colonialist,' the 'Psychological-Orientalist,' and the 'Fantastic'. Each category will be presented and discussed in a separate chapter; presently, a brief introduction may suffice.

1) The Realist-Colonialist Category

Major distinguishing elements of this group of films are a high degree of realism, a preponderance of action over psychological development (as is clearly indicated by the majority of the titles, see relevant chapters), and most significantly, a clear pattern of confrontation between Western and Oriental characters. The confrontation, be it over a kidnapped Western woman or some contested space, enacts the overt or implicit Western wish to conquer and rule; hence the term 'colonialist' in the label. Concerning the Western and Eastern characters, their numbers are nearly always balanced; however, while there may sometimes be more Oriental participants, it is the Western team which always initiates the better part of the action, and is always privileged with the superior moral point of view. Furthermore, because the films of this group strove to achieve some 'realism' —usually understood at the time as a combination of credible action and locations– they are usually set in the traditional Orient, where some of contemporary action-inducing conflict is never far away from the center of the films' concern (e.g., the Spanish Rif War in Morocco, the French Legionnaires in Syria and North Africa, etc).

2) The Psychological-Orientalist Category

Films of this group are also concerned with East/West confrontation; but the clash here is one of character rather than a physical one. What this group lacks in dashing physical action it makes up for in character development. Here, in lieu of one simple formula (Arabs initiate crisis/Westerners restore order) dominating the films of the first group, the plots demonstrate a degree of sophistication matching the relative depth of the animating characters. Since the films' scripts were nearly always based on well-known novels –written mostly by Westerners– this should be not be surprising. The novelists deserving of mention here are Robert Smyth Lichens, whose screen-adapted works include *Bella Donna* (E. S. Porter, 1915; George Fitzmaurice, 1923), *Barbary Sheep* (Maurice Tourneur, 1917) and *The Garden of Allah* (Colin Campbell, 1916; and Rex Ingram, 1927); and Edithe Maude Hall, whose much-awaited literary Sheiks made a swift transition to Hollywood on at least four occasions before 1930. Drawn from such works, the films of this category demonstrate a sophisticated, albeit far from balanced, approach to the Orient. True, they all take for granted the widely held assumptions about the inferiority of the East, but they do venture relatively deep into the East to give Orientals at least a measure of dimensionality. Curiously enough, though for the audiences it undoubtedly was a source of immense pleasure, the contest between Western characters and Orientals nearly always hinged on a beautiful woman, nearly always a Westerner. Unlike the frail Western maid in the realist group who hates the soul of her wicked Arab captor, the lady here is often tossed in a game of emotional and sexual brinkmanship that underscores the white male's fear of miscegenation and confirms the male-gender specificity of the Orientalist system. All throughout, the dominant theme is a time-honored one; namely, not only have Orientals lost their position of power and subsequently the claim over their territory and people, but in attempting to seduce and corrupt Western women they are also proving their moral villainy.

3) The Fantastic Category

The films of this category operate within a far-removed time and a quasi-mythical space, as in mythical Baghdad and the *Arabian Nights*. This book from which they nearly all derive, furnish them with their popular fantastic plots and the important doses of humor and laughter. Unlike the two previous categories, both the characters and the setting are entirely Oriental and both are equally essential to the story development and atmosphere. The domed Baghdad, the sultans, the wicked viziers, and the usual iconography of the East (camels, baggy trousers and robes, scimitars, and deserts) are no less important than the action, indeed they are inseparable from it.

Though not overt, the clash between East and West manifests itself in sundry subtle ways. The comic nature and escapist intent of these films notwithstanding, movies such as *The Thief of Baghdad* are not devoid of ideological statements. At the least, in reducing a geographical and ethnic reality into a no-man's-land of genies and ethereal treasures, these films enact the old Western communal wish to dissociate the Orient from the Orientals as a step to its possession. The fact that some of these films were fantastic and also enacted by children is, barring the obvious consideration of the industry's desire to cater to an all-inclusive audience, further illustration of a major tenet of Orientalism: namely, the infantilism of the East. Throughout this seemingly inoffensive category, the East is denied maturity, and the whole Oriental universe is presented as still steeped in that inchoate state of logic and behavior that universally characterizes children.

The Genre's Iconography, Plots, Characters and Setting

All narrative films involve tension and are about some sort of conflict. The centuries-old political, religious, social, moral, and intellectual conflicts embedded in the system of Orientalism stand at the core of the three categories of the Oriental genre. The ideological tug-of-war between the two hemispheres had started long before and continued well past the Crusades, had already found expression through the traditional channels of Western lore and popular imagery as well as in the elitist but influential media of drama, poetry, novel writing, painting, the scientific disciplines, and the official discourse of the church and the state. The new cinematic medium, coming at the close of a tumultuous century for non-Europeans and the beginning of another, could not hope for a better quarry of stereotypes or a more colorful and ready-made array of villains and heroes, ranging from the Elizabethan Saracen and Moor to the contemporary Legionnaire and the Paris-educated Arab prince.

There was, however, very little doubt about who would be the villain when Hollywood turned to Arab themes. The outcome or resolution of an Oriental film, whatever the category, was never an issue as the Western side always prevailed. Of the four-stage plot structure of a genre; namely, the establishment, the animation, the intensification, and the resolution (as outlined by Schatz), only the second and third permitted any some variation in the Oriental formula. The establishment phase usually celebrated the collective stance vis-à-vis the threatening "Other," and served to allay the common fear associated with the loss of control. As such, the establishment and resolution phases perform one and the same ideological function; namely, the celebration of Western identity achieved by the negation the distancing of the Oriental and his world. It could therefore be said that the plots' first and last stages were basically the people's (and culture's) gift to the film industry; while the animation and intensification phases were the film industry's technical gift to these audiences.

The plots of the Oriental genre have generally been perceived and were therefore reviewed in the trade press in a manner corresponding to the main characteristics of each category: action for the first, psychology for the second, and fantasy for the third. For *Love in the Desert* (George Melford, 1929), a film from the first group, the plot was described in *Variety* as "usual desert stuff. The young American sap, sent to Arabia to keep away from the girls, is kidnapped. He is saved by Zarah, Arabian chieftain's daughter. That promotes a war. Abdullah, vicious turbaned gangster is bumped (*Variety* 8 May 1929). The review even went on to lament the fact that the action was slowed down by the film's involvement with character and setting: "Preliminaries, introductions, overdrawn scenes and character delineation slow everything. And the hero never gets a chance to work at his job of fighting and saving anyone."

Quite differently, *Barbary Sheep* (Maurice Tourneur, 1917), from the second category, was judged by a contemporary reviewer as possessing "fascinating psychology...especially where it revealed the effect of primitive passions on the refined mentality of a modern society woman" (*Variety* 8 May 1929). *The Sheik* (George Melford, 1921) was presented as a film of relationships rather than action: "A photoplay of tempestuous love between the mad English Beauty and a bronzed Arab Chief" (*The Moving Picture World* 7 22 Oct. 1921).

On the other hand, the 'fantastic' films comprising the third category neither strive for realistic action nor exclusively seek to explain or explore relationships. It is for their technical, magical, and stereotypical aspects that most of these fantasies were appreciated; as the following commentary on *Aladdin and the Wonderful Lamp* (C. M. Franklin and S. A. Franklin, 1917) demonstrates: "The production is elaborate, several scenes having marked beauty. The magical effects demanded by the story have been supplied by the resources of the screen, no task imposed on the slave of the lamp being beyond the skill of the producer. The palace of the sultan, the scenes in the desert and the interiors of Aladdin's magic palace are all fine examples of their kind, and the atmosphere of the East is never lost" (*The Moving Picture World* 13 Oct. 1917).

While the plot lines of the genre's three categories varied markedly, all utilized the stock of characters produced by the system of Orientalism. The traditional types, such as the Sheik, the Pasha, the Sultan, the vizier, the palace guard, to name only a few, spearheaded the male side of the Oriental threat; while the sultan's wife, the dancers, the harem dwellers, and the beautiful princess represent their gender counterparts in the unending drama of Oriental intrigue, violence, and untrammeled sexuality. The Western camp was animated by such heroes as the time-honored Christian Crusader, the diplomat, the missionary, the Legionnaire, the female Western tourist, and an assortment of military characters –captains, lieutenants, sergeants, marines. Other Western characters include Egyptologists and their daughters and wives, Western hermits escaping the harsh demand of an increasingly materialist West, adventurers, treasure seekers, American journalists (on whom sometimes fell the task of rescuing maidens of their own race), female romantics, game hunters, and thrill seekers.

According to genre critic Edward Buscombe, the setting of a genre is an integral part of its "outer forms," and therefore is no less important than the "inner form," or subject matter (14). In Oriental films, the Oriental setting defines and stands as the most obvious part of the generic contract between the films and their viewers. The titles of the films themselves reflect an unmistakable foregrounding of the Oriental setting, either directly through the use of specific places, such as Baghdad, Egypt, the Sahara, or by association through the use of such words as 'Arab,' 'desert Sheik,' and 'harem.' Accordingly, from the fictional entries alone (see Filmography) the terms 'Arab' and 'desert' appear fifteen times each; twelve titles incorporate Arabic names (such as Allah, *Kismet*, Fazil), while precise geographic designations (e. g. Egypt, Morocco, Baghdad, Cairo) appear in thirteen titles. The term 'Sheik,' first appearing in the 1894 Kinetoscope shorts, *Sheik Hadj Tahar and Hadj Cherif*, enjoyed its greatest prominence or notoriety in the 1920s, appearing in no less than seven titles.

The system of Orientalism and the traditional literary discourse it engendered loaned the films the elements and details of the Oriental setting, the urban as well as the desert one. Palaces, massive walls, meandering streets, a skyline of minarets, bazaars, coffee houses and slave markets are just a few recurring urban locations, all contributing to the 'Eastness' of the East. Beyond the huge city gates lay the eternal and vast Arabian Desert; the ultimate test of endurance, a space for healing but also a virtual vortex of destruction. The desert's shifting sand and blinding sandstorms on one hand, and on the other its life sustaining oases, symbolized its dual function as a destroyer and a life giver. Some potent films of the genre tried to communicate this dual role; the least imaginative ones were content with its use as an exotic backdrop.

Not surprisingly, the native masses were rarely seen or distinguishable in the Oriental films; when they entered the films it was as an extension of the setting. In Rex Ingram's *The Arab* (1924), for example, the Oriental natives were objectified and collapsed into the stylized background, made to move in the same picturesque fashion of a palm tree under a desert breeze. A reviewer attested: "There are impressive stretches showing Arabs in white burnous seated on the hot sands in the scanty shade of a few palm trees. The sight of the great wall of striking length is compelling, as are also the scenes of low white buildings, the odd, narrow streets and the interiors where one sees the Mohammedans sipping their Turkish coffee from their tiny cups as they play chess, or pulling on their narghiles" (*The New York Times* 14 July 1924).

Sand, palm trees, coffee, narghiles, Arab dress (or in the case of the last film, the Arabo-Berber burnous) furnish the formal elements that help advance and define the action as well as reinforce the "genre-ness" of the film. Costume is as integral to the Oriental genre as to any generic regime. When Tom Mix was cast in *Arabia* (Lynn Reynolds; 1922) (a film spoofing Valentino's *The Sheik*) costuming was relied upon to dispel the effect of Mix's typecasting as an American cowboy. That perhaps was the aim of *The Moving Picture World* as it advised exhibitors that "it will be effective to treat the idea of Mix in burnous in semi-kidding style to match the general idea of the production" (*The Moving Picture World* 11 Nov. 1922: 184).

As some Oriental films moved to ossify animate objects and animate physical ones, the end result was an extremely "iconized" genre, but one that is perfectly decoded by viewers, for whom the iconography, action and theme were inextricably linked. A *Chicago Daily Tribune* critic praised *The Arab* (Rex Ingram, 1924), and in so doing lumped the people and the objects together into one colorful and complex icon: "[*The Arab*] is beautifully done, with colorful scenes of the Orient–patriarchs with long beards and flowing robes– broken walls and white stones road–mosques and temples–Turks with cruel scimitars–Bedouins on eager steeds (*The Moving Picture World* 13 Sep. 1924: 131).

As in the Orientalist system, there was no conscious desire on the part of the makers of Oriental films to humanize the Orient. The film, *The Corsair* (Frank Powell, 1914), a dramatization of Lord Byron's Oriental poem of the same name, mirrors the tendency of Orientalism to itemize and label an entire region. A review of the film remarked: "Turks, pirates, veiled ladies from harems, dancers, eunuchs and soldiers pass in kaleidoscopic disorder on the screen, and when the end comes we are mildly wondering how so much trouble could originate in such a short time (*The Moving Picture World* Aug. 1914: 708).

The whirlwind of images and types is testimony to the ability of the Western system of Orientalism to re-invent itself in Oriental films. If the audiences were not wearied by repeated exposure to it, it is because of Orientalism's status a collective cultural myth, and also because of film genres' uncanny ability to offer diversity in sameness. The next chapters will demonstrate this paradox of genres: generating diversity in sameness, or spinning few formulas into limitless colorful tales.

Chapter Five

THE ORIENTAL GENRE: REALIST-COLONIALIST FILMS

In 1921 French General Gouraud declared on the tomb of Saladin in Damascus: "Nous revoilà, Saladin!" emphatically reversing, on behalf of the West, the defeat the Europeans had suffered during the Third Crusades as well as sealing the *de facto* reality of conquest. To a great extent, realist-colonial films act out the triumphant and unconciliatory statement of the General, through the action of the Westerner heroes, be they Foreign Legionnaires, British soldiers, marines, traders, tourists or diplomats. Commenting in 1975 on the majority Western films on North Africa (and most of them belong to the realist-colonialist category), French critic Guy Hennebelle warned that their war-like mentality make them unbearable for viewing today: "La plupart d'entre eux…sont devenus des films partiellement insupportables à cause de leur racisme latent, de leur paternalisme ou de leur mentalité guerrière." (Translation: "Most of them … have become nearly unbearable to watch because of their latent racism, paternalism, and war-like mentality") (qtd. in *Le Cinema colonial* 5). Whatever the verdict today —that most of these films are racist, paternalistic and war-like, and I grant that some of these films are what Hennebelle thinks and more— the films constitute a significant portion of the Western film heritage and therefore merit public attention and scrutiny. For those outside the film discipline, discounting these texts as raw and demeaning to a people is choosing to turn away from valid cultural evidence.

In this chapter, I will introduce a few films that are most

representative of the popular plot directions of this category and the general concerns of the Oriental genre. To better seize and manage the differences and the nuances, the films belonging to this category (constituting more than the third of this study's fiction films entries) are organized into four plot types: 1) those centering on a Western female engaged in physical and/or sexual conflict with an male Arab; 2) those dealing with a Western male involved in a romantic/sexual relationship with an Oriental female; 3) those portraying some sort of conflict between a Western army and Arabs; and 4) those recounting the exploits of the Foreign Legion in Arab lands. Naturally, the types do overlap sometimes; but stopping at each one should make this analytical exercise both orderly and rewarding.

1. *Bound in Morocco:* Western Women vs. Arab Males

The following might be a fit-all summary of the action characterizing this sub-group of films: an American/European female tourist, wife or daughter of a diplomat, an Egyptologist or a businessman arrives in an Oriental setting (mostly North Africa) where she is sighted by a male Arab. The latter, may be a Sheik of a tribe, a powerful merchant, or a nondescript Bedouin, subsequently kidnaps the white female for sexual motives, ransom, or both. A Western male, who may be a soldier, a fiancé, a fellow countryman, or a co-religionist, always finally saves the kidnapped female. The intervention always results in the defeat of the Oriental male and in the romantic or conjugal union of the Western male and the rescued Western female.

The following films all recount the events, the adventures, and the narrow escapes that usually arise when a Western lady is in distress. The titles almost announce the nature of the plots: *In the Sultan's Power* (1909), *Won in the Desert* (1909), *Captured by the Bedouins* (1912), *Into the Desert* (1912), *A Prisoner of the Harem* (1912), Fire and Sword (T. Hayes Hunter, 1914), *The Arab* (Cecil B. DeMille, 1915), *The Arab's Vengeance* (1915), *Saved from the Harem* (William Melville, 1915), *A Sultana of the Desert* (1915), *Bound in Morocco* (Allan Dwan, 1917), *Flame of the Desert* (Reginald Barker, 1919), *Her Purchase Price* (Howard Hickman, 1919), *A Cafe in Cairo* (Chet Withey, 1924) and *King Cowboy* (Robert De Lacy, 1928).

Bound in Morocco (Allan Dwan, 1917) is a film involving an American male character fighting his way to the whereabouts of a young and endangered American lady. The film's beginning is explosive enough: Douglas Fairbanks (as Western male hero and rescuer) is bound to a prison wall facing a bomb with a lighted fuse which two Moroccans have just hurled at him. Fairbanks, of course, weathers this initial difficulty, and with typical aplomb he is soon seen scurrying across the Moroccan hot sands in a motorcar followed by a native policeman. As he reaches a city, he is faced by still more adventures and narrow escapes before the girl is saved. The beautiful girl (played by Pauline Curley) has been taken by a Pasha (a title given to powerful rulers of certain cities) to increase his harem. All ends well as the girl and her mother are loaded into a Ford and the three disappear into the desert amid clouds of sands. With typical Fairbanksian humor, the film ends with the title, "One Hundred Years Later" and a flash of a quiet corner of a cemetery, suggesting an obvious matrimonial union between Fairbanks and the girl.

Given the prevailing taste for Fairbanks-style adventure and swashbuckling, *Bound in Morocco*'s story and plot were bound to please. Yet, despite the immense popularity of Fairbanks, part of the appeal of the film has to be sought and attributed to the generic and broadly cultural contexts surrounding Oriental films. The following advertisement headlines clearly point out to this context: "Hopping through Morocco while the wild tribes battle/ Fairbanks acrobatics from the harem to the hot sands." Then, there was this piece of advice to the exhibitors enjoining them to anchor the film in its Oriental context: "Tell your patrons that as an American boy in Africa, Doug excels his previous records in acrobatic activities, and tell of the harem scenes and his rescue of the unfortunate maiden. Use plenty of paper and don't expect the mere name of Fairbanks to enable you to dispense with advertising" (*The Moving Picture World* 10 August 1918: 888).

To rescue the girl from the Pasha's harem, Fairbanks has to resort to a trick used again and again in Oriental films; namely, the disguise and substitution of the male hero for a woman or a servant to gain admittance to the ferociously guarded Oriental harem. Fairbanks's penetration results in his and the audience's voyeuristic feasting on a spectacle offering sensual bathing scenes, various degrees of nakedness, and, as a reviewer put it, plenty of "cooch" dancing. The harem scenes and the rescue of the unfortunate maid would become centerpieces in the majority of films about the Orient, for at least the triple attraction of polygamy, sexual titillation, and the fear of and curiosity about miscegenation.

The routing of the "wild tribes" by Fairbanks is more than an affair of agile acrobatics; it is also a matter of national, racial, psychological, and moral survival. The East, muted and unable to represent itself, repeatedly loses as it is pictured as criminal, morally decadent and war-like (the name of the fictitious city "Al-Harib" is a slight deformation of the Arabic word for war). *Bound in Morocco* did not evidently invent the images of the Oriental woman abductor and white slaver; it merely borrowed, refurbished, and enacted them. Similar re-enactments with modernized weapons and props would continue well through the twentieth century and afterward, as outrageous terrorists and harem-addicted Arabs are churned out by Hollywood and television.

Bound in Morocco, like other Fairbanks' early vehicles, also played its part in galvanizing post-war American males and society at large (perhaps comparable to the role played by Valentino with regard to the female element in American society). Fairbanks' optimism, extraordinary physique, and agile acrobatics presented the audience with, in the words of Alistair Cooke, "a beautifully deceptive act of flattery, suggesting that all that is needed to clear up the stagnation of city life, a capture by Moroccan bandits, or a Cabinet crisis in a South American republic, is the arrival of an average healthy man" (Alistair Cooke 126). This myth is also known as the American mission to save the world.

2. *The Song of Love*: Western Males vs. Oriental Women

Western literature dealing with the Orient abounds in situations where languorous Oriental courtesans and wives have turned against their cruel and swarthy Arab husbands and masters for the fulfillment and protection guaranteed by the white male. Edward Said has explained Flaubert's narration of his explicit sexual encounters with Egyptian courtesans in terms of power relationships. Echoing Said, Rana Kabbani elaborates: "Since Victorian imagination could not conceive of female eroticism divorced from female servitude; since in the core of nineteenth-century sexuality there lurked all the conflicts of power and powerlessness, wealth and poverty, mastery and slavehood, the spectacle of subject women (and boys) could not be but exciting. The western male could possess the native woman by force of his dominion over her native land; she was subjugated by his wealth, his military might, and his access to machinery. She was his colonial acquisition, but one that he pretended enjoyed his domination and would mourn his departure." (Kabbani 80-81)

The sexual exploitation of Oriental females has resulted in a redefinition of their role and identity. For ideological and scopophilic considerations, films have frequently objectified Oriental women, stripping them of their role as individuals, mothers, and nurturers and casting them as providers of sexual pleasures and entertainers of Western troops in military camps, clubs, and Kasbahs. French critic, Pierre Boulanger, enumerates some of the Arab women's occupations in these films: "Quant à leurs femmes, du moins celles que l'on voit, elles sont généralement danseuses (les Ouled-Naïl), prostituées dans quelque kasbah ou tireuses de cartes au regard insondable" (Translation: *As to their women, at least the ones we see, they are generally dancers (the Ouled Naïl), prostitutes in some Kasbah, or fortune tellers with an unfathomable look).(Le Cinema colonial* 7)

Unlike the previously discussed formula ("Western Female versus Oriental Male"), where the ending is nearly always "happy," culminating in the Western couple's living in a continuum of bliss and happiness ever after, not all the films involving Western males and native females end in marriage. Inter-racial marriages and miscegenation were rarely if ever tolerated in Western societies. Guy Hennebelle, in his introduction to his book, *Le Cinema colonial,* remarked that mixed marriages were treated negatively and deemed impossible in many early French films on North Africa. In these films, he remarked, the Moorish woman's chief engagement was reduced to "spicing up the sexual life of members of the superior race" ("épicer de temps à autre la vie sexuelle des ressortissants de la race supérieure") (9).

Oriental films made in the United States likewise retained a high degree of discomfort regarding mixed relationships. What is significant, however, is that the majority of the films belonging to this group do indeed end with marriage, or the prospect or promise thereof, overriding somehow the grip of the miscegenation taboo. I may suggest here a couple of explanations to this quite surprising loosening of a societal grip. First, the ethnic groups who lived in the United States between 1900 and 1930, and who constituted a sizable part of the motion picture audiences, were engaged with various

46

degrees of intensity and success in the process of integration and assimilation which often meant marriage across ethnic, racial, national and religious lines. This fact did not accord with the miscegenation interdiction. The second explanation may be found in the nascent star system and the special hold a few film stars exercised on the audiences as a result of their frequent film appearances. Normally, within the compass of a single year, audiences encountered a Norma Talmadge, a Theda Bara, or a Lillian Gish in a big assortment of roles; a fact capable of short-circuiting any lasting identification with a particular role, whatever the cultural and ethnic dimensions or risks. Indeed, many went to the movies primarily to see their favorite female stars in exotic or dancing garb, rather than as an Arab or a Mexican girl. In *The Song of Love* (Charles Franklin and Francis Marion, 1923) Norma Talmadge was viewed and relished first as Talmadge in various poses of semi-nudity and then perhaps as an Arab girl inciting the tribes to revolt.

The Song of Love, from the novel of Margaret Peterson entitled *Dust of Desire* (*The New York Times*, 1922), encloses a rather familiar plot, shared by the following films constituting this grouping. These are: *The Pasha's Daughter* (Thanhouser Co., 1911), *The Next In Command* (J. Searle Dawley, 1914), *The Rug Maker's Daughter* (Oscar Apfel, 1915), The Road to Love (Scott Sidney, 1916), *The Lad and the Lion* (Alfred Greene, 1917), *The Sixteenth Wife* (Charles Brabin, 1917), Eye for Eye (Albert Capellani, 1918), *The White Man's Law* (James Young, 1918), *The Song of Love* (Charles Franklin and Francis Marion, 1923), *The Forbidden Woman* (Paul L. Stein, 1927), and *Two Arabian Knights* (Lewis Milestone, 1927).

In *The Song of Love*, the owner of a gambling house in a North African French desert colony has a niece who possesses such beauty and skill as a dancer that many Arabs are drawn to her, including the fierce Arab chieftain, Ramlika. The chieftain is believed to be planning a revolt against the French, and the French commissioner in the region sends a spy, Valverde (played by Joseph Schildkraut), to gather intelligence. Feigning indifference, Valverde wins the beautiful dancer's love. When the Arabs finally revolt, the spy nearly perishes but his life is saved only because the dancer agrees to marry the Arab chieftain. In the end, as is customary in films of this group, military reinforcements arrive and the Arabs are routed. Valverde, who now realizes that he is in love, is united with the Arab dancer.

The double source of appeal in the role of a dancer did not go unnoticed by *The Moving Picture World*: "The star [Norma Talmadge] has a role which gives her good chances for effective emotional scenes and also the opportunity to appear in very scant raiment of an Oriental dancer" (19 Jan. 1924: 218). Titling its piece, "The Biskra Dancing Girl," *The New York Times* chose to emphasize the Oriental setting: "[Talmadge] appears as a tempestuous brazen Ouled Nail dancing girl in a locale scorched by Algerian desert suns (25 Feb. 1924)." (The Ouled Nail dance, from the eponymous Algerian tribe, was featured in many films of the teens and twenties, gaining some notoriety as is attested by its frequent —and unexplained— use by film reviewers and reporters). Commenting on the change of role of the highest salaried actress of the time from costume dramas to dancing girl, *The New York Times* reviewer tantalized readers with these delectable prospects: "Imagine passing in the Rivoli with a vague impression of Miss Talmadge in…voluminous skirts that jealously guard even her slender ankles from view, and suddenly beholding a startling vision of undeniable beauty, clad expensively, but not extensively".

Other thrills were duly noted; "especially where Arabs sweep on in their attack against the French garrison," and about the scenery, as the "splendid shots of desert caravans [are] silhouetted against the evening skies." Mentioned as memorable also was the scene where the Western hero feigns nonchalance to the degree of yawning as the native girl "tries to lure him with passionate glances and rolling head" (*The New York Times* 25 Feb. 1924). It is impossible not to imagine the power of a scene where the promises of love and pleasure are tantalizingly offered and refused in the style described above. The image of an Oriental female in an attitude of submission, writhing before her Western master, is sensual if not outright erotic. Literature and travel accounts of the nineteenth century have left no doubt as to the veracity of these pleasurable experiences: the East was perceived as a land of untrammeled sexuality, where the sexual act is committed without the slightest sense of guilt.

Film historians who have ignored films like *The Song of Love*, or committed them to the meaningless category of films of adventure, have not gone beyond the chases, the dagger throwing, and the heroics of the sieges and counter-attack. In this action-filled group, Western Male/Oriental female relationships are particularly significant in so far as they reinvent and reinforce the traditional treatment of women fixed by the system of Orientalism. The late realization in this film that the Western male loves the native woman is in no way a happy ending: the native girl does not attain a level of dramatic gravity until she forsakes her native suitor, and more importantly, thwarted a political rebellion of her people against the foreign invader. As previously stated, Western Medieval literature based on conflicts with the Muslim East, often wove plots which were part wishful-thinking about the defeat of the enemy, and part expression of pent-up sexual desires, all involving native women turning against their husbands, fathers, or tribe in favor of white Western knights.

The Song of Love then belongs to the Oriental genre by dint of its plot, themes, characterization, and outstanding visualization. The reviews singled out, along with the not too discreet Arab dress of the dancer, the desert caravans silhouetted against the evening, the luxurious tents, the garrisons, the dashing Arab riders, the intense desert sun, and the famous Algerian locale of Biskra (labeled by one hyperbolic reviewer 'the Monte Carlo of Africa'). As genre films often borrow and exchange motifs and images, *The Song of Love* reused some outstanding scenes of silhouetted caravans, Bedouins' attack on the Western garrison, and the Biskra locale prominent in the famous first Valentino Sheik vehicles.

3. *The Dishonored Medal*: Western Armies Confront Arabs

Early films depicting wars in the Arab lands generally remain inarticulate about the causes of the involvement, beyond the colonial motive, or leitmotif, of the "pacification" of natives. Typically, an attack from the colonized side supplies the pretext and the trigger; and the ensuing war is seen as justifiable self-defense. Expectedly, the white boys shine in battle and few of them end up elevated and romanticized in their home countries' salons or press reports. Despite the prevailing muteness about the political and moral dimensions of the conflict, it is hard not to see that the films of this category respond in one way or another to Chateaubriand's paradigm. A century ago, Chateaubriand regarded the modern Crusades in the Orient justified because they were "not only about the deliverance of the Holy Sepulcher, but more about knowing which would win on the earth, a cult [Islam] that was civilization's enemy, systematically favorable to ignorance, to despotism, to slavery, or a cult [Christianity] that had caused to reawaken in modern people the genius of a sage antiquity, and had abolished base servitudes?" (Said 172)

There were of course other more immediate realities to which the films of this category were responding. By 1912 nearly the entire non-Western world was under some form of European occupation or mandate. It was also a period which ushered in numerous movements of independence. These wars of independence or "trouble spots," whichever the perspective, sprung up all over the globe and led to sustained coverage in the press. The nascent film industry, as though on a predetermined rendezvous with modern conflicts, duly capitalized on the action and emotions these wars engendered. Filmmakers had recognized the financial attractiveness of war films as early as the American-Cuban and the Boer wars. They were no doubt encouraged in their endeavor by the colonial powers, which saw their objectives furthered by essentially cost-free propaganda. In the Arab region, trouble spots were legion and some of them have riveted the attention of the West, namely the Gordon-Kitchener British wars in the Sudan of El-Mahdi, the Italo-Libyan war, the armed resistance against the French in Algeria, and the Abdelkrim-led Riff revolt in northern Morocco. Interestingly, while some films capitalized on famous conflicts and settings; the majority resorted to the use of fictional wars in nondescript Arab settings, where the discontented Arab tribes usually supplied the casus belli for a demonstration of Western valor.

Whether they were made during a time of peace or war, the following films pitted the French or the British army against Orientals subjects: *Lost in the Sudan* (1910), *Arabian Infamy* (1912), *The Guerrillas of Algiers* (1913), *The Next in Command* (J. Searle Dawley, 1914), *The Dishonored Medal* (Christy Cabane, 1914), *The Light That Failed* (Edward José, 1916), *Eye for Eye* (Albert Capellani, 1918), *The Man Who Turned White* (Frank Frame, 1919), *The Man of Stone* (George Archaimbeaud, 1921), *Burning Sand* (George Melford, 1922) and *Fighting Love* (Nils Olaf Chrisander, 1927). These titles need to be added to the list of films involving the Foreign Legion (the subject of the next group).

Although the action in these films centers essentially on an armed conflict between Western armies and Oriental natives, the narratives are usually spiced up by romantic liaisons, stories of courage and camaraderie between the Western participants, and extensive vignettes of Arab life. As it deals with romantic liaisons, revenge and honor, *The Dishonored Medal* exemplifies the balance between action on a battlefield and tension on the love front.

Produced by Reliance Company, under the supervision of D. W. Griffith and the direction of Christy Cabane, the story of *The Dishonored Medal* revolves around the experience of the French army in colonial Algeria. French Lieutenant DuBois makes love to a beautiful native girl, Zora, whom he forsakes as he is ordered to move to another station. Before he secretly departs he gives the girl the cross of the Legion of France. When later Zora gives birth to the Lieutenant's son, an old Sheik offers refuge to the grieving mother and her son. The mother is killed in an attempt to rescue her from an Arab abductor, and her son, Al-Rabb, is raised with the Sheik's own son, Bel Kahn. Twenty years later, Dubois returns as a General to the village of Bel Kahn and Al-Rabb. One day, he sees Anitra, a young girl recently promised as wife to Bel Kahn, and forces her to his tent. Upon hearing of this outrage, the natives become furious and a state of strife begins, during which the General's command is nearly annihilated. Then, reinforcements arrive, and the Arabs are defeated. The brothers escape slaughter and find their way to DuBois' tent just as he is about to ravish the young woman. Al-Rabb plunges a dagger into the General. As he sinks, the General notices the medal of the Legion of France on the Arab's breast and realizes that retribution has been dealt to him by his own son. The son then tears the medal from his breast, tramples it, and instead of escaping, awaits the deadly arrival of the soldiers.

Reviewers received *The Dishonored Medal* warmly, commending the direction of Cabane and appreciating the Griffith touch. One reviewer picked up "the unmistakable Griffith trademark in the frequent employment of the dissolver [sic] for dimming in and out and the handling of the mobs in a highly effective battle scene." (*The Moving Picture World* May 16 1914: 942) Cabane was congratulated for the "successful simulation of the manners and customs of the Orient," and for the choice of his locale and Arab characters who, according to the reviewer, are "sufficiently characteristic to be types from that mysterious country: Brown men of the hill country, all of them, turbaned and sandaled and solemn."

Although American reviewers sometimes reflected the general American unease with European colonial practices, they rarely disputed the concept of European hegemony. This hesitation was reflected in the film: while Griffith's southern sensibilities may have led him to sanction a European despoiler of innocence, the massacre of Arabs and the final triumph of colonial justice go to reinforce the traditional position of Western moral superiority. The first to be punished and disappear is Zora, perhaps the most innocent and suffering. The retribution against the General and the death of Zora are in keeping with the prevalent fear of miscegenation, particularly as understood by D. W. Griffith.

The film industry has traditionally adopted a double standard regarding miscegenation, when dealing with ethnic types. The prohibition of inter-racial sex was strictly observed if involving a white female and a non-white male. However, a white male's sexual exploitation of a non-white female was viewed in a more permissive light. Thus, despite the fact that DuBois had committed miscegenation, he still got promoted. His second such act however brings about his destruction (It should be pointed out that this punishment is dealt to him by his son, the fruit of his first liaison). It could be argued that the punishment was intended for the criminally lustful character of the French General rather than for the common practice of the white males' rapport with non-white females. According to this reading, the title, "The Dishonored Medal," might be interpreted as follows: the General has dishonored the French medal in becoming a criminal and a liability to the empire. It could also be that the medal had been dishonored when it was initially offered to the native girl. As such, the medal represents the rape act. Here, the role of D.W. Griffith is perhaps central.

Griffith, who was skillful in appealing to an audience rooted in the ideals of prewar America, had an essentially nineteenth-century view of sex and morality, which would have pitted him against the leanings of libertine DuBois. In addition, Griffith was essentially a non-male-hero director. As a modern critic observes, "the moral dimension of his work is best revealed by the characterization of the heroine since the hero was an accessory to the plot. The focus upon woman's essential goodness and purity reflected Griffith's Southern background and sentimental Victorian temperament, but it was a concept of woman very much in vogue during the nineteenth century" (Higashi, 3). Fittingly, the character of Zora was played Miriam Cooper, whom Griffith believed represented the "perfect type of the beauty prevalent below the Mason and Dixon line" (Slide 1973:132). Thus, what a reviewer considered to be deficient acting in Cooper as she played Zora was very much the incarnation of the Griffith heroine, innocent and vulnerable beyond redemption: "The Algerian girl had about as much expression as an Egyptian mummy. When the Frenchman made love to her; when she was abandoned with her baby; when she was dying; and at all other times, she was always pretty but devoid of creating any illusion of emotion by pantomime" (*Variety* 4 May 1914). Perhaps because feminine innocence was at stake, Griffith chose to sacrifice the male hero, damning him for the sin of rape. In this case, *The Dishonored Medal* may be regarded as an original blend of Oriental discourse and Southern sensibilities.

4. The Foreign Legion Films: *Under Two Flags*

In 1915, an American reviewer gave the following romantic and widely accepted definition of the Foreign Legion: "The Foreign Legion is a military sanctuary, stationed on the edge of the desert, where men who have met with misfortune or disgrace may redeem their past by bravery and honorable service. No questions are asked and no papers are required to explain who or what they are when they make the application for membership. A man is taken for what he is and not for what he was." (*The Moving Picture World* 4 Dec. 1915: 1855)

Only the phenomenon of colonialism could have given rise to the unique institution of the Foreign Legion. Literature and cinema have played a major role in romanticizing its harsh, painful, and contradictory realities. The Legionnaire, as the films and novels of the period have presented him, is usually a bad boy, compelled to flee home, family, and country because he had committed a dishonorable act or had been chagrined by a romantic misfortune. On the sands of Arabia, where he is set loose in the hot pursuit of natives ("chasse au salopards," in the ironic words of Hennebelle) he gains redemption and rejoins his home country; misunderstanding cleared, stock raised, and honor restored. One cannot but note with Hennebelle the strange purpose of this recurring myth of redemption which leads "les rejetons de la société française en rupture de ban avec la morale bourgeoise à tenter d'obtenir leur rachat en servant " la plus grande France,' c'est-à-dire le colonialisme." (Translation: *"those rejected and banished by French society's bourgeois morality as they attempt to seek rehabilitation through serving the 'Greater France,' that is, colonialism"*). (*Le Cinéma colonial*, 8)

As a body or institution, the Legion may be viewed in metonymic relation to the collective European power, discordant and speaking in many tongues (the Legionnaires were recruited from diverse parts of Europe and North America), but united in the service of the colonial objective. That few or no questions were asked of its members parallels the mutedness surrounding European colonial ventures. Following their passage through North Africa and then back home with changed skin tone and full honor, one cannot but be reminded of Medieval knights riding back from the Holy Land to the princely courts of Europe. The checkered past of the Legionnaire and how it is bleached clean through trial by fire is the stuff out of which these films were made. It is strange how a group of bad boys fighting a bad war for a largely unknown cause can be so appealing, as exemplified by the Legion films. It is interesting to observe that some World War II films, such as Robert Aldrich's *The Dirty Dozen* (1967), have also used the technique successfully; assembling the most degenerate and unfit renegades to undertake the most dangerous missions behind German battle lines.

The story lines of the Foreign-Legion films are so similar and the variations so minor that film industry often stayed with one title, which they remade every few years. *Under Two Flags*, from the popular novel of Ouida Bergere, was remade four times before 1930; first in 1912 by Gem Company (Harry Nichols), then in 1915 by Biograph, a year later by Fox (J. Gordon Edwards), and by Universal in 1922 (Tod Browning). *The Unknown* (George Melford, 1915) was not dissimilar in its plotline to *Under Two Flags*. *Beau Geste* (Herbert Brenon, 1926) was one of the top-grossing films of 1926, succeeding in exciting a half-jaded audience at this late date. *The White Black Sheep* (Sidney Olcott, 1926), *The Four Feathers* (M. C. Cooper, 1929), and *Plastered in Paris* (Benjamin Stoloff, 1928) were directly inspired by the success of *Beau Geste* (the first two are serious melodramas while the third is a hilarious burlesque).

Although the Legion films have always used the Arab setting as both a romantic background and an arena on which redemption is gained, the increasing appeal of the Oriental genre in the twenties meant that the scope of these films would be expanded, particularly in the direction of more varied Oriental settings and exotic images and themes. Comparing the first *Under Two Flags* to many of its remakes after 1921, for example, one notices a major transfer of the action from the inside of a Western military camp to the outside of it, into the deserts and mountains where exotic characters initiate the action.

The Legion film, *Under Two Flags* (Tod Browning, 1922) incorporated many of the most popular features of the Oriental film, including a womanizing Sheik, tents, attempted rape, double identities, and primitive Bedouin life. The film begins with the arrival in Algeria of an English nobleman, compelled to leave England because he has been embroiled in some financial fraud. In Algiers he joins the Foreign Legion as a private. As he declines to give his real name, he comes to be known as Victor by all the members of the regiment. Cigarette, a half Arab, half French vivacious girl, referred to lovingly as "the daughter of the regiment" is disappointed that the Englishman does not respond to her charm, and is further aroused by the arrival of an English princess who in the past has known Victor. An Arab Sheik, Ben Ali Hammed, is also attracted to Cigarette. The latter, suspecting the Sheik is plotting against the French, goes with him to his harem to learn about the details of the scheme. In the meantime, and as a result of some machinations, Victor is convicted for treason. Cigarette begins to gather evidence to clear him of the charge. Victor is to be executed after sunset, and in a daring race to rescue him, Cigarette is followed by the Sheik and his tribe, who in turn are followed by the French cavalry. Cigarette reaches the fort in time to hurl herself in front of Victor, fatally receiving the bullets destined for him from the firing squad., Realizing that the girl has always loved him, Victor holds the dying Cigarette tenderly; his kiss upon her lips.

The role of Cigarette became popular as early as 1901, when Blanche Bates introduced it to the theater. After *The Sheik* (1921) had intensified the craze for things Arabian, Universal signed in 1022 popular actress Priscilla Dean and director Tod Browning for Ouida's story. Previously, Dean and Browning had teamed for another Oriental film, *The Virgin of Stamboul* (1920). For *Under Two Flags* the director was commended for having "taking full advantage of the stirring dramatic situations, picturesque background of Algiers, the interesting character development, and the stirring climax in the wild ride of the girl across the desert to save the man she loves" (*The Moving Picture World* 7 Oct. 1922: 505). Also noted as highly effective were the "numerous striking scenes in the streets, bazaars and cafes of the Oriental city." The film exhibitors were given assurances that the film should offer excellent possibilities, because, "in addition to containing a Sheik element, it is based on a novel which is a classic of the romantic literature, [and] has been widely read for more than a generation." Coming in the midst of a spate of Sheik films, *Variety* magazine predicted that the film "will compete with any of the more recent desert pictures and more than hold its own." (22 Sep. 1922). It was also noticed that actor John Davidson "tries hard with the eyes to make his Sheik a Valentino, and to some slight degree he succeeds in putting it over in the harem scenes with Miss Dean." One reviewer, however, feared the sad ending might not appeal to some film devotees and complained about the "over-frequent use of punctuation in the titles;" but, he added, all that was atoned for by "the sand storm scenes" (*The New York Times* 4 Oct. 1922).

The sandstorm scenes were an important aspect of the Oriental film's iconography. In 1915, *The Moving Picture World* praised Biograph's *Under Two Flags*, stating that "the sandstorm in the desert is in itself enough to distinguish the production as something out of the ordinary" (*The Moving Picture World* 3 July 1915: 78). By 1926, the sandstorm has become all but a cinematic cliché, frequently assigned by editors to the cutting room floor. Before that however, audiences loved the blind and mysterious force of the desert storm, and so did directors who often went to great lengths to produce them. Rex Ingram, the subject of the next chapter, agonized about them for days, carting heavy airplane propellers to the Algerian desert to create them, not without blinding and causing great pain to his actors and crew.

Chapter Six

REX INGRAM AND HIS NORTH-AFRICAN FILMS: IS INGRAM HOLLYWOOD'S LAWRENCE OF ARABIA?

A foremost aim of this book is the establishment and elaboration of the characteristics and confines of the Oriental genre along clear generic guidelines. It has being largely accepted that film directors are less visible in genre films since the genre's iconography and formalized structure smother individual directorial expressions. Yet, a genre approach ought to not completely disregard the contribution of a director to a genre film, particularly if his/her input significantly rearranges the pre-established generic elements of the film. Depending on each specific film, directorial influence on the Oriental genre may range from significant to no more than a slight twist on a jaded plot line meant to keep audiences interest. However, with regard to director Rex Ingram, it is safe to say that his directorial contribution to the Oriental genre was both extraordinary and far-reaching.

Rex Ingram by no means started the Oriental genre, nor did he make the genre's most famous or commercially successful films. Yet, no other American film director dedicated entire decades of his life to the making of Oriental films in authentic Oriental settings. After 1924, Ingram's life simply became inseparable from his North African films, which he completely dominated from inception to exhibition, making him thus a textbook *auteur*. This chapter will explore the effect that this extraordinary film director had on the Oriental film genre, and in the process bring him to the attention of film enthusiasts who had undeservedly ignored him for too long.

Ingram's North African Film Experience

Born Reginald Hitchcock in Dublin in 1893, Rex Ingram arrived in America in time for the nickelodeon era. He first acted for Edison and Vitagraph for a few years before directing his first film, *The Great Problem* (1916) at Universal. The subsequent colossal critical and financial success of his next films *The Four Horsemen of the Apocalypse* (1921), *The Prisoner of Zenda* (1922) and *Scaramouche* (1923) earned Ingram a place, according to film critic Tamar Lane, among the four leaders of the film industry, along with D. W. Griffith, Cecil B. DeMille, and Marshall Neilan (Koszarski 238). Emboldened by these successive money makers, he lobbied for and received permission to make *The Arab* on location in Tunisia in 1924. The film was the first in a series of others made throughout North Africa and in part in his French studios in Nice, the Victorines, acquired for him by M-G-M and later coming under his own control. The most important of these films are: *The Arab* (shot in Tunisia and released in 1924), *Mare Nostrum* (1925-26), *The Magician* (1926), *The Garden of Allah* (shot in Algeria and released in 1927), and his last film and first in sound, *Baroud* (shot in Morocco in 1932, and released in America under the colorful title, *Love in Morocco*).

The Irish newspaper that carried the notice of his birth also carried this item: "The Ultimatum to Morocco; Sultan consents to pay indemnity for the murder of Juan Trinidad" (O'Leary 10). Ingram was destined to have his fate and that of North Africa intertwined for many years. Liam O'Leary, in his excellent biography of Ingram, noted that Ingram and his brother had visited the International Exhibition at Cork in 1902, during which Ingram's first interest in the Arab world was perhaps first stirred. (O'Leary 19). In fact, it hardly had to take an international exhibition for this young man to become interested in the Orient; since nineteenth-century romantics and Europe's continuing colonial involvement in the region had created in the West what Raymond Schwab had labeled an "Oriental renaissance." When Victor Hugo was composing the *Orientales*, "the entire left-wing element of his audience was composed not of poets but painters; young people expecting Hugo to deliver them from Greco-Latin formalism" (Schwab 411). Hugo had reopened the vast Eastern vistas and legitimized the Oriental experience in art; after that, the traditional voyage to the Orient was duly made by Delacroix, Lamartine, Chateaubriand, Gautier, Nerval, Flaubert, and others. The position of the Orient for the romantics, whatever the medium of expression, was so central and indispensable that in 1840 Maxime De Camp, referring to the previous generation's mediated approach to the Orient, wrote: "To make up the *Orientales* without knowing the Orient is like making rabbit stew without the rabbit" (Schwab 411).

Furthermore, the diffusion of the popular and oft-translated *Arabian Nights*, the accessibility of Indian and Persian lore, the diverse accounts of travelers and histories about the East, and to a certain extent the translation in 1859 of the poetic work of Omar Khayyam, the *Rubaiyat*, literally made of the Orient for the romantics what Rome was for the classical Renaissance. The general pervasiveness of the East in the arts and even in the national mood during the second part of the nineteenth-century was acknowledged by none other than Rex Ingram's father, Dr. Hitchcock, a religious scholar in his own right who had published many works. Dr. Hitchcock once wrote to reassure the British public that "the sense of society may be titillated with the poisonous perfume of the *Rubaiyat* but it is not permeated by it for there is always the virile optimism of Tennyson and Browning to act as an antiseptic in stirring the hearts and kindling the enthusiasm of our people" (O'Leary 34).

Ironically, just as he would later resist the logic of Hollywood, the son, Rex Ingram, rejected the balanced rationality of Browning and fled to the perfume and lure of the East. In a letter to his aunt, dated 17 March 1915, Ingram, now a Vitagraph boy, wrote of his artistic preoccupation with Oriental themes: "I am working the finishing touches to another version of the *Rubaiyat* of Omar Khayyam – you know it– this is my first verse – I'll send you a copy when it is published. I am going to illustrate it myself.... I am going to illustrate it in a rather unique way –illustrating the underlying thought, rather than the literal verse" O'Leary 31). The letter in fact included three quatrains from the poem as well as some sketches.

Perhaps a keen sense for the exotic was behind Ingram's decision to leave the Fox studios early in his career, when his request to make a Chinese film had been denied. Shortly after moving to Universal, he was able to make two Chinese films: *Broken Fetters* and *The Flower of Doom* (1916). The eventual success of *The Four Horsemen of the Apocalypse* permitted Ingram to pursue his interest in the Orient. His immediate task was the making of *The Arab* (1924) on location in Tunis. More than a mere location for his films, North African provided a permanent home for Ingram, which he could access easily from the French Riviera where his Nice studios were located. Even after he quit making films after 1932, the Oriental city of Cairo provided temporary quarters. When he returned to California in the late thirties, the Orient accompanied him in the form of hundreds of objects d'art, sketches, sculptures, and other paraphernalia.

It is perhaps stating the obvious to say that Ingram's immersion in the East informs his Oriental films. No Western film director was more devoted, fascinated, or changed by the East as Ingram was. Arguably, if his Oriental films failed to repeat the success of his previous Hollywood productions it is because of Ingram's peculiar understanding of, and interaction with, the Orient. This reason underscores rather than contradicts the other reasons; namely, Ingram's protracted absences from Hollywood, his loosening grip on the taste and desires of American audiences, and the great changes that befell the medium of film itself, in particular the sudden and disorienting onslaught of sound.

When Ingram left the staged reality of Hollywood he substituted it not only with the make-believe reality of his Nice studio, but with another staged reality, that of colonial North Africa. For many years, North Africa had been occupied with varying degrees of intensity and pain. French colonial philosophy mandated that Algeria should become assimilated into the mother country; while Tunisia and Morocco would endure the realities of colonialism under the euphemistic "protectorate system." The French campaign of submission was referred to as "pacification" of the wild tribes; while Arab efforts of self defense and nationalism were interpreted as acts of incomprehensible defiance. When Ingram chose Nice as his headquarters and North Africa as his theater of operation, he was in a sense adopting the posture of the colonialist master. The symbolism was further reinforced by Ingram's long friendship with Lyautey, the great colonial conscience with Napoleonic visions. Ingram's novel, *The Legion Advances* (1932), a colorful and violent tale of Arab life, was dedicated to the Maréchal. The friendship reflected similar frames of mind and a developed romantic temperament. Both men, for example, professed great respect for the Islamic Orient and were fascinated by its people. However, despite the Maréchal's unrivaled knowledge of the details of the colonial territories and Ingram's avowed Oriental inclinations, neither managed to transcend their elitist European vantage point to establish a genuine rapport with Arabs and develop an understanding of their needs and aspirations.

Furthermore, Ingram's filmmaking activities and generally his movements throughout North Africa owe a great deal to the blessing and encouragement of the colonial authorities and their native allies. For instance, in order to scout locations for *Baroud*, Ingram set out on a journey throughout Morocco, armed with a safe conduct signed by French General Catroux. It was this trip to the Atlas Mountains that provided satirist Windham Lewis with the opportunity to lampoon Ingram as a "Sheik faker." In his collection, *Journey into Barbary*, Lewis called Ingram "one of the first men to fake a Sheik, an old confederate of Valentino and he had been in it at the birth of the tradition" (Lewis 93). Lewis shrewdly recognized the value of Ingram, the master filmmaker, to the colonial administration in Morocco and the French empire in general. With caustic effect, Lewis lashed out at Ingram: "From the point of view of the French Colonial Authorities....this Sheik-complex must have been fairly handy, and this "Sheik" of the Riviera certainly was afforded every facility with his vulgarization of the Berber Steppes. When he built himself a Kasbah in the Provençal Bled... they must have been rather pleased than otherwise. It would be like an annex of the Colonial Exhibition" (Lewis 93.

Inevitably, Ingram's relationship with the people of North Africa was filtered through this colonial reality. Not that he did not possess some affinity, albeit abstract, with the Arabs; his biographer believed that Ingram "felt a strange affinity with the Arab people, approving of their rather passive attitude to life, contrasting it with the rush and bustle of American habits" (O'Leary 129). In point of fact, during his long sojourn in the Arab lands, it is disputable if he hardly had any real and mutually satisfying contact with ordinary people. His friendship with the Bey of Tunis during the making of *The Arab* resulted in the latter offering him his personal jester, a dwarf by the name of Ben Mairech, who made frequent cameos in many of his films and was all along the butt of Ingram's temper. A similar paternalistic concern for the East made him adopt a Tunisian boy, Abdelkrim, who also figured besides the dwarf in his film, *Mare Nostrum*. Another Arab and an extraordinary actor, John George, had met Ingram earlier and appeared in some of his early films. This deformed young man, originally named Tufei Fatella, came from Syria to the United States in 1911 in search of his mother and sisters, who had previously settled in Nashville, Tennessee. Like the other two Arabs, George would become a characteristic feature in Ingram's films, and even appeared with Lon Chaney in the Unknown. The list of vulnerable Arabs also included Rebha, the Tunisian female dancer, whose Tunisian husband Ingram had to compensate for divorcing her before she could dance in his film, *The Garden of Allah*. The amount paid to the husband was reportedly taken from the wage of the dancer. Ingram later took Rebha to his Nice Studios, from which she was one day seen riding away on a bicycle into the French countryside, her fate forever changed. In sum, the Arab people Ingram enjoyed and with whom he was intimately involved included one dwarf, a deformed actor, a child, and a female belly dancer; a foursome characterized by deformity and extreme dependency.

A sense of romantic exaggeration also marks Ingram's acquaintance with another Arab figure, El Glaoui, the great feudal lord of the Atlas and Marrakech. El Glaoui showed great support for Ingram in the making of his last North African film, *Baroud*, supplying men, arms, horses, costumes, and protection. There was perhaps more to the relationship of Ingram with this tribal chief, other than the supply of logistic aid and props. El Glaoui wielded great power in Morocco's south, and was therefore a source of immeasurable fascination for Ingram and Western visitors and readers alike. In 1920, the Tharauds published a book in which they "picture the Great Caids [El Glaoui was perhaps the greatest] as typical representations of ancient nobility, warrior princes who carried the finest traditions of medieval chivalry into the prosaic twentieth century" (Bidwell 113). A lady novelist even reported, or perhaps invented, the legend that the name El Glaoui was derived from Goliath (Bidwell 113). Ingram's keen romantic individualism and a characteristically romantic yearning for the past brought him under the spell of this legendary native; the friend of the French and a controversial figure in the eyes of Moroccan nationalists.

Like Lyautey, the French administrator of Morocco, Ingram learned to write Arabic and took pleasure in signing his acquired Muslim name, Bib Alim Nasr El-din, in Arabic. Also, following an Orientalist tradition honored by Napoleon and Gerard De Nerval,

Ingram reportedly became a Moslem and donned the emblematic native Arab garb. News of his conversion caused a stir in Hollywood and Ingram had to explain: "For many years I have been interested in things Arabic and have always had a profound respect for Islam. I admire much in Islam as I do in Christianity and Buddhism but my sympathy for Islam is rather a question of philosophy of life than faith" (qtd. in O'Leary 176).

Ingram's conversion constituted interesting material which Ingram's publicity agent, Gabriel Costa, duly relayed to fans in the United States and elsewhere. In an article in *The Film Pictorial of London* (15 October 1932), Costa reported "Ingram's adoption of the Islamic faith and that he [Ingram] was received by Abdul-Mejid, ex-sultan of Turkey and Caliph of all Islam." Both Michael Powell, who worked under Ingram in Nice, and O'Leary, think his conversion was real. The former, however, retained a dose of unease about the conversion as late as the 1970s, when his autobiography was published: "Unfortunately Rex loved North Africa and was becoming fascinated by Mohammedanism" (Powell 162). Ingram's Islam, as all the signs indicate, was not more than skin deep, coming more from an idealized view of the life of the Bedouin than a result of a crisis of faith. When it came to religion, Ingram adopted an eclectic and comparative stance, symbolized by one of his clay statues of Christ in the arms of Buddha. His positive views about the desert nomad and his life's style, however, were genuine and seemed to grow in proportion to his increasing dislike for Hollywood and its practices. "The desert nomad," he said, "can pack all his earthly goods in a couple of camel bags. He is richer, more free and happier than the richest man in the world. In the desert all men are free and equal. Their code is the unwritten law of hospitality. Nothing can threaten this freedom, not even Bolshevism, because in threatening there is nothing material to gain; so the personal freedom of the nomad will continue indefinitely" (O'Leary 173).

Ingram's conversion to Islam did not go unnoticed by lampoonist Windham Lewis who offered this explanation: "He said he had become a Mohammedan—at least his publicity-staff interpreted his fascination for Islam and for Islamic Sensations in that way. For the public of the Sheik-fans at all events he was a follower of the Prophet. He had built himself a Berber *Timgremt* or Kasbah, upon the Riviera…. Yes, not content with living amongst sham-Sheiks, false

Palace-guards, Mokhaznis, and Viziers, for a few months every year, he actually wanted to *be* a Sheik forever" (Lewis 93).

The Kasbah Lewis refers to was Ingram's villa in Nice, which he decorated with Moorish objets d'art and a collection of paintings by Dinet, a French painter who had also given up Western ways to live as a brother among Arabs. Clearly, Ingram has carried his novel Sheik status seriously as far as his residence at Nice; where, many have observed, he was not above acting as sultan to his guests and to the Niçoise bathing girls.

Inevitably, Ingram's life-style, his publicized conversion to Islam, and in particular his unfavorable remarks about Hollywood as an enemy of artistic creation, made the people at M-G-M uneasy and the Hollywood colony in general suspicious and angry. When in 1926 M-G-M refused to renew Ingram's contract, Louella Parson, the sharp voice of the industry and the reflector of its mood, wrote in The *American* (23 July 1927): "No one can deny that the officials of M-G-M have had the patience of Job with Rex Ingram. Mr. Ingram refused point blank to make his pictures in America, although Marcus Loew pleaded with him to come to Culver City where he would have every facility and co-operation." She added: "As I remember the situation, Mr. Ingram did a lot of talking about Bourgeois America and Hollywood conditions.... My only surprise is that M-G-M did not take this stand a long time ago." (qtd. in O'Leary 169) Ingram, however, was certain he was the target of this criticism because "the Americans are sick with [him] for producing out of Hollywood. They like money to come into their country, not to leave it." (Ibid)

Ingram's North-African Films:

The Arab (1924)

Although Ingram operated within an Orientalist world-view and produced films that could be placed at the center of the Oriental genre, there is no doubt his intense, intimate, and peculiar relationship with the Orient had resulted in a vision very much his own. In large measure, this relationship was characterized by the ambiguous and shallow rapport with the common Arab, an ideological alliance with the region's colonial rulers, a fascination with local feudal lords, his conversion to Islam, his perceived status as Sheik and demigod, and a romantic predilection toward the deformed and exotic. Ingram's relationship with the Orient simply failed to connect. It is symptomatic that the myriad relationships depicted in his North African films, in particular those concerned with inter-racial love and marriage, themselves tell of a similar story of unconsummated rapports. To a large extent, the failed relationships, the cinematic as well as the personal, stand in metonymic relation to the wider and more violent colonial reality in the region. Ingram's film, *The Arab*, is an apt demonstration of this.

The Arab (1924) was probably intended to invoke the Sheik/Valentino formula, a successful and proven recipe no Oriental picture in the few following years after *The Sheik* of 1921 could afford to ignore or go against. According to one reviewer, "the picturialization of Mrs. E. M. Hull's novel, *The Sheik*, started a craze among film producers for Sahara photoplays in which the beguiling beauty of Anglo-Saxon maidens wrought havoc with handsome Arabian chieftains." (*The New York Times* 14 July 1924)

Based on the Edgar Selwyn play (first made into a film in 1914 by Lasky with Selwyn himself in the lead), the story revolves around a love relationship between a Christian missionary's daughter and the son of an Arab chief, Jamil, culminating in the latter rescuing the Christians from a massacre on the hand of the natives. Jamil (played by Ramon Novarro) likes to describe himself as "the best dragoman in the world," and is therefore proud of, and often shows, a testimonial written for him by an American which he thinks contains his praise but actually reads thus: "Jamil is the finest little liar in this country of liars, and as a dragoman he is a bunco artist." To a white girl, Mary Hilbert (played by Alice Terry, Ingram's wife), the manners of this indigenous Arab are peculiar, since his sole interest in having the Bible read to him by pretty Mary Hilbert comes from listening to the sweet voice and watching the fair face before him.

Despite saving the white girl and the Christian mission (brazenly erected by the side of a mosque, as a reviewer was able to remark) from destruction by marauding Arabs, Jamil and the girl do not unite in the customary Hollywood salute to the divinity of love and family. The ending is strategically left open; yet, the traditional attitude to miscegenation leaves no doubt that this relationship will go unconsummated. *Variety* gingerly but tellingly approached the point: "The 'happy ending' is wisely left 'open' –it is asking too much for her to dismiss the handsome noble Moslem who has saved her and her whole white family and flock, given up his indigenous rascalities for her and fallen in love with her; yet he is 'tan,' by birth and tradition, and she is white –oh, so white" (*Variety* 16 July 1924).

The romantic relationship does not mask the longstanding state of conflict between West and East; in fact it dramatizes and re-enacts it, as is further symbolized by the Christian missionaries' and the colony's attitudes and actions against the Muslim Arab tribes. *The New York Times* was able to discern the colonial drift of the film in a statement that may be taken to reflect America's post-war sense of restraint and feeling that the Europeans' involvement with the colonies is not beyond questioning: "The tale is spun around the hatred of the Mohammedans for the 'infidels,' and consequently one is surprised at the temerity of the missionary, Dr. Hilbert, in setting up the headquarters in a house contiguous to a mosque" (*The New York Times* 14 July 1924).

Made in Tunisian Gabes and Sidi Bou Said, *The Arab*'s iconography and general atmosphere responded to Maxime de Camp's previously cited injunction to the romantics to seek the real Orient for their artistic productions. As such, Ingram crammed in as much atmosphere and local color from the East as possible, commandeering, among other Oriental paraphernalia, about 800 camels and 400 horses (O'Leary 134). Reviewers approved of Ingram's insistence to go on location, as is evident from this endorsement by *Variety*: "there is a complete illusion of being there with the events. *The Arab* gives the truest impression of the great desert that this reviewer has ever enjoyed, even when in the desert himself, for Ingram is a better picker than this reviewer and a more inspired translator of symbolisms into concrete picturialization" (*Variety* 16 July 1924).

The famed American poet Carl Sandburg, also a fine critic and apologist of the new motion picture medium, was cited in *the Chicago Daily News* article, "Chicago Critics Applaud Rex Ingram's *The Arab*," as saying that "in several of its scenes [*The Arab*] delivers sketches of Arabia that are the work of genius" (qtd. in *The Moving Picture World* 13 Sep. 1924). In the same article, another Chicago critic, Bob Reel, lauded Ingram's direction: "*The Arab* is great. Of the Sheik type of photodrama it rises above its class. In the first 100 feet you are given more genuine atmosphere of Algiers (sic) than is to be found in the entire seven or eight thousand feet of any of its competitor."

Similarly, Maurine Watkins of the *Chicago Daily Tribune* was impressed by the "colorful scenes of the Orient, patriarchs with long beards and flowing robes, broken walls and white stone roads, mosques and temples, Turks with cruel scimitars, Bedouins on eager steeds." Virginia Dale's endorsement in the *Chicago Daily Journal* was spontaneous and perhaps representative of female reactions to Oriental pictures: "Once again an Arabian Knight flies over the moonlit desert, a white girl standing enthralled and the audience ready to jump out of its seat. This is Rex Ingram at his best and I would walk a mile for a camel, a hero and a lady as he presents them."

Ingram's excessive (romantic) attention to detail, his skill as a master pictorialist and his staging abilities were visible to all. Ingram's production manager in *The Garden of Allah* offers a glimpse of a meticulous master at work: "We had a set in a deserted town in the desert. The prop man shot spider webs around the interior. Rex looked at the set and asked if there could be spiders in the desert. I checked this out and there could not be. So out came the webs.... He made drawings of the sets with details of the furnishings. We had to find out just such pieces, sometimes going to Paris to rent them." (Qtd. in O'Leary 174)

Heightened attention to detail did cost Ingram precious time resources; and if he were not now independent of Hollywood, this luxury would have been certainly denied him. Often, he would spend months, and in the case of *Baroud*, even years scouting locations in North Africa. It is therefore illegitimate to ask what for Ingram came first: making films, or living in Arab lands, or filtering the Orient through his peculiar lenses.

The Garden of Allah (1927)

The Garden of Allah (1927) was indeed the type of picture many other filmmakers wanted to make, but none was more naturally or publicly drawn to it than Ingram. Frank Scully, the publicity man for the film, advanced in his book *Cross my Heart*, the theory that Ingram wanted to make The Garden because the monk in it has a bastard child (O'Leary 172). My view however is that the parallels between Ingram and the monk are legion; chief among them is the monk's repudiation of monastery life, a move which should bring to mind Ingram's grappling with the issue of faith, his abandonment of

Christianity in favor of Islam; and most importantly perhaps, a vicarious return of Ingram to the Christian fold, just as the monk returns to the vows and the monastery after the temporary lapse.

The Garden of Allah, based on the popular Hichens novel, had previously been filmed a decade earlier (in 1916) by Colin Campbell, with Helen Ware and Tom Santsci in the lead. The tale seemingly continued to fascinate, as Richard Boleslavsky later filmed it in 1936 as a sound film featuring Marlene Dietrich and Charles Boyer. The film recounts some events in the life of Boris Androvski, a rich novice who has embraced a religious career and become a monk in the Trappist monastery of Staoueley, in southern Algeria. The young monk, now Father Adrien, finds the monastic regime too severe. After being kissed by a girl whom he has saved after falling from a tree, father Adrian becomes tormented and finally decides to quit the monastery. After regaining his liberty, he becomes an elegant man of the world. Traveling in the Biskra region he helps save an English lady, Dominique, from being robbed in a native dance hall. After a period of friendship comes their marriage. Dominique is extremely religious, but somewhat eccentric as she insists on passing the honeymoon in the desert. During a sandstorm, Boris confesses his former calling to his wife and his dislike for modern civilization. Dominique recognizes that her husband is not shaped for society and concurs with his decision to return to Holy orders. As he enters the monastery for the rest of his life, the 'widowed' Dominique decides to live alone in Algeria, consoled in her solitude by a child, the fruit of her brief marriage to the monk.

The film, premiering on 2 September 1927 at the Embassy Theatre, New York, achieved some commercial success but attracted some mixed press. The beauty of the desert and the North African setting, rendered faithfully by Ingram and photographer Lee Garmes, were singled out for praise. *The Moving Picture World* believed it to be "a picture that for sheer beauty of scene has never been equaled" (3 Sep. 1927) but felt that atmosphere and pictorial qualities were achieved at the expense of character. *The New York Times* was guarded but reflected a general mood of the audience weariness: "the effect of the many desert romances that have preceded [*The Garden of Allah*] have undoubtedly made Mr. Ingram's task a very difficult one. *The Garden of Allah* is a picture which one regretfully finds to be a series of scenes which in themselves are pleasing to the eye, but which do not often engender much in the way of suspense or drama, except in individual episodes. And the characters, with the exception of Boris, are lacking in vitality" (*The New York Times* 3 Sep. 1927).

In its comprehensive review of the film, *Variety* similarly observed that the film is somehow dated in both subject matter and technique; defects feared traceable to Ingram's absence from Hollywood. Specifically, the failure is to be attributed to Ingram not keeping up with new developments in film technique and audience taste. Here are some of *Variety* explanations: "What faults *The Garden of Allah* has may either be attributed to the making or the cutting. No question that in certain passages the story becomes dull as it pauses. Running 90 minutes, there is much that the program houses will delete and which should be of advantage to the picture. At odd moments some of the photography is beautiful as regards desert scenes. Yet the sandstorm, the kick of the play, doesn't impress as much more than a flurry against the big stuff that has been hitting the screen of late. A main idea again is that possibly Ingram has been staying away from this country too long" (7 Sep. 1927).

Ingram did not seem to heed the critics' and the audiences' shifting alliances and tastes, as these were exactly the same criticisms leveled later at his last and first sound picture *Baroud*.

Baroud (or *Love in Morocco*, 1932)

Baroud was made at a time when Ingram's Nice studios had already slipped away from his control, and most importantly after his Hollywood backers had either died or ceased to be supportive (for example, Marcus Loew, the only friendly executive at MGM; Rudolph Valentino, his friend and protégé; and June Mathis, his favorite scriptwriter, all died in 1926). Therefore, financial backing for the film came from an English producer, United Artists only undertook distribution. An assortment of international actors with varying degrees of experience was used, while hordes of Moroccans supplied the needed local color. It was by then apparent that Ingram lacked confidence in native talent, a feeling which coheres with his Orientalist paternalism. After all, the Orient for Ingram was largely a palette of vivid and exotic colors to be dished out to eager Western audiences.

The plot of *Baroud*, involving the familiar love relationship between a native female and a Western male, was based on a story by

Ingram and Benno Vignay, whose novel, *Amy Jolly*, later provided the material for Von Sternberg's Morocco. A French officer falls in love with a female native, who happens to be the sister of the officer's native friend and the daughter of an Arab chief. The brother disapproves of this relationship and, as custom dictates, decides to kill his French friend. The Arab chief in the meantime comes under attack from a bandit and the French officer and the brother rally to his support. The film ends with the French lover riding off with his regiment as the native female lover bids him farewell, in a gesture reminiscent of the finale of *The Arab*.

Of the three film versions announced to be made (in English, French, and Arabic) only the English and French materialized –the significance of the omission hardly needs underscoring. The film(s) took a year to prepare and another to make, costing $1 million. For the French version, Rolland Caillaux played Ingram's part and Colette Darfeuil that of Rosita Garcia.

Baroud was released in France by Armor Films and in Britain by Ideal Films. Its reception was mixed at best. The film's international cast did hurt the film, as did Ingram's unease with the new sound technology. Reviewers invariably and rightly noted the weaknesses in characterization and the excessive concern for local color. *The New York Times* thought the film "pleasantly amateurish in its acting, juvenile in its story development and definitely charming in its creation of the Moroccan atmosphere and the dark beauty of its people as idealized by Mr. Ingram's canvas. The pastel skies, the mountains and the desert country, the narrow winding alleys of Marrakesh, the flat white houses and the Moorish civilization make a fascinating background" (*The New York Times* 20 March 1933).

Variety, on the other hand, was exasperatingly damning. Ingram, it noted, has become incorrigible in his superficial rendering of the East: "It is all Ingram. He retains his looks, but what he's actually done is to take a good old-fashioned western and transpose it to Morocco. Two tribes are warring, and in the usual way, the good tribe is surrounded in the fortress, while a messenger is dispatched for aid. The bad boys are closing in, the good boys run out of ammunition, it looks like finis. But in the distance, a blare of trumpets, a roll of drums—the marines…. Feeling throughout is that the film is merely a shell. No warmth and no fire" (21 March 1933).

And, it was Ingram himself who played the role of the French officer, in front of Rosita Garcia who played the native girl. Windham Lewis, who deemed the director-turned-actor excellent fieldwork for a psychologist, wondered with characteristically biting rhetoric, "why at this distant date from such epical events [Ingram's successful past] this wire pulling dictator should wish to take a hand himself in the sets, at the dead end of the wire, where the automatons capers–and smile out in debonair close-ups, or prance in wistful middle distance shots, for the benefit of a gum-chewing World-pit– that was difficult to see" (Lewis 94).

One ought to agree with Lewis: it is surely difficult to comprehend why the celebrated director of The Four Horsemen of the Apocalypse, (labeled once one of the four, never however outside the ten, best directors of the silent era), suddenly opted to appear in a film like *Baroud* at a time when his career was on a clear downside trend. One answer, or rather an impetus, could be his admiration for the colonial mission in general, turned into support through the adoption of the colonial uniform.

Those who came into contact with Ingram were usually struck by his colorful, yet also discordant, personality. The man who chose to stay in Europe and North Africa, away from the Hollywood that bestowed fame and power upon him, appropriated and came to exercise extraordinary princely qualities and capabilities. Ingram was a self-idealizer who was not beyond preaching what he rarely practiced. His strutting and posing throughout Morocco earned him the label of "Sheik faker". More important to comprehending his downfall is his failure to take seriously his own recipe about filmmaking. He once wrote: "There is a tendency in film production when one is striving to make something of beauty, to sacrifice, or lose sight of, story theme. In moving pictures, this is particularly dangerous…" (qtd. in Koszarski 88). In his Oriental films, Ingram did not attend to the choice of story and characterization, privileging instead photographic detail and artistic design. Moreover, although he believed that a successful director is one who enjoys a broad familiarity "with the world at large; an intimate knowledge of the races; an understanding of how people live in the countries throughout the earth," he himself was never able to perceptibly delve into the mindset, the practices, and the aspirations of his Oriental subjects. Notwithstanding his professed love and respect for the Arabs, "for they are the most sincere people in the world," as he said in an interview in 1926 (*The*

New York Times 19 Sep. 1926) the Arabs in Ingram's films emerge either as romantic oddities (dwarfs and hunchbacks), violent marauders, or lifeless shadows, as expressive and one dimensional as their spears.

In fact, in reducing the conflict between the natives and the French into the terms of Barbarians versus Civilized, in adopting a paternal and essentially Romanticist and Orientalist view, and in staging and managing the East for export, Ingram wound up caricaturing the Oriental instead of understanding him. By secluding himself in Nice and North Africa, Ingram also failed to keep track of shifting Western tastes as well as the rapid and far-reaching technical and aesthetic advances brought about by the sound film. Like Griffith, Ingram simply had become dated. *Variety*'s comment on *Baroud* sums up the failure of Ingram's Oriental mission: "Someday somebody will make a good picture of, about, or, in Morocco. This one, like its predecessors, has some beautiful scenery and costumery, with its authenticity, but that is all" (21 March 1933). Many today would agree with this feeling, deeming it applicable to past and present attempts at the cinematic representation of the Arab.

Ingram: Hollywood's "Lawrence of Arabia"?

Throughout this section, I delayed succumbing to the temptation to label Rex Ingram "the Lawrence of Arabia" of cinema. Indeed, the commonalties between Rex Ingram and T. E. Lawrence are legion; some go beyond the fact that both lived in the Orient for a considerable period of time and had significant and far-reaching contacts with its inhabitants. Curiously, Ingram's biographer does not mention whether Ingram had met Lawrence or, like so many of his contemporaries, he at least followed and admired the famed heroics and singular adventures of Lawrence of Arabia. Be that as it may, it is safe to say that Ingram could not have been oblivious to the legend of this British adventurer, particularly as cinema has done so much to boost his myth. Before David Lean's *Lawrence of Arabia* (1962), T. E. Lawrence had himself recognized the mythologizing power of film, and when the chance had come, he was eager to pose for Lowell Thomas' successful film/lecture "With Allenby in Palestine and Lawrence in Arabia" (1919-1920). Thomas' 1926 book, *With Lawrence in Arabia*, is credited with the glorification of Lawrence, but it was the film/lecture, and particularly the photography of the Arabian scenes, including a moonlit evening on the Nile, which made Lawrence, in his own words, "a kind of matinee idol." This is not surprising; between 1919 and 1923, the film/lecture was shown about four thousand times to four million people around the world (Anderegg 106).

Both Ingram and Lawrence lived in the East amongst the Arabs; and both used them for their own purposes. Both were admired and hated, both became god-like figures; neither British nor American nor Arab. Both represented the British Empire, becoming apologists and admirers of European colonialism; yet both became victims of imperialism, in the sense that none was able to transcend the political realities of the region to be able to express their intimate views or reach their individual potential. Also, both were outstanding actors, performing on a larger stage called the Orient, recycling its inhabitants, plants, and artifacts into props and spectators for their itinerary shows.

In a chapter on "Lawrence of Arabia", Michael Anderegg advances three paradoxes having marked the life of T. E. Lawrence. Of these Ingram could comfortably share two: the "Good/Bad Imperialist paradox" and "The Paradox of Self-Promotion/self-Abnegation"

With regard to the first, Lawrence loved the East, its desert nights, and its people. He longed and worked hard to lead an oppressed people out of bondage; but he also sold out the Arab cause at the Peace Conference. Worse, he could write the following about the Arabs he proclaimed to love: "for an Englishman to put himself at the disposal of a red race is to sell himself to a brute, like Swift's Houyhnhnms" (qtd. in Anderegg 107). Similarly, Ingram loved the Arabs, admired the Oriental space and its inhabitants, enjoyed the translation and worked on illustration of the Khayyam's *Rubaiyat*, made of North-Africa and Egypt a home for more than a decade, sacrificing the luxury and fame Hollywood had bestowed upon him. Yet, Ingram is also the man who treated the East as a huge bazaar, strutting across its mountains and plains with spectacular arrogance and detachment, playing master to the deformed and the weak, and allying himself to local potentates (the Bey of Tunis, the Pasha El-Glaoui in Morocco....) and to French colonial masters in North Africa, on whose behalf he was content to relay to the world pictures of exoticism, beauty and primitiveness, in lieu of championing self-determination for those he repeatedly called the "most sincere people in the world". In David Lean's *Lawrence of Arabia* (1962), Prince Feisal tells Lawrence: "the English have a great hunger for desolate places." Both Ingram and Lawrence have labored to satisfy this imperial hunger: actively in the case of Lawrence, vicariously in Ingram's case through his films and in particular while in the uniform of the French officer in the film, *Baroud*.

As to the "Paradox of Self-Promotion/self-Abnegation," Lawrence of Arabia enjoyed posing for Lowell Thomas' photographer in the flamboyant white robes of the Arabs in an attempt to consolidate his own myth. He also constructed for himself a palatial literary edifice, *The Seven Pillars of Wisdom*, where he recounted his real and imaginary exploits. Yet this demigod sometimes shunned publicity, and even chose to enlist in the Royal Tank Corps as a private under a false name. Likewise, Ingram converted to Islam admittedly on the strength of the simplicity of the Muslims, and at times donned the humble Arab dress in Rabat to pass as a native. At the same time, Ingram was indeed overpowered by a Sheik complex. An indefatigable self-promoter, he often acted as a royal or sought the company of the great, the rich and famous. The greatest highlight of Ingram's career perhaps, and his closest brush with hubris, may have been his self-imposed righteous mission to speak for, present, and represent an entire people living in a space a hundred times bigger than his native Ireland. For, in this he seemed to reiterate that opening quote to Said's *Orientalism* from Karl Marx's *The Eighteenth Brumaire of Louis Bonaparte*: "They cannot represent themselves; they must be represented."

Chapter Seven

THE ORIENTAL GENRE: THE PSYCHOLOGICAL-ORIENTALIST CATEGORY

Many Western romantics and travelers into the East have made of the expression, the "rape of the East" more than a metaphor for economic exploitation; for, in pursuit of sexual gratification the expression too often became a description of a Western male's dream-come-true. The fantastic accounts that resulted from such journeys provided exotism and titillation to a male and female readership chafing under a restrictive Victorian order. Flaubert's Egyptian journey, particularly the graphic description of his own amorous dealings with Egyptian courtesans, exemplifies these pleasurable, real or imagined, sexual trips. In film, as the examples discussed in the previous chapters demonstrate, adventurers and Legionnaires availed themselves of wives and daughters as freely as they dispensed with the lives of husbands and brothers. The grab for women continued well into this century, as former Legionnaire Jean Martin remembered, in a telling description of the sexual frenzy surrounding the "mobile" brothels set up for the French troops in Morocco. Martin recalled: "The females following the military columns were generally Mauresques; sometimes a European woman who had reached the last degree of decadence mixed with the crowd of colored whores ... [These] numbered ten or twelve, exposed to the fury of 5,000 solid young males, bubbling over with ardor and vitality.... In order to avoid bloody fights it was necessary to reserve one day for each corps: Legion, Spahis, tirailleurs.... On pay nights the guards made the clients line up in front of each tent where they patiently awaited their turn as in civilized towns and cities one lines up at a bus stop" (qtd. in Mercer 244-245).

Martin's description was avowedly in praise of this unique military institution; as such, it bespeaks complicity, even a sense of vicarious pleasure derived from the recollection of the delectable memories of rape. In the excitement of recollection, Martin's language escaped self-censorship, becoming therefore highly expressive. So, not only is the gang-rape spectacle incongruous with the triumvirate virtues of "honor, courage, and *'patrie*,'" which the Legion's romanticizers advanced as the philosophical bedrock of the Legion's mission, but the use of "bus stop" reveals, in addition to recurrence and guaranteed availability, an extremely unbalanced relationship between the Western male and the Oriental female victims. More significant, and somewhat pertinent to the discussion below, is the characterization of the odd European woman who chanced to throw her lot with the herd of native women. Clearly, the passage stresses, only extreme decadence explains a European woman's lapse into what is by definition the Oriental woman's duty and fate.

Bella Donna and *Barbary Sheep*: The Thrills and Risks of Miscegenation

A the Western male saw in the Orient his sexual animus, the Western woman was made to undergo a parallel journey into sexual oppression and devaluation, accompanied by the opposite wave of protectionism and idealism. To a great extent, this protectionism explains the solidification of the taboo of miscegenation in Western societies. In film, the fear of miscegenation would engender a systematic vilification of the non-white male in general, an anxiety about inter-racial sex, a concomitant mistrust of colored, and a sexual craving of non-white females by white males. The angst-ridden situation would give rise to a set of different standards of sexual do's and don'ts; in perfect harmony with the Western patriarchal culture, as well as Orientalism, itself "an exclusively male province" (Said 207). Film, a cultural vector and a reflector of social moods, had to abide by these restrictions.

With regard to Oriental films in general, one may discern three attitudes. First, inter-racial sex between a white male and a non-white female is permissible (the better part of the Realist-Colonialist films discussed in the two previous chapters enact this trend). Second, inter-racial sex between a white female and a non-white male is prohibited (the films treated in this chapter show various degrees and forms of this prohibition). Third, inter-racial sex, or the prospects of it, is permissible on the condition that the ending brings the disclosure that the non-white male partner is actually white and/or Christian (the Sheik films to be discussed later are situated within this pleasurable seesaw of sexual promise and prohibition).

In addition to these three patterns, there exist, at least, three corresponding variations. First, sex between Western males and non-white women, although permissible under the industry's conventions, may at times engender trouble and disaster (for instance, the case of *The Dishonored Medal*, discussed earlier). Second, interracial sex between a white female and a non-white male may be shown and treated as long as the end of it is total destruction and death (*Bella Donna*, discussed below is a poignant demonstration). This variation is rare but the very powerful lesson it imparts goes to reinforce the taboo of miscegenation. Third, inter-racial romance and the possibility of sexual contact between a white female and a non-white male are allowed; yet this permission usually turns out to be a mere ploy, the purpose of which is the vilification and eventual destruction of non-white males by their white counterparts (*Barbary Sheep*, treated below is an example). The above variations in the end all serve the societal taboo of inter-racial sex; thus, by rebutting all sorts of attempts at encircling the interdiction they forcefully remind everyone of the inherent dangers attendant on any possible infringement.

The above standards and variations on a single sexual theme cut across all Oriental films involving contacts between Westerners and Orientals. What distinguishes the films of the psychological category from other Oriental films is that the sexual interest in the former accounts for the entire psychological interest and therefore constitutes the centerpiece of the drama. The steady development of the inter-racial sex theme and, most importantly, the forceful enactment of the interdiction become for that reason more culturally significant and psychologically complex than the simple statement of prohibition present at the endings of the realist-colonialist films.

Furthermore, since the love interest between Westerners and Orientals constitutes the main burden of these films, the psychological and cultural dimensions of each camp are usually extensively explored and more subtly delineated. However, the forcefulness of the statement against inter-racial sex notwithstanding, the nature of the film medium as a complex cultural text speaking in many codes and sub-codes often made it possible for some films to take culturally significant detours. Thanks in part to the visual, iconic, diegetic and extra-diegetic elements, these films were able to sometimes subvert the traditional codes of the Hollywood film industry and of the wider dominant culture (for more on this point, refer to the discussion of Sheik/Valentino below).

Case Study: *Bella Donna* (1915) and *Barbary Sheep* (1917)

In the tradition of Orientalist mistrust, both *Bella Donna* (E. S. Porter, 1915) and *Barbary Sheep* (Maurice Tourneur, 1917) enact the curse and fear of miscegenation. Importantly also, both are based on popular novels by Robert Smythe Hichens, who, together with novelist Edithe Maude Hull, indefatigably churned out dozens of tales about the Orient and its extraordinary but false romance. It was this huge captive readership of these romances which Hollywood duly exploited as a pre-sold market for its frequent Oriental productions.

The title character, Bella Donna, has been an enduring presence in American stage and film. The Russian-born actress Nazimova first created it on Broadway in 1912. In film, the role first went to Pauline Frederick in the E. S. Porter's version of 1915 (the one discussed here), and Paula Negri in George Fitzmaurice's in 1923, both versions produced by the Lasky Company.

Bella Donna relates the exploits of its main character, Bella Donna; a beautiful English adventurer who goes to Egypt with her husband, Nigel Armine. There in Egypt, the English lady falls quickly and deeply in love with a handsome native, Baroudi. A clandestine relationship quickly develops and intensifies to the point that the Egyptian lover suggests to Bella Donna that she should poison her husband. This she immediately begins to do by placing small doses of sugar of lead in his coffee. The husband's condition soon worsens as a result the poisoning and, and just as she is beginning to foresee her immediate release, Dr. Isaakson, an old friend of her husband and an enemy of Donna, arrives and discovers the foul play. Dr. Isaakson immediately denounces her to her husband, who, unbelieving, angrily orders him out of the house. Later, when the husband tries innocently to explain to Donna what has transpired between him and Dr. Isaakson, the wife loses her temper and pours on his astonished head a barrage of abuse, culminating in a decision to leave him for Baroudi. When she arrives at her lover's, Donna is shocked and overpowered by his statement that she is too dangerous a toy for him. With the door closed upon her, she falters back to her husband's but is met by her enemy, Dr. Isaakson, who in turn shuts the door in her face. With everything gone, she wanders into the desert. The last pictures show her body in the sand, followed by cut-in of a jackal, suggesting the ultimate ignoble disposal of her carcass.

Despite the film's unmistakable treatment of the taboos of adultery and miscegenation, the reviews of the period went to great lengths to avoid reference to the unambiguous sexual content of the film. This they did through trivializing, glossing over, or simply distorting the message of the film. For example, *Variety* believed that "women will be especially interested in this photoplay, not only for its intrinsic merit, but by reason of the vast quantity of dresses which Miss Frederick is called upon to wear. She looked most enticing in Egyptian garb" (19 Nov. 1915). George Blaisdell of *The Moving Picture World* was not distracted by the star's costumes, but his pedestrian morality was rather lame: "It [*Bella Donna*] is the straight tale of a woman who saw only herself, who has eye for no one who stands in the way of her ambition, who hesitates not to sacrifice her best friend, her husband, when she thinks her fortunes will be furthered by attaching herself to the Egyptian Baroudi (20 Nov. 1915).

Some reviewers have inadequately interpreted *Bella Donna*'s interest in Baroudi as blind pursuit of wealth, power, and luxury. Blaisdell, however, was forced to obliquely refer to the sexual nature of the drama, grudgingly pointing out to the fascination the Oriental Baroudi exercised on this Western woman: "Mr. L'Estrange is Baroudi, the Egyptian, one of whose chief fascination for women is said to be his direct, brusque, even brutal manner of manifesting his attention. Baroudi and Bella Donna have the same code of morals..." (*The Moving Picture World* 20 Nov. 1915). The circumspect reviews, however, were often belied by the public's very enthusiastic reception of the film. A reviewer attested: "There was pronounced applause from a great house at the Strand Monday afternoon at the conclusion of *Bella Donna* –by no means an every-day occurrence. Three thousand people by their deep silence attested the dramatic quality of the Hichens-Fagan story...." (ibid)

Although some reviews did not directly blame the tragic fate of the heroine on Baroudi, he, and through him perhaps the entire East, emerged battered. Not only is Baroudi a rascal, a liar, and a coward; but the idea of the romantic opportunities customarily associated with the Orient are proven to be dangerously false and downright destructive. In finally committing Bella Donna's body to the desert to be fed upon by jackals, the film is in fact forcefully rebutting the enduring romantic image of the Arabian moon-washed desert as a space for romance, freedom, and mystery. Here, the desert instead spells perdition. In other words, by allying herself with a native male in defiance of all the dictates of traditional morality, Bella Donna is not after all dissimilar, in the Western perspective, to Jean Martin's European woman who had reached so low a degree of decadence when she mixes with the crowd of colored whores. There is no doubt, therefore, that the deep silence of three thousand people referred to above was wrought more by the myriad psychological and social contradictions inherent in the issue of miscegenation than by a combination of exotic dress and a facile interest in crime and punishment.

The next film, *Barbary Sheep* (based on the Hichens' novel of the same title) treats of a similar story. Lady Wyverne, or Kitty, grows bored and restless with her placid English countryside life and a very prosaic husband. As she listens to the stories about the Orient from a family friend, she pictures the desert as a land of mystery and magic, and soon develops a strong desire to go to the desert. Appealing to her husband's love for hunting (and stalking Barbary sheep), she prevails upon him to take her to Algeria. Immediately after she arrives there, Kitty begins to find adventure. During a dinner, she catches the admiring gaze of a handsome Arab chieftain, Benchalaal. That night, before she goes to bed, she wanders onto the balcony to enjoy the moonlight. There, in the courtyard below, she sees Benchalaal, who, sensing her fascination, begins a desert love song: "Oh, that my blood were water, thou athirst,/ And thou and I far in the desert land,/ How would I shed it gladly, if but first/ It touched thy lips, before it reached the sand."

Enchanted, Kitty allows the Arab to show her the moonlight-washed desert. As they are walking, they meet an old man who has gone mad with grief over the murder of his only daughter, strangled apparently for a diamond necklace she wore. That night, Benchalaal gentlemanly escorts her back to her hotel. The following morning, the grief-stricken old man discovers that Benchalaal is the murderer of his daughter, and from that moment he begins to stalk him. Benchalaal arranges for another tryst with Kitty, and for that he bribes a guide to persuade Sir Claude to spend the night hunting in a distant village. Kitty is now gnawed by incessant temptations; as, in the words of reviewer Louis Reeves Harrison, "the conflict between her civilized nature and her primitive passions grows more intense" (*The Moving Picture World* 29 Sep. 1917). After a brief moment of hesitation, the "primitive passions" prevail. Serenaded by another desert song, she goes into the desert with the Arab, a diamond necklace around her neck.

In the meantime, Sir Claude is told of Benchalaal's bragging about his conquest of French officers' wives. Suspicious and increasingly uneasy, Sir Claude decides to return home. On his way back, he nearly surprises the wife and her Arab companion, but the two quickly huddle behind a rock. Back in the hotel, Sir Claude notices the empty bed but retires to his bed. The following evening, Kitty fights her desire for the Arab; yet again she is unable to get rid of her fantasies and goes with him into the desert. As the Arab starts to make advances towards her, she recoils; then, the Arab goes for the diamond necklace around her neck. At this moment, Sir Claude, who has been watching from the cliffs above, aims his rifle at the Arab, then at his wife, unable to decide whom to shoot first. However, when he sees Kitty repulsing the attacker, he senses that there is still some love for him. Before he can switch his aim to the Arab, the crazed old man who has been seeking revenge leaps onto Benchalaal's back and stabs him to death. Sir Claude rushes down to take Kitty in his arms for the predictable happy but unconvincing ending.

The reviews of *Barbary Sheep*, like those of *Bella Donna*, were evasive, more so this time about the degree of the sexual involvement than about the sexual nature of the relationship between Kitty and the Arab. A reviewer from *Variety* was a trifle over-confident about what had transpired between the Western lady and her Algerian friend: "The story is of the wife of a British sportsman, the chap who neglects his wife for the rod and the gun. A trip to Algiers results in her infatuation with an Arabian chieftain. Nothing happens, but she treads dangerous grounds" (*Variety* 14 Sep. 1917). The conclusion of Reeves Harrison of *The Moving Picture World* is also remarkable for its protectionism and the choice of the blame target. The film, for him, is about the "inner struggle of the civilized woman with the fragmentary remains of barbarous instincts still lingering in her soul," and this, he went on to reassure, "is very well done in a ladylike way" (19 Sep. 1917).

How much of Kitty's momentary lapse into the clutches of primitive passions was deliberate, and how much of it was precipitated by the lethargy of her husband, are questions clouded further by the film's insistence on incriminating the Arab and completely absolving the English lady. It seems the film's ending had to be forced to toe the acceptable limits set by the sensors, resulting in a palpably artificial and ludicrous denouement reminiscent of the ending of the famous *The Sheik* (see the film's analysis below). The tempering did not go unnoticed at the time, and Director Maurice Tourneur, although praised for his direction, was singled out for the blame: "Maurice Tourneur deserves high commendation for his work. It is to be deplored, however, that he could not attain something with more zip in it for the last scene rather than the conventional ending. The play is strong enough throughout to deserve something more effective at its conclusion." (*The Moving Picture World* 19 Sep. 1917)

This unconvincing but happy ending stands in sharp contrast to the distressing but more convincing fate of *Bella Donna*. One might find some explanations for the two films' oscillation between salvation for one heroine and utter damnation for the other. One difference could be sought in the fact that, with regards to Kitty, the sexual act has not been consummated (diegetically at least). Many in society understood sexual intercourse with a non-white male native as a point of no return –and Hollywood had to agree. While both heroines are technically guilty, Lady Wyverne finds herself absolved from all charges on the grounds that she is acting under the force of the remnants of a primitive psychology. It is interesting to note that this "call of the wild" first emerges as a result of hearing about the Orient in her native England, but intensifies and becomes irresistible as she arrives in North Africa. Now that the "barbarous instincts" are at home, as it were, it is too late or of little use to try to suppress them. In this regard, the happy ending is an acknowledgment that Sir

Claude is as guilty as anyone else in coming to hunt Barbary sheep in the East, not heeding the traditional Orientalist wisdom that classifies Arab land as a treacherous and pathologically over-sexed world.

As in all films from this category, the dramatic tension arises not from some dashing villain soon to be overpowered by a charismatic Western hero, but from a carefully arraigned opposition of imagination and reality; the first represented by the Western female participants, the second as defined and instituted by the male Western hero. It is interesting to observe that Orient in these films is initially portrayed positively, either in the form of a romantic and charming male or as an idyllic and invigorating setting. The tension develops and intensifies only with the discovery, usually by a Western male and almost always narratively unconvincing, that what the hapless Western females have believed to be romantic males are in fact cowardly liars (the Egyptian Mahmoud) or murderous thieves (Benchalaal). Obviously, with such discoveries come the collapse of the entire edifice established by women's imagination and their experience of the Orient, and inevitably the realignment of their perspective along conventional Orientalist views.

Because the Western female in the Oriental film is either physically destroyed or ideologically absorbed, she invariably loses. One might advance that the subjugation of the white female by the Western male in many ways parallels the supremacy of the West over the East. It may therefore be argued that the sexual leaning of the Western female toward the Arab male is a gesture of sympathy for a fellow-oppressed, and as such an act of sabotage on the male-centered edifice of mistrust and hate towards the Oriental. When Sir Claude points his gun at both his wife and the Arab lover, the two are physically and morally placed on the same footing in the face of his impending aggression. The twist in the plot that allows the woman reprieve and forgiveness from the husband –and by extension society–, while at the same time condemning the Arab lover to death, comes out poorly patched onto a hitherto logical and homogeneous thematic and narrative progression. Through the sub-plot of the extra-diegetic murder and robbery of an old man's daughter, the film tries to sidetrack the issue of sexual desire by incriminating the Arab male and interpreting for him the object of desire: Kitty's diamond necklace. The attempt is not however entirely successful, for the violent ravishment of the diamond necklace gracing the alabaster neck of Lady Wyverne connotes sexual aggression and rape –another necklace was the object of the Arab's murder of a virginal native. Lady Wyverne's final efforts to disentangle herself from the sexual assault/robbery have been unconvincingly interpreted by the film as remaining love for the husband. This unlikely elaboration, avoiding a frontal treatment of the explosive theme of miscegenation, was surely intended to placate the censor. *Bella Donna*, however, benefited from no such forgiveness; indeed the film turns her into a moral and ideological *persona non grata* through the constant harping on her greed and lust, which have led to her committing the final heinous act of miscegenation. The severe punishment was, in the view of society, measured and justified; because, by slowly poisoning her husband with drops of lead, she was in a sense fouling up his blood, in the same manner that miscegenation is a contamination of racial purity.

The Positive Orient: Neutral Film Arabs

One is tempted to write off Hollywood's portrayal of minorities and ethnic characters as one dark, monolithic blanket without a single motif for variation. However, to accept this as true –and there is ample evidence to support this– and still go on reading about or studying so called "image studies" is tantamount to protracted self-flagellation. Fortunately, and perhaps problematically, Hollywood representations were frequently more varied and nuanced than believed. Exceptions or slips, the fact remains that a number of film texts have gone against the dominant trend dehumanizing the ethnic other; and therein reside their significance and hidden force.

For some examples of positive filmic texts, we may cite the some titles, all made between 1912 and 1914. Although few in number, they are exceptional for their balanced, intelligent, and sensitive treatment of the Arab and Oriental themes. To illustrate this idea, here is a brief review of the following films: *An Arabian Tragedy* (1912), *Fatima* (1912), *The Moorish Bride*, (1912) *Tragedy of the Desert* (1912), and *A Princess of the Desert* (1914).

In An Arabian Tragedy, an Arab by the name of Ayub Kashif becomes embittered toward his wife, Fatima, because their union has been childless. He eventually divorces her and marries her slave. Fatima's love for her husband is so great that when she hears the news he has a child from the slave, she writes to him asking that she becomes the slave of her former slave. Ayub refuses. On one of his trading trips in a caravan across the desert some time later, the husband is smitten by a disease, and, according to custom, he is left to die in the desert. In her dreams, Fatima sees that Ayub is dying. Haunted by this vision, she decides to go to his wife and asks her to rescue her husband. The wife laughs indifferently. Fatima then takes some slaves with her and goes on an exhausting journey across the hot desert where she finds her former husband digging his own grave. Realizing how much she loves him, the sick husband asks forgiveness and dies in Fatima's arms.

Technically, the film belongs to the early teens, taking full advantage of the dream as an editing and narrative technique used frequently after Edwin S. Porter introduced it to great effect in his 1906 film, *The Dream of a Rarebit Fiend*. Unlike the majority of the films in this chapter, the action is entirely carried through by Oriental characters developing in an Oriental setting; but, like all Oriental films, it is supported by the usual iconography of the genre: camels, desert, slaves, and a strong patriarchal order. As the title indicates, the tale is a tragic one, involving the universal emotions of love, treachery, repentance, and death. The Oriental setting could be easily interchangeable with another setting, being less a value-laden space than a viable arena for action. In fact, similar denouements where husbands are finally faced with their wrong decisions –having run away with destructive vamps or leaving the virginal small town sweetheart in favor of the rich but faithless city girl– were as common in the teens as they are now in Turkish or Mexican soaps. The story of An Arabian Tragedy was certainly a fresh twist on a perennial formula, pitting the two powerful instincts of love/desire and family against each other. In this instance, the harsh desert provided the test for love to come out triumphant. Again, the desert plays its dual role of life and death provider, destroying the flesh but allowing a wellspring of love to gush out from its barren sands.

Love, betrayal, and death are also the subject of another Kalem film, *Tragedy of the Desert* (1912). In this film, Dr. Franklin Cochran is a European doctor practicing in Luxor, Egypt. His wife, Miriam, is attracted to an Oriental diplomat. Seeing that his wife is neglecting him, Dr. Cochran decides to leave her after generously providing for her in a will. He then buys a camel and rides into the desert. The camel takes him to an oasis, where he is rescued from exhaustion and taken care of by Bedouins. He later adopts Islam and falls in love with an Egyptian girl, Zenab, whom he later marries. The two live happily ever after, until Miriam and a group of tourists come upon the oasis. Recognizing her former husband, Miriam implores him to go back with her but the doctor refuses. Zenab sees the two talking and, thinking that her husband is betraying her with the woman, she commits suicide. The doctor is overpowered with sorrow, and kneeling at the edge of his dead and faithful wife, he cries in supplication: "Allah preserve us, for we are but the Dust of the Desert."

Tragedy of the Desert is one of about a dozen narrative and documentary Oriental films made by Kalem Company in 1912. These were the outcome of a trip the Kalem players had made to Palestine and Egypt, and judging from the present and previous film, the treatment of Oriental subjects is markedly positive (is it because the players had close and fulfilling contacts with Easterners during their trip?). There is no doubt that, while watching the film, the audience' sympathy was with the wronged but now blessed and transformed Dr. Cochran and his native wife, and not with the materialistic and faithless European wife. The traditional East/West polarities have been dramatically and sensitively used to describe the increasing alienation and estrangement between the doctor and his first wife. The desert marks the end of one existence and the beginning of another, the death of old love and the birth of a new one. It also serves as a barrier between an old material world and a new spiritual beginning. Yet, once the barrier is crossed disaster ensues. The ending is truly original: unlike classical tragedies where the hero is forced to blaspheme and call the cosmic order into question, the now Muslim Dr. Cochran falls back on Oriental resignation and religious stoicism. The return-to-dust ending has Christian as well as Muslim overtones, bringing together the two faiths into a rare and positive synthesis as a counter-balance to the nihilistic Greco-Latin tragic finality.

Love which transcends religious enmities between Christians and Muslims is part of the concern of another film, *Moorish Bride*. Clare, the daughter of a rich Moorish merchant has two suitors: Tuzani, a Moor; and Mendoza, a Spaniard. The girl chooses the Moor and the Spaniard vows vengeance. Days pass, and the Spanish soldiers retake and sack the town where Clare and her father live. The father and daughter fall into the hand of the cruel Spaniard, Mendoza, and when

Tuzani secretly tries to get into the camp to rescue Clare he is captured. At the end of the film, the hapless Arab lovers are brought before the Christian Commanding General, John of Asturia, who, touched by their story, graciously liberates them.

It is rare in an Oriental film that a native woman is allowed to choose a native in preference of a Christian suitor; the traditional formula being that the Christian usually wins the native girl and, together, they set out to thwart the opposed forces represented by the family, the tribe, or the country. Here, surprisingly, love has been allowed to play its course irrespective of racial might, taboo, or artistic conventions.

Released by Cines Company in the same month as *The Moorish Bride*, *Fatima* (1912) offers a uniquely Oriental story of love and sacrifice. The narrative, which has the feel of an Oriental folk tale, involves the time-honored formula of two brothers in love with the same girl. Malik, a powerful magistrate, is betrothed to Fatima, a beautiful girl living in a distant land. Malik asks his younger brother, Omar, to bring Fatima to him. During the journey, Fatima becomes strongly infatuated with the handsome Omar. Although he returns her admiration he is faithful to his trust and delivers her safely to his brother. Omar confides his hopeless love to his mother, who in turns informs Fatima, much to her happiness. As time passes, Malik tries to win Fatima's love with gifts and attention, but realizing he cannot win her love, turns her to his young brother, the man of her choice.

The Oriental participants in *Fatima* share little with the typical Oriental individuals animating most Oriental films in this study. Instead of a polygamous, sensual and cruel magistrate, the film presents a respectful and respecting individual whom emotional setbacks do not cause him to behave irrationally. His brother also shows enough honor and self-restraint to retain audience sympathy. Fatima, on the other hand, is not the harem dweller typically pictured for Western gaze. There are no secret musings, no dangerous trysts, no fatal potions, and no hidden daggers; only passionate love trusted to Oriental resignation for the most appropriate moment of requital.

The few films discussed above are extraordinary on more than one account. They show a positive treatment of the Arab and the Oriental settings, possess a sensitive style, and avoid the stereotypical and the racially and culturally derogatory. The films also give rise to some questions. Why did these films forsake the traditional unbalanced Orientalist treatment of the Orient in favor of a less ideologically motivated, more neutral treatment of the Arab and his world? What motivated the choice of the Oriental setting and the Oriental characters to discuss universal virtues and emotions such as love, faithfulness, honor, and pain? Finally and most importantly, why did films of similar subject matter and style suddenly cease to be made after 1914?

At the outset, it should be reiterated that the traditional view of the Orient, a legacy of centuries of coexistence, mistrust and conflict, has always contained a streak of positive feelings towards the Orient. After all, the religions that fueled the antagonism and kept it alive for so long had began and propagated from virtually the same geographical location among the same peoples. The Muslims' ascendance to power in the Middle-Ages, evident in marked economic, cultural and technological superiority, caused the West to sometimes assume an attitude of wonderment and respect to things Islamic and Oriental. European travelers usually recounted stories of luxury, civility, and prosperity of Oriental cities such as Cairo, Damascus, or Baghdad. I had previously noted here the degree of ambivalence in the attitude of Western Crusaders towards the Muslims and their culture. This ambivalence is exemplified by Dante's total condemnation of the Prophet on the one hand, and an acceptance and embracing of Saladin and some Muslim philosophers as redeemable and essentially virtuous on the other. Furthermore, the Romantic Movement's involvement with the Orient, despite the eventual exploitation, would not have been possible without a high degree of fascination with the positive experiences it could provide. Even the imperialistic intentions towards the Orient (Napoleon's, for example) revealed a sense of awe about it, at least at its golden and prosperous past. Finally, the wide circulation of the translated *Arabian Nights*, in its integral form or in bowdlerized editions for children, had all but created a positive and empathetic attitude towards the magical Orient. In sum, due to all the above, there never ceased to exist, side by side with the traditional and largely negative perspective about the Orient, a positive and respectful attitude to what many Westerners continued to consider as sacred lands.

Finally, even in the most negative Oriental film, a degree of fascination was always present, if not in the Oriental characters, at least through the exotic settings and the iconography. In the 1920s, due to the interplay of such factors as the sophistication of the Oriental genre, the significant change in the mood of post-war American society, the female demographics in the composition of the audience, and the consolidation of the star system, it was even possible for Arab characters to outgrow their negative and one-dimensional attributes to begin to reflect the ambiguous and sometimes positive attitudes towards the Orient. This ambiguity was perfectly served by the ambivalent figure of the twenties' most celebrated star: Rudolph Valentino. The adulation reserved to his Sheik persona, as will be detailed later, is in great part an illustration of the continuance of the positive streak in an overwhelmingly tumultuous and largely negative West/East relationship.

Chapter Eight

VALENTINO AND THE SHEIK FILMS: THE ARAB
AS ROGUE SUPERSTAR

The Sheik (1921) did not start the Oriental genre, nor did it single-handedly generate the craze for things and themes Arabian in evidence during most of the 1920s. However, the manner in which this film has organized and deployed the fundamental elements of the Oriental genre has made of it not only an immense screen success but also a true social event. French film director and critic, François Truffaut, once aptly remarked: "When a film achieves a certain success, it becomes a sociological event" (Truffaut 100). *The Sheik* (George Melford, 1921) and *The Son of the Sheik* (George Fitzmaurice, 1926), both Valentinian vehicles, were by all standards huge and resounding successes.

The Sheik (1921)

Few people, not even the film makers themselves, could have anticipated the spectacular success of *The Sheik*. Surely, the film intended and set out to recapture some of the palpable effect that Edythe Maude Hull's Oriental romance had generated within the increasingly powerful female readership. Hull has claimed that her eponymous novel was written in India for the purpose of her own relaxation while her husband was in the war. It seems the desire for this type of relaxation was a collective one; as the exoticism of the book and her inscription in it of her own views about the role of men and women heightened the overall fascination with the Orient as a space where suppressed sexual desires may roam unchecked and even be fulfilled.

Paramount, the production company, shrewdly recognized the psychological impact of Hull's book on women. Specifically, it set out to exploit the female readership, and the flapper element in it, as a pre-sold audience (the book circulation had been in the hundreds of thousands), as is evident from *The Moving Picture World* cover advertisements presenting the film as the much-awaited picturialization of the novel: "They can't print the book fast enough for the demand. It's the big conversational topic of the year. Everyone has read it or heard of it or wanted to borrow it or discussed it or wanted to read it or hid it or wondered when it would be made into a picture..." (6 Nov. 1921). A week after its release, *The Sheik* was already a record-setting picture. According to Paramount, 112, 625 people saw *The Sheik* in New York in one week; that is 14, 912 more than the record audience for Cecil B. DeMille's *The Affairs of Anatol* and 22, 625 more than the attendance to the famous Dempsey-Carpentier fight. The record, the company claimed, had never been equaled in a single city in all the history of entertainment. (*The Moving Picture World* 26 Nov. 1921)

The Sheik is an avowedly Oriental picture. Its opening title promptly places the viewer in the exotic atmosphere of the Orient: "In this world of peace and flame lies a palm garden of the Sahara –a blessed oasis of the sand." The scene is a marriage market in Biskra, Algeria, where wives are bought by wealthy men. In this gateway to the desert, the English Diana Mayo gives a dance party to celebrate her farewell to Biskra, because the following day, she will travel through the desert. Her decision to be accompanied by only one Arab guide flies against the wishes of the members of the English community and that of her brother in particular. Diana is undaunted; she says she lives for adventure and considers the other alternative, marriage, as "captivity –the end of independence." The young and energetic Sheik Ahmed, who has seen Diana in a dance before, bribes the guide to steer her to where the Sheik and his men are hiding, intent on kidnapping her. The plan succeeds and Diana is taken captive. Once in the Sheik's tent, Diana asks her captor: "Why have you brought me here? The Sheik replies with the classic line: "Are you not woman enough to know?"

Weeks of "sullen obedience" pass before Ahmed's novelist friend from Paris, Raoul de Saint Huber arrives for a visit. Raoul (played by

Adolphe Menjou) persuades his friend to let Diana leave, and the Sheik agrees reluctantly. On her way back through the desert, Diana is kidnapped by an evil Sheik, Omair. But, before she disappears, she manages to write the following inscription on the sand: "Ahmed, I love you." In the ensuing attempt to rescue her from the evil Sheik, Ahmed is wounded. While Diana is sitting at his beside, watching over him, and fondling his hands, she discovers that "His hands are so large for an Arab." Raoul agrees, explaining that indeed the Sheik "is not an Arab. His father was an Englishman, his mother a Spaniard."

Just as the novel was a success because, as one reviewer impatiently remarked, it "dealt with every caged woman's desire to be caught in a love clasp by some he-man who would take the responsibility and dispose of the consequences," the film played to larger women's desires and fantasies. The following snippets, culled from a poster, are only part of a veritable Oriental discourse accompanying the film's release: 'when an Arab sees a woman he wants he takes her!' Ancient Proverb of Arabia/ Don't miss the thrill of seeing the proud mad-cap English girl snatched from the sand by the hard-riding Sheik of a hundred tribes/ You will see love making by the handsome Rudolph Valentino as the Sheik, which is in the full torrent of Oriental tradition. (*The Moving Picture World* 22 Oct. 1921)

The film was indeed a much tamer offering; no doubt due to the fear of censorship. To subvert societal and psychological interdictions, Valentino tried some suggestive antics, like rolling his eyes and showing his teeth; practices which proved more comical than effective (these Valentinian trademarks would however be reproduced by most Sheiks of the 1920s, in serious films as well as in the spoofs). *The Sheik*, however, pleased and delighted everywhere it was shown, despite its muted sexuality. Like the audiences, the critics were drawn to the Oriental atmosphere, commending director George Melford for his direction and special handling of the Oriental tale and theme. The Orient was dished out in the form of an assortment of Bedouin horsemen on Arabian steeds, a sensational harem scene, an Oriental dance staged by Margaret Loomis (a famous dancer as well as an actress), and the indispensable animated representation of Biskra, made famous by the Hull novel. The oasis as the star scene was there also, complete with Sahara palms manufactured in the Lasky workshop and trucked to the California desert where the film was being shot. As expected, the desert occupies the center-piece in the film, prompting a praising reviewer to advice people who planned to see the film to bring with them amber glasses so that their eyes would not give up at the glaring scenes" (*The New York Times* 7 Nov. 1921). The windows designed by movie theaters to accompany the exhibition of the film reflected a similar penchant towards sand, romance, and local color. One such 'model' window, as described in a trade magazine, was "filled with fine sand. At the rear was a tent made of colored tissue paper and small sticks, and in the foreground a cut-out from the stills showed Valentino taking his daily exercises with Agnes Ayres. In the background, a bunch of horsemen, also cut from the stills, watched their chief at his simple love-making." (*The Moving Picture World* 11 Feb. 1921)

Although fear of censorship steered the film from a more explicit exploitation of sexual situations, the most intractable form of censorship was exercised by society and culture at large. This involved the societal taboo of miscegenation, and the ending of the film was where it is most evident. The late discovery that Sheik Ahmed Ben Hassan is actually not an Arab but only brought up as one is, in my opinion and that of many contemporary viewers, pleasantly fantastic as a censor pleaser ploy, with regard to both the manner as well as the time of discovery. The following excerpt from *The New York Times'* review is particularly perceptive, commingling humor and light chiding with a rare punch: "here's the picture tale of a nice Sheik and his agreeable English girl. And you won't be offended by having a white girl marry an Arab either, for the Sheik isn't really a native of the desert at all. Oh, no; he's the son of a Spanish father and an English mother who were killed when he was a baby so the old Sheik could raise him as his son. These Arabian romantic movies, you know, never have the courage of their romantics." (7 Nov. 1921)

On the other hand, one could read in the English lady's peculiar observation, "His hands are so large for an Arab," (instead of other, perhaps more effective, cinematographic techniques which could have been used to reveal the Sheik's identity), an oblique gesture of social defiance, even mockery at the expense of the taboo of inter-racial sex. In the same way that Valentino deflected censorship through rolling his eyes, grinning suggestively, and expressing his decisive sexual one-liners, the film keeps the sudden 'discovery' till the end, couching it furthermore in a farcical style of delivery, in order to chip away from the weight of the societal interdiction. There is in cinematic representations of interracial sex, as the phenomenon of the foreign lover indicates, a significant degree of appeal and titillation, and *The Sheik* plied this emotional seesaw most effectively. The film's multitudinous audiences, in particular the female segment of it which included the norms-flouting flapper contingent, may well have been humming Richard Koszarski's apt observation: "Who cared if Sheik Ahmed Ben Hassan had been a European all along?" (Koszarsky 301)

In electing to substitute an Arab for a European, *The Sheik* was willing to operate within the purview of the Oriental film genre; itself structured along the Orientalist ethos. However, the subversive personality and gaze of Valentino, the predisposition of the largely female audiences to accept and allow the full growth of an Arab character, and the age-old coexistence of a core of sympathy for the Orient have made *The Sheik* yet another example of the trend toward a more nuanced treatment of Arabs and Oriental themes. At the minimum, by retaining the traditionally negative view of the Orient (a site of kidnapping, rape, bandits, lawlessness, and slavery) on the one hand, and introducing the positive and invigorating aspects of the Sheik persona on the other, *The Sheik* is as ambiguous and ambivalent as the history of contact between East and West.

At the exhibition end, *The Sheik* benefited from the combined talent of scores of musicians, who went on to reinforce the Oriental character of the picture with mostly Oriental and Orientalist musical compositions. The musical accompaniment to *The Sheik* consisted of passages from over thirty different selections, each of which the orchestra conductor had to perfectly time and tie to the titles and actions flashing on the screen. As described by Norman Mackenzie, when at a particular performance the curtain would rise and the credit titles begin to be shown, the orchestra leader would be waiting ready with raised baton for the sub-title, "Evening at ..." to signal for the orchestra to start the program by playing six minutes of Ring's *African Dances*. This would change to two and a half minutes of Siede's *Orientalische Streifwache* as the heroine enters and is shown in close-up. On her appearance in a bedroom scene, appropriate atmosphere would be created by playing two minutes of the Arabian dance, Mystic Shrine, by Cameron, followed by a minute and a quarter of Rhode's light intermezzo, *Tricks of the Gnomes*, and one and a half minute of *Hula Hula*, a Hawaiian dance by *Tompa*. For Omair, the bandit, there would be strong musical support with an *agitato* from the Berg Series and a slow dramatic from Czardas by Monti. The seductive harem scenes would be accompanied by Gregh's *Oriental suite*, *Nuits Algeriennes No. 1* followed by the sad *Chanson Triste* by Beaume. As the wounded Ahmed lay between life and death, a heavy piece from the *Berg Series* played like a funeral dirge, doubtless with some effect on even the most hardened males. (Mackenzie 177)

It is a unique testimony to the huge effect of *The Sheik* that it not only started a series of about two dozen films, closely modeled on the original, but the word "Sheik' and the behavior and ideals this character stood for managed to enter American vocabulary and seep through popular lore. It was noticed for example that women and girls wanted their husbands and boyfriends to act like, and be, "Sheiks". Popular songs, such as *"The Sheik of Araby,"* and *"The Sheik of Avenue B"* further exemplified the fascination with the Sheik type. So did fashion with its popular desert capes and headdresses; and interior design, as the Arabian look touched many movie theaters and homes.

The Son of the Sheik (1926)

With such favorable and wide reception as *The Sheik* had received, it was only a matter of time before a sequel would be made, with the great Valentino securely in the lead. Whatever eroding effect the multiple imitations, remakes, and parodies may have had on the successful formula, Edithe Maude Hull obliged with a second and equally popular novel, appropriately titled *The Sons of the Sheik*. As with her first work, Hull has again touched the right nerve of post-war American society, with its contrasting moods of Jazz Age swinging and Prohibition; a fertile ground for flappers who reveled in twisting the dominant conservative social and sexual norms. The masses of liberated women took to her message, and her contrived flights of fancy offered the needed freedom that previously had been the acquired realm of the flapper element only. Scriptwriter Francis Marion also helped the novel make a successful transfer to the film medium, as she is credited with combining the Sheik's two sons in the novel into one film character, played by Valentino.

Predictable and even by then antiquated, the plot hardly explains the eventual huge success of *The Son of the Sheik*. Ahmed, the son of a Sheik, is strongly attracted to Yasmin, the daughter of a renegade Frenchman and leader of a band of thieving desert entertainers. Ahmad's father opposes the relationship and so does a member of an enemy band of Bedouins who later captures and tortures Ahmed. The latter wrongly assumes that the girl has betrayed him and caused his capture. He therefore resolves to take revenge on her; subsequently abducting and taking her to his tent, a conscious parallel to a similar scene in the first Sheik picture. Ahmed's father is outraged by his son's behavior and orders him to release the girl. Then, a friend of Ahmed informs him that the girl has played no part in his capture. One way to amend to the girl was to engage in a rescue action, clinching the girl from the grip of some evil characters in a dancing hall. The fight, which his father also joins (like father like son, a gesture intended to link the two Sheik films), results in Ahmed's walking away with the girl in his arms.

Beyond the acrobatics, the fights and narrow escapes, lies a backdrop of rape, seduction and eroticism. One erotic scene involves Valentino being savagely whipped by a gang; hands strung up above his head and stripped to the waist while a dwarf sadistically touches the wounds (Valentino's exposed flesh was an offer to a section of the audience to indulge its fantasies). Another "Sheikish" approach to sex is to be found in the scenes involving the abduction of Yasmin. As the girl is brought to the tent, the Sheik lights a cigarette, removes his robes and begins to unbuckle his belt. Referring to her presumed betrayal of him, he says: "I may not be the first victim, but, by Allah, I'll be the one you remember." Then, as the Sheik savagely pushes her backward the camera reveals a bed. The scene, mixing hate and love, humiliation and submission, is not atypical. It was perhaps what a contemporary reviewer had in mind as he predicted that the film would have a special effect on women in general and flappers in particular: "Valentino's love-making is of the passionate sort —the kind adored by flappers and even the more mature patron…. in this picture most of his work is devoted to a passionate love" (*Variety* 14 July 1926).

Not all the interest in *The Son of the Sheik* was motivated by the fascination with rape and seduction. As the title proclaims it, it was also a picture about the Orient. As such, it packed in and made effective use of the conventional and predetermined cultural and generic properties. As a genre-minded reviewer noted, the film was "a 100 per cent Sheik picture, in theme treatment and locale," and made according to the "excellent recipe" of the Oriental film tradition (*The Moving Picture World* 7 August 1926). Needless to say, the director who was a noted picturialist as well as an experienced hand in Oriental subjects deftly utilized the repertoire of images traditionally associated with the Orient. These included oases, desert sand, palms, tents, camels, long robes, Arabian horses (Valentino insisted on having, and managed to obtain, a true Arabian steed for the part), marauding Bedouins, and desert chiefs whose single passion was the abduction of white maidens.

Valentino and Film Audiences

It has been customary in genre criticism to view the contribution of artists and stars as of no great significance to the individual films, since these were generally considered to be predetermined texts. Here, despite the firm grip of generic determinism upon *The Sons of the Sheik*, part of the success and appeal of the film resides in a choice cast (Valentino in particular) and the excellent technical support of other artists.

One member of the collaborative group impacting the shape and fate of this film was director George Fitzmaurice (1895-1940). An Irishman born in Paris, Fitzmaurice became a major Hollywood figure during the silent era. As a friend of Valentino –who was particularly happy when he heard that Fitzmaurice was assigned the direction of *The Son of the Sheik*– it must have been of benefit to the film that there was complete understanding between two continental artists. An added asset for the film was Vilma Banky, the Hungarian-born actress, for whom Goldwyn hired a publicity director to capitalize on her romantic appeal and in particular on a presumed relationship with Valentino. Banky was not only a radiant beauty, but also an actress who performed with ease and charm. Multiple reviews talked about her loveliness, and Elinor Glyn stated that she "has IT!" a cryptic reference to a combination of sex appeal and star quality (qtd. in Scott Berg 151). When Valentino suddenly died after the completion of *The Son of the Sheik*, Goldwyn not only reaped the benefits occasioned by the publicity surrounding this death, but was also able to stage one of his many publicity stunts around Vilma

Banky, announcing he was insuring her for $500,000. No less important a factor in the success of the film was George S. Barnes, a talented and experienced cameraman who had before worked with Fitzmaurice and Banky in *The Dark Angel* (1925). King Vidor said of this cinematographer: "George Barnes was one of the first cameramen to be subjective with his instrument" (qtd. in Scott Berg 149). Barnes was also among the first artists to work with the new panchromatic stock, one of the few real technological breakthroughs in the history of cinema. *The Son of the Sheik*, one of the earliest films to use this technology, benefited from the range of sensitivity the new film stock offered for outside photography.

By far the most crucial contribution to both the first and second Sheik films is that of the male lead, Rudolph Valentino. Valentino was an Italian immigrant who had worked as a taxi driver in New York before going West and appearing in few films as an extra, a dancer, and a gangster. His torrid tango dance in Metro's The Four horsemen of the Apocalypse (1921) won him the attention of both critics and female audiences. The good looks, muscular build and flashing eyes made him a perfect choice for *The Sheik*. The casting was a stroke of destiny: Valentino, like a magnet, attracted and engaged the myriad complex and conflicting desires of an entire generation.

To showcase the Valentino phenomenon, critic Richard Koszarski offers a pertinent analogy: "As Theda Bara brought the Kohl-eyed vamp into the culture of the teens, so Valentino, riding the crest of an incipient vogue of Orientalism, launched the twenties passion for Sheiks. The difference was, of course, that to love Valentino was not to die but to be reborn in a paroxysm of liberated bliss" (Harpole 301).

Through his "structured polysemy," to use Allen and Gomery's expression, Valentino crystallized American society's "collective needs, dreams, fantasies, and obsessions" as only great stars can (173). George Melford, director of *The Sheik*, had earlier acknowledged the females' intense fascination with Valentino: "I often believe that Valentino's popularity is largely due to the intuition of women. They see something in him that is not apparent to men" (Mackenzie 167). Asked by a reporter about the source of his fascination for women, Valentino confirmed with measured humility: "I don't know. This is a matter-of-fact age, and everyone is starving for romance. I suppose they like me because I bring that romance into their lives for a few moments" (Mackenzie 167). Male spectators, as well as male critics and reviewers, were not unaware of the effect Valentino had on society, evincing no small amount of uneasiness and cynicism with regard to Valentino, much to the actor's discomfort. A writer in the *Chicago Tribune* launched a vicious attack on Valentino, casting doubts on his sexual integrity, and accusing him of effeminacy. The journalist editorialized acidly: "Is this degeneration into effeminacy a cognate reaction with pacifism to the virilities and realities of the war? Are pink powder and parlor pinks in any way related? How does one reconcile masculine cosmetics, Sheiks, floppy pants, and slave bracelets with a disregard for the law and an aptitude for crime more in keeping with the frontier of half a century ago than a twentieth-century metropolis? (*There is a New Star in Heaven* 106). Valentino was deeply hurt by this assault on his manhood, particularly as news began to circulate that both wives he had married (Natacha Rambova and Jean Acker) were lesbians and were romantically involved with his friend, Alla Nizimova, the famous designer and actress who launched their careers.

Valentino's relationship to the audience is unique; neither replicated by later stars nor adequately explored by critics. Allen and Gomery have rightly pointed out that the movies' audience is "really only an abstraction generated by the researcher, since the unstructured group that we refer to as the movie audience is constantly being constituted, dissolved and reconstituted with each film-going experience" (157). This may shed light on an early instance of significant structuring of the audience around the Sheik texts and in particular the Valentino Sheik persona. According to critic Miriam Hansen, in her colorfully titled essay, "Pleasure, Ambivalence, Identification: Valentino and Female Spectatorship," women spectators at the time of Valentino were perceived for the first time in film history as a group of social and economical significance. The ascent to stardom of Valentino coincided with the ongoing crisis in the American post-war social values, resulting in his body becoming the site of the many contradictions reflecting the ongoing upheaval in gender relations. The orientation of the market towards a female spectator/consumer, Hansen argues, opened up a gap between traditional patriarchal ideology on the one hand and the recognition of the female spectator, her needs and fantasies on the other –albeit, to a great extent, for the purpose of immediate commercial exploitation and eventual containment. Valentino's appeal for a woman audience depended, to a large extent, on the manner in which he combined masculine control of the look with the feminine quality of "to-be-looked-at-ness". The feminine connotation of Valentino's "to-be-looked-at-ness," to borrow a term from another feminist critic, Laura Mulvey, destabilized his own glance in its very origin, making him vulnerable to temptations that jeopardize the sovereignty of the male subject. The erotic appeal of the Valentinian gaze, staged as a look within the look, is one of reciprocity and ambivalence, rather than one of mastery and objectification. Thus, the threat posed by Valentino's complicity with the woman who looks is not a threat merely of sexual difference but of a different *kind* of sexuality, different from the norm of heterosexual, genital sexuality.

It may be said then, in the same way that *The Sheik* has made it superfluous for the audience, in the words of Koszarski, to care if Sheik Ahmed (Valentino) had been a European all along, *The Son of the Sheik* managed to some extent, through Valentino's special control of the look and his charged and polysemic persona, to subvert the sexual and racial norms of patriarchy. Like the character of Bella Donna that flaunted the Victorian values of womanhood with the act of miscegenation, Valentino's female fans, goaded by his destabilizing look and androgynous make-up, were in a sense revolting against a system that has codified sexual norms and assigned women to the same category of otherness as the Oriental foreigner. Unlike Bella Donna, who was condemned and completely crushed by Victorian morality, the female audiences in the mid-twenties were finally coming into their own, demanding through box office clout the kind of sexual mythologies that would liberate their fantasies. A significant side effect of the rise in power of the female audiences, boosted by a highly visible and influential flapper fringe, was that the Arab would transcend multiple generic and Orientalist restraints; a situation which translated into a more complex and less negative characterization, albeit not necessarily a less stereotypical one.

The Sheik Film Formula
The ambiguous, mixed and at times positive portrayal of the Arab in the Sheik films of Valentino was not replicated in the cluster of films revolving around a Sheik figure. Generally, films of the Sheik

group overused the crude plots revolving around Sheiks kidnapping American women; in particular those whose fascination with Arab Sheiks (or their celluloid counterparts to be exact) had blinded them to the danger these desert creatures represent to them and to their civilization core values. Of course, the dashing fiancé, the husband, and the compatriot were always there for the heroic rescue and the unmasking of the false romance and the ghoulish charm of the East.

For a definite sign of maturity and saturation of the Oriental genre one has to look at the degree of reflexivity and consciousness involved amongst its individual films. As with other popular generic formulas, the audience of the Sheik films did not tire of the repetition; on the contrary, it called for more. And there was a great deal of repetition and imitation, surprisingly, only eight months after the 1921 *The Sheik*. A reviewer wrote in 1922, "There seems to be more Sheiks around now than you can shake a stick at. These warm-blooded gentlemen are enjoying wide popularity in both literature and pictures.... As a matter of fact, this Arabian type of lover appears to have found unusual favor with picture patrons (*The Moving Picture World* 13 May 1922).

One of the first films to capitalize on the great popularity of Sheik characters is Arabian Love (Jerome Storm, 1922). The Sheik in this film is actually an American (played by John Gilbert) who joins a band of desert outlaws, graduates into a Sheik, and of course saves the life and honor of a white woman (actress Barbara Bedford) kidnapped during a raid on a caravan. The industry's desire to turn the huge demand in its favor is further evidenced by another 1922 film, *The Sheik of Araby*, advertised as re-edited and re-titled but essentially the same as the 1919 film, The man who Turned White (directed by Frank Frame). Since revivals were rare during the silent era, *The Sheik of Araby* constitutes further indication of the popularity of Oriental subjects with strong Sheik elements. The film also capitalized on the very popular song of the same title, as this advertisement attests: "*The Sheik of Araby*: 'On every lip–on every phonograph–on every screen'" (ibid).

Despite being dubbed by *Variety* as a "shameless lift from *The Sheik*," (1 Feb. 1923) the film, *One Stolen Night* (Robert Newsmonger, 1923), offers a fascinating commentary on the presumed effect of the Sheik persona on women. The story is of a lovesick American girl from a conservative Boston family who ventures out on the Arabian

Desert alone. In a moonlit night, she visits an Arabian camp in disguise as a native woman. There, she falls in love with an Arab horseman. During a desert love scene, bandits attack the couple and the man is left for dead, while the girl is taken to the tent of a monstrous and evil Sheik. The kidnapped girl is later rescued by the Arab horseman, who later turns out to be not only white, but the very man the girl is engaged to back home in Boston. When later he appears at her hotel in European clothes to introduce himself, the girl refuses to meet him in "regular shirt and pants of civilization." However, once in their full desert disguise, they go out into the desert for further sentimental wooing.

Another Sheik film, appropriately named *A Son of the Sahara* (Edwin Carew and René Ploiesti, 1924), deals with a story that is "nothing new as Sheik stories go." The film is in fact very similar to the Hull story, in the choice of the Algerian setting, the psychological interest, and in particular the sudden switch in identity of the main character, Prince Cassin. When Cassin's father is killed in an attack on a French fort, Cassin vows vengeance on Colonel Barnier. As he grows into a polished westernized gentleman, Cassim falls in love with Barbara, the colonel's daughter, who spurns him when she learns he is Arab. Rejected, he kidnaps her and subsequently sells and buys her in a slave auction. Days pass, and then Cassim and his people are attacked by the French army under the command of Barbara's father. The father is badly wounded; yet before he dies he gives Barbara a letter written by Cassim's mother, revealing the fact that Cassim is not an Arab as his father was French. Now becoming the French Raoul, he and Barbara find happiness together.

In its insistence on racial purity, armed conflict, and the stereotypical slave markets, *A Son of the Sahara* is far more negative in its treatment of Arabs than any other film from the Sheik group. On the other hand, the film has the questionable distinction of presenting a soft and sentimental Sheik –a wrong decision, according to one reviewer: "That Mr. Carewe should have insisted on the Sheik weeping copiously on one or two occasions is a mistake, for the average Sheik would, we imagine, be able to keep control over his emotions, even if they represented acute affections" (*The New York Times* 27 May 1924).

The Sheik Films Parodied

Thanks to its phenomenal success, Valentino's 1921 *The Sheik* not only spawned numerous imitations, but has attracted the inevitable attention of parodists. However, the numerous takeoffs on the Sheik persona, the over-exploitation the Oriental elements and the incessant humorous attacks on the Sheik figure ironically served to keep the Sheik theme relevant and popular for nearly the entire decade.

Film parody, according to genre critic Wes D. Gehring, is "a comic, yet generally affectionate, and distorted imitation of a given genre, auteur, or specific work" (145). It is additionally recognized as an educational tool, a kind of "creative criticism" (Davis, in Gehring 146). For instance, it has been acknowledged that to better understand Griffith's *Lonely Villa* (1909) one is advised to see Mack Sennett's spin-off, *Help! Help!* (1912). By the same token, Sennett's parody, *The Shriek of Araby* (F. Richard Jones, 1923) is not only one of the many films that owe their existence to the success of the Sheik films, but it is also an eloquent critique and commentary on the famous Valentino's *The Sheik* (1921).

The hilarious *The Shriek of Araby* features the cross-eyed Ben Turpin, as the Sheik, and Sennett in an ingeniously crafted story. The film begins with Ben passing out handbills for a Sheik show in a picture house where a handsome Arab is riding a horse as ballyhoo. The Arab in the Sheik clothes outside the movie theatre proves such a hit that the audience will not go inside to watch the fictional Arab, instead "all the flappers fall for him, seeing in him the real hero of the story." The disappointed theater manager fires the "Arab" and gives Ben his job and clothes. Ben straddles the horse and in no time becomes bored. Suddenly, he is seen onboard a boat where he meets a girl, an artist specialized in painting the desert. After all sorts of scrapes, Ben is thrown overboard; but manages to land on a desert island. In the Arabian Desert, he befriends an Arab Sheik (the Arab of the ballyhoo), who gives Ben his place before going on a vacation. The girl, whom Ben has met before, is subsequently kidnapped by an evil Sheik; and saving her finally wins Turpin her love. When the girl is retaken by the evil Sheik, Ben rescues her again and rides triumphantly away. At the end of the film, a mounted traffic cop rudely awakens Ben, who has been on a horse outside the theater all along. He then discovers that his tumultuous journey into the desert has been but a dream. (*Variety* 14 June 1923)

Early previews of this parody found it extremely funny but too long, wondering if in fact comedy could be sustained for five reels. Length was apparently no obstacle to success, as the film played in first-run houses and even made it to the Capitol; an achievement for early comedies.

If parodies work it is chiefly because they trigger a viewer's prior knowledge of a given genre or auteur. In *The Shriek of Araby*, the Oriental iconography is effectively utilized, emphasizing such well-known features as tents, camels, sand, horses, and evil as well as less evil Sheiks. The film covers a wide range of themes and situations, taken mostly from the parodied Valentino film. To a large extent, the comic effect is created by twisting and ridiculing the very images and themes made memorable by Valentino's vehicle. Thus, in lieu of a lovesick and serious Sheik, the Arab in this film prefers to take a day off to go trout fishing. This Sheik's tent is even equipped with a telephone, has fresh milk and the morning newspaper (*The Daily Camel*) delivered to it every morning. Perhaps the harshest and most effective ridicule is the one dealt to the figure of the Sheik, as the cross-eyed Ben Turpin replaces the good-looking and virile Valentinian Sheik.

A radical reversal of the role of Valentino appears in another famous Sheik parody, *She's a Sheik* (Clarence Badger, 1927). Here, a female Sheik lords over the desert and its men in the same decisive Valentinian way. A biting satire on Valentino-Hull's, this film displays more raciness and not a streak of the positive aura of the Orient.

She's a Sheik opens with two Arabs discussing the charms of Zaida (Bebe Daniels), the Spanish-Arabian granddaughter of Sheik Yussuf Ben Hamad. Zaida's motto, not unlike that of Valentino in *The Sheik*, is: "When I see a man I want I take him." This female Sheik, however, is rather particular about the man she wants: he must a Christian and not a bronzed desert chief. When she later discovers that a handsome Legionnaire is interested in a blonde European, she kidnaps him and puts him in an empty animal cage. After a few days of taming, Zaida orders that the Legionnaire be cleaned and brought to her. The two fall in love and begin to woo in the Sheik fashion. Meanwhile, a native suitor, anxious to get Zaida, is growing more threatening. The female Sheik, who knows how to fence, rips off the Arab's garments with her rapier. The humiliated Arab gathers some tribesmen and attacks a garrison where Zaida and a couple of traveling film showmen are hiding. The showmen have come to the desert to exhibit films to the tribes in the oases. The fort was nearly overrun by the tribesmen when the two men save the day by projecting into the screen of night a film featuring marauding Arabs. The sight of the phantom army of desert Bedouins caused the attacking Arabs to flee. Zaida and the French Legionnaire resume their romantic affair.

Like Sennett's *The Shriek of Araby*, this film effectively uses cinematic reflexivity. In both films, Arabs in previous strips of celluloid jostle for position with the other Arab characters about to be in their turn embalmed in film cans. The strip of film projected into the screen of night by the showmen in *She's a Sheik* saves the people and the garrison, delivering at the same time a real blow to the famed courage and intelligence of Bedouins. Shooting back at the shadowy army in the empty night sky, the Arab characters in Bebe Daniel's vehicle must have come through like infants fighting their mirror reflection.

She's a Sheik achieved a measure of financial success, doubtless due to the title's promise of parodic comedy. Widely circulated picture posters, with Bebe Daniels ensconced in flowing Sheik clothes and head cape also helped. By this date, only a female playing the desert Sheik was able to rekindle the interest of a saturated audience. One reviewer discerned the usefulness of the ploy: "Placing the girl in the position usually taken by the male, as the physical aggressor in love maneuvers, is not exactly unique in the annals of film production. Giving the girl color as the lady Sheik, however, furnishes as suitable idea for putting the story over along novel lines (*Variety* 23 Nov. 1927).

In addition to the dramatic gender reversal, two themes were emphasized: first, coercive love making; and second, the racial identity of the main character. Thus, like the Valentinian Sheik, Zaida seeks danger and sadistic sexual experiences. Like Diana Mayo, whose will is broken by isolation in the tent, the Legionnaire is assigned to a leopard cage for appropriate taming. Yet, whereas Diana only indirectly proclaims her love for Ahmed by a hasty inscription on the sand ("I love you, Ahmed"), the Legionnaire is only too happy to oblige his female captor. As much as it was intended for fun, this reversal is in line with the traditional order of sexual situations in Oriental films, with the Western male availing himself of the half-Oriental female.

If it is only at the end of *The Sheik* that one receives the disclosure that Ahmed is not an Arab but a European, Zaida, it is established from the outset, is a half-breed (half-Spanish, half-Arab, but completely exotic) who, in addition, insists that she seeks no swarthy native Sheik for a lover. Only a European would do; a Legionnaire in a position of (colonial) authority is preferable. It is significant that this parody singles out for rebuttal the very idea that I argued constitutes a clear, positive shift in the portrayal of Arabs in *The Sheik*; namely, Sheik Ahmed's European identity is narratively delayed to the extent that it does not greatly matter, allowing thus the audience to somehow share in and accept an inter-racial sexual saga. In contrast, *She's a Sheik*, as though to signal society's continuing refusal to allow sex across ethnic lines, moves to forcefully reshuffle things back to the accepted, more 'natural' order. As a contemporary reviewer assured, a tinge of irony, Zaida "would marry only in the Christian faith, declining to choose from the swarthy brethren among whom she had always lived." (*Variety* 23 Nov. 1927)

The societal taboo of miscegenation, then, plays itself in a predictable fashion in this parody as well as in most of this category's films, the serious and the less serious ones. The destruction of Bella Donna in the eponymous film analyzed earlier, underscored by the ultimate disposal of her flesh to desert jackals, served as a warning and an example of the consequences of defying an important societal injunction. The dramatization of the difficulties facing the multiple heroines who have allowed themselves to be beguiled by the false charm of Sheiks or the East also functions as a reminder that the Orient is not a site of adventure, exoticism, and sexual promise, but the source of innumerable threats and dangers. Only Western males, these films seem to solemnly imply, can fathom the depths of the Orient, partake of its erotic pleasures, and more importantly, neutralize and prevent its contagious and falsely alluring perfumes from reaching the impressionable women; the West's only guarantors of racial purity.

Chapter Nine

ORIENTAL FILMS: THE FANTASIES

At first sight, mirth-filled *Aladdin* and *The Thief of Baghdad* appear to share little with the war-like *Under Two Flags* or the tragic psychological romance, *Bella Donna*, exposed in the previous chapters. The differences run the entire gamut of visualization, drama, style, characterization, and even the specific audience targeted, explaining in part why this study has subsumed each of these titles under a distinct category. Yet, despite the apparent lack of common elements, these films do partake, respond, and are better understood in reference to the Orientalist system; that inexhaustible pool of knowledge, views and perceptions which I argued is essential to the formation, consumption and understanding of the Oriental genre.

The present chapter will present and discuss some of the films constituting the fantastic category, a group of films forming, with the realist-colonialist and psychological categories that ensemble of films labeled in this book as the Oriental genre. In particular, it will map the network of relationships these films entertain with each other within their generic grouping, as well as within the cultural context surrounding their consumption. Films like *The Thief of Baghdad* and *Aladdin*, all deriving from the popular collection, the *Arabian Nights*, have been an enduring presence in the annals of Western cinema, and will continue to interest and entertain audiences everywhere. The ideological and political content of these films should never be discounted however, even though all too often these films had for expressed goal the entertainment of children. Indeed, the political charge of these films resides exactly in their alleged escapism and the rejection of the overriding empirical and realist dimension of modern experience. For the Orient and its inhabitants, the implications go beyond the allegorical or the fleetingly therapeutic; since, in reducing a geographical and ethnic reality into a no-man's-land of genies and ethereal treasures, these films could be seen to enact the old communal practice/wish to dissociate the Orient from its people as a step to its (re)possession. The fact that some of these films were often enacted by children is, barring the obvious consideration of the industry's desire to cater to an all-inclusive audience, further illustration of a tenet of Orientalism: the infantilism of the East. The Orient in this seemingly inoffensive category is denied maturity, presented as still steeped in that inchoate state of logic and behavior that universally characterizes children.

The *Arabian Nights* as Super-Script

The *Arabian Nights* translated by Antoine Galland in the eighteenth-century so enchanted Europe that for many Westerners the work either adequately substituted for the entire Orient, or at least was deemed the key to its understanding. Interestingly, for some Western travelers in the East, the verification of the *Nights'* authenticity constituted an immediate goal. Lady Wortley Montagu, wife of the British ambassador to Turkey (1716-18), alluded to this interchangeability in one of her letters home: "This is but too like (says you) the Arabian tales; these embroider'd Napkins and a jewel as large as a Turkey's egg! You forget dear Sister; those very tales were writ by an Author of this Country and (excepting the Enchantments) are a real representation of the manners here..." (qtd. by Fatma Moussa-Mahmoud, in Caracciollo 96). Similarly, as late as 1907, the introduction to the Nister-Dutton edition of the *Nights* judged that the work reflects faithfully the life and concerns of the Eastern peoples, and therefore its reading could advance the interests of the British empire: "For Englishmen, whose empire contains so many millions of Muslims, this study of the Night is of high importance; it is not possible to govern well without understanding of the governed and sympathy with their feelings and thoughts, and only through knowledge can come that wise tolerance which wins trust and enables the ruler to control, to improve, to reform." (Qtd. in Caracciolo 41)

A brief survey of the Western reception of the *Arabian Nights* confirms the extraordinary grip of its tales on the imagination of the young and the adults alike. Galland's Mille et une nuits (1704-17) was the first translation of *The Nights*. In England, a translation from Galland (known as the "Grub Street version") by an unknown hack-writer reached its third edition by 1715. The London News, a thrice-weekly newssheet, began serializing the *Arabian Nights'* Entertainment in 1723, running 445 installments over three years (Caracciolo 2). The success of this early translation, in book form or serialization, was huge and the effect on children as well as adults remarkable. Gibbon remembered: "Before I left Kingston school I was well acquainted with Pope's Homer and the *Arabian Nights'* entertainment, two books which always please by the moving picture of human manners and specious miracles" (Caracciolo 2).

Ever since its introduction into Europe, the *Arabian Nights* has undergone remarkable economic and media exploitation. The multiple editions and translations (Henry Torrens, 1832; E. W. Lane, 1839-41; John Payne, 1882-4; and Sir Richard Burton, 1885-6) often included illustrations and wood engravings. The practice of excerpting individual stories from the collection brought further popularity to the tales as well as financial benefits for the publishers. The tale, "History of Sinbad the Sailor," for instance, underwent many "picture book editions ... versions in words of one syllable, and movable adaptations such as harlequinades and pop-up books" (Caracciolo 91). For young readers, the relevance of the *Arabian Nights* continued unabated into the twentieth-century. The selections and abridgments peaked in 1907 and 1908 with half a dozen or more juvenile versions a year; most of these were decorated with attractive pictures and importantly were "reasonably cheap" (Caracciolo 39). Unabridged and adult-oriented editions were also made available for clubs and male literary societies in Victorian England; these contained explicit lengthy commentary on the presumably peculiar sexual mores of Oriental men and women.

Furthermore, originally the creation of more than one author, the *Arabian Nights* has grown "both by accretion and by self-replication" (ibid 5). The potential for self-multiplication, which ensured the survival of the tales, also explains why its motifs, characters, plot, and themes moved into other media, both popular and highbrow. Thus, by the turn of the century, the *Arabian Nights* began to eclipse the Commedia dell'Arte as a source for pantomime (ibid 44). In the

1910s and 1920s, some famous theatrical treatments of the *Arabian Nights* were undertaken to outstanding critical acclaim. In 1911, Max Reinhardt brought his Arabian fantasia, Sumurûn, to London for six weeks; that same year Scheherazade of the Ballet Russe played to outstanding success in London in a production which "fused Rimsky-Korsakov's music, Bakst's design, Fokine's innovative choreography and the genius of Nijinsky as a dancer" (Caracciolo 44). The dazzling ballet enchanted artists and intellectuals, influencing such things as "poster design and interior decoration, and accounting for the Persian look increasingly evident in the work of book illustrators such as Dulac, René Bull, E. J. Detmold and Kay Nielsen." With similar success, Oscar Asche's and G. F. Norton's musical *Chu Chin Chow* (based on pantomime's use of the *Arabian Nights)* ran for almost five years from 1916. In 1923, James Elroy Flecker's *Hassan* (the basis for the film version, *The Lady of the Harem,* discussed below) began its London run of 281 performances. Basil Dean (a disciple of Reinhardt) directed, Delius supplied the music, and Fokine took charge of the choreography for what was then considered "the most significant musical production the London stage had seen for many a day, opera not excluded." (Ibid 44)

The Orient constructed in the Western mind and imagination through these tales was as contradictory, ambivalent, and fantastic as the tales it was equated with. The Arabs and Muslims animating the translations and adaptations were no less fantastic or colorful. In an essay accompanying his voluminous translation, Richard Burton painted a contradictory picture of the Medieval Arab. The *Arabian Nights*, he believed, has shown the Arab both "at his best" and "at his worst." On the positive ledger, the Arab is "courteous and affable, rarely failing in temperance of mind and self-respect, self-control, and self-command; hospitable to the stranger, attached to his fellow-citizens, submissive to superiors, and kindly to inferiors.... As a friend he proves a model ... as a lover an exemplar to Don Quixote.... As a knight he is the mirror of chivalry, doing battle for the weak and debelling the strong, while ever 'defending the honour of women'.

After this laudatory inventory, Burton moves to describe the Arab at his worst: "[*The Arab)* is "a mere barbarian who has not forgotten the savage. He is a model mixture of childishness and astuteness, of simplicity and cunning, concealing levity of mind under solemnity of aspect. His stolid instinctive conservatism grovels before the tyrant

110

rule of routine .... His mental torpidity, founded upon physical indolence, renders immediate action and all manner of exertion distasteful...." (Burton Vol.VIII: 59-61)

Worthy of mention here is, among other things, how Burton elected not to attach the list of virtues and vices to the fictional characters of the Arabian tales, but to the ethnic Arabs, among whom the tales have originated and who indeed enjoyed them for precisely this multifaceted and colorful treatment of the human condition. When the film medium was born, this assortment of characters, which more than anything else, account for the popularity of the *Arabian Nights*, provided the palette for scores of colorful popular heroes and villains pitted against each other in various "good" versus "bad" configurations.

Early Oriental Fantasies: *The Rummy Act of Omar K. M.,* and *The Harem Scarem Deacon* (1916)

There exist, according to Todorov, four types of the fantastic, or as he called it, the marvelous; these are, the hyperbolic marvelous; the exotic marvelous; the instrumental marvelous; and science fiction (Todorov 54-55). In the first type, "the phenomena are supernatural... by virtue of their dimensions, which are superior to those that are familiar to us." In the second, the supernatural events are reported without being presented as such; and "the implicit reader is supposed to be ignorant of the regions where the event take place, and consequently he has no reason for calling them into question." In the third type one finds "gadgets, technological developments unrealized in the period described but, after all, quite possible." For an example this, Todorov mentioned the "Tale of Prince Ahmed" from the *Arabian Nights* –on which *The Thief of Baghdad* (1924) is largely based– where some of the marvelous instruments are a flying carpet, an apple that cures diseases, and a pipe for seeing from great distances.

The films to be introduced here somehow reflect Todorov's definition and categories. *The Thief of Baghdad* (Raoul Walsh, 1924) and *Aladdin* (C. M Franklin and S. A. Franklin, 1917), while clearly hyperbolic and exotic, may be labeled as instrumental in view of the many gadgets and devices relied upon to advance the action. The second set of films, *The Rummy Act of Omar K. M.* (Mutual, 1916) and *The Harem Scarem Deacon* (Allen Curtis, 1915) are hyperbolic and exotic in the presentation of the Oriental setting, in particular their depiction of harems. The last pair, *Kismet* (Louis Gasnier, 1920) and *The Lady of the Harem* (Raoul Walsh, 1926), while not relying on gadgets and magical instruments, utilizes the notion of Oriental fate (*Kismet*) to explain the sudden change in the heroes' fortunes. A further division according to the source of the six films may also be made: except for *The Rummy Act of Omar K. M.* and *The Harem Scarem Deacon*, the films considered here, and indeed most films of the category, derive more or less directly from the *Arabian Nights. Aladdin* and *The Thief of Baghdad* are based on well-known stories from the collection, while *Kismet* and *The Lady of the Harem*, were written initially for the stage; yet were modeled after *The Nights'* stories and therefore labeled *Arabian Nights'* tales by their creators.

As their synopses show, *The Rummy Act of Omar K. M.* and *The Harem Scarem Deacon* successfully blend the fantastic, the exotic Oriental, the topical, and the innovative in film technique during the early teens. Both films allot a dual identity to their main characters. Beginning as Westerners, their dream or hallucination transports them to Oriental settings where they are transformed into Oriental figures: the famed poet Omar Khayyam in the first; and a powerful Oriental Pasha in the second. Both films used the dream (or daydream) technique as a narrative and framing device (a prevalent practice in the teen), as well as a means to transport the heroes into a new world. Alcohol abuse and drug addiction, subjects treated in many films of the period, also tie the films to their era. Diegetically, alcohol and opium serve to catapult the heroes to the land of their choice. Significantly, the preference for these hallucinating agents is not gratuitous; the Orient setting which the films take as subject matter has long been associated with sensual pleasures akin to those induced by these substances.

In *The Rummy Act of Omar K. M.*, a man named Omar K. M. has just finished reading Persian poet Omar Khayyam's, the *Rubaiyat* (the English translation of which by Fitzgerald in 1859 was feted in England as a literary event). His wife, displeased with both his drinking habit and literary taste, hits him with a broom, precipitating him "to the sphere of the Persians." In the Orient, Omar meets Thou (of the poem) and goes to a winery, as in "a jug of wine, a loaf of bread and thou." He buys some more wine and rides with Thou in a chariot that takes them to a cottage in the woods. While Omar is whispering sweet things to Thou, telling how much he loves her, Mrs. K. M. talks the chariot driver into disclosing the whereabouts of her husband. When Mrs. K. M. arrives at the cottage, she fails to enter, for "There was the door to which she found no key, and there was the veil thru which she could not see!" Circling the cottage, she manages to crawl in through an opening in the rear. Once inside, she takes a jug of wine and hurls it at Omar, who is in the midst of a poetic outburst with Thou. The wetness brings Omar back to his yard, where he has initially received the broom blow. As he is dragged by the wife, he philosophizes about fate, life and death: "when we reach the spot where he made One, –we turn down an empty glass!"

Similarly, in *The Harem Scarem Deacon*, the hero's trip into the pleasures of the Orient is precipitated by a hallucinating agent: opium. In the 1910s, films began to treat of the effect of drugs on health and families; but the actions taken by some anti-drug societies against substances abuse were crudely insensitive to Asian ethnic groups, in particular the Chinese who were blamed for the scourge (as in this film). In *The Harem Scarem Deacon*, Deacon Stillwaters is the agent sent by the Anti-Sing League to investigate the vice conditions in the dens of opium in Chinatown. On entering this part of the city, Deacon is warned by Celeste, a flower girl, of the dangers of his mission. As he enters an opium den, Deacon is convinced by the owner that there is no harm in opium and therefore accepts a pipe. Smoking causes him to sleep, dreaming himself being the Pasha in a large harem; the den's owner his Grand Vizier and the League's president, Miss Crobar, his wife. The flower girl he has met before is brought to him by the Vizier as a dancing girl and an addition to his harem. The Pasha falls in love with the dancer and this arouses the jealousy of his wife, who incites the women of the harem to a revolt. The Pasha flees, pursued by the women who corner him and pummel him mercilessly. The scene then fades to the den where the president of the League and other scandalized women are shaking Deacon back to consciousness. He tries to explain what has happened but there was no sympathetic listener. However, as the flower girl is still by his side, he does not care what the others think or say.

In both films, the heroes' journey begins from a cloistered and prudish existence: the bullied husband in the prison of his courtyard in the first, and the lifeless, dull, and aptly named Stillwaters taking orders from a prim and prying Miss Crobar (read crowbar) in the second. The wine and opium trigger, as by association, the escape into the semi-mythical space of the Orient. As in the Land of Oz, the wicked intruders interrupting the heroes' flight into joy and freedom emerge from the "old," black-and-white world of the humdrum existence of home and coterie. Yet, unlike Dorothee who personally chooses to go back to Kansas, Omar K. M and Deacon Stillwaters have their trip brutally shortened by the intimidating Mrs. K. M. and the meddlesome Miss Crobar. The flight into fantasy land, however, enriches the heroes' outlook on life and self: for Omar K. M., there is the belief that life without imagination is synonymous with death; and for Deacon Stillwaters, the pleasures and experience he gained as a Pasha survive his rude awakening (he keeps the flower girl, Celeste, confirming his passage from still waters to celestial heights).

In both films, the adoption of the East as the setting of choice, instead of the gnomes- and witches-infested heaths and vales of traditional fantasies, is as significant as it is narratively expedient. To begin with, the heroes' means of escape —hallucinating agents— are suggestive of the Orient as a land of sensual pleasure, freedom, and reverie. Furthermore, the strong sexual component of Deacon's flight fits the established pattern of the sexual voyage made by Westerners into the East. As used in these films, the dream technique was not only a deft cinematic ploy destined to save filmmakers costly transition film footage, but a trope of considerable psychological and cultural density. In a study of dreams experienced between 1830 and 1870, it was noticed, for example, that dreams depicting harems or orgies where the dreamer could possess a multiplicity of women were rather frequent (Jacques Bousquet 498).

Aladdin and the Wonderful Lamp (1917)

The magical and technical possibilities offered by the new film medium were a worthy match to the wonderfully fantastic Arabian collection, the *Arabian Nights*. Aladdin's fabulous palace destined for his beloved Morgiana, the daughter of the Sultan, was completed overnight by the genie of the lamp to the astonishment of the ancient world; a few centuries later, it would take less than a second for the same feet to be accomplished through the cinematic process of pixilation. When Fox undertook in 1917 to bring the stories of *Ali Baba* and *Aladdin* to the screen, the *Arabian Nights* at last found a total medium. This review of *Aladdin* and the Wonderful Lamp clearly shows why early audiences were thrilled; as: "the magical effects demanded by the story have been supplied by the resources of the screen, no task imposed on the slave of the lamp being beyond the skill of the producer. The palace of the sultan, the scenes in the desert and the interiors of Aladdin's magic palace are all fine examples of their kind; and the atmosphere of the East is never lost." (*The Moving Picture World* 13 Oct. 1917)

Aladdin appealed to the audience also on account of its humor, theme, and Oriental atmosphere. Newspapers advertising the film tagged it as "spectacular ...more exciting than the biggest screen 'thriller,' and a thousand percent, more wholesome, [having] more humor to the fifty feet ... than the funniest farce of the screen" (from a poster in *The Moving Picture World* 13 Oct. 1917). A reviewer in *Variety* magazine was similarly impressed: "As a spectacular production it is little short of stupendous" (28 Sep. 1917).

Although *Aladdin* in the original tale was no kid, the Fox production used mostly a cast of children. Yet, the main didactic purpose of the tale suited all kinds of audiences; namely, Aladdin has the right intentions, and deserves to acquire and enjoy wealth, unlike the evil sorcerer who seeks to obtain wealth by wicked methods, and is unworthy to enjoy it. The story of *Aladdin* is well known to be retold here in detail. In brief, the film's Aladdin finds himself destined for great fortunes, unwittingly aided by the evil Moorish magician who leads him to the cave containing the enchanted lamp and many other great treasures. After he becomes rich through the magical intercession of the genies of the ring and the lamp, Aladdin shows the contrasting emotions of humility (he initially asks the genies only for food) and overarching ambition as he sets his eyes on the beautiful Morgiana, sole daughter of the good Caliph. His lowly station –being the son of a poor tailor– together with the evil intentions of the Vizier make his wish to marry Morgiana a difficult one to realize. Yet, since his love is pure and absolute, he does everything in his (and the genies') power to satisfy the Caliph, from offering him loads of huge diamonds to the construction overnight of a fabulous palace for his beloved Morgiana. In the end, Aladdin gains the princess, the satisfaction of the Caliph, wealth, knowledge, wisdom, and happiness. After the Caliph dies, he and the princess live happily ever after, ruling with mercy and compassion over large and prosperous lands.

Aladdin is no doubt a fantasy; in the sense fixed by Todorov. Aladdin goes on a quest, procures the magical instruments of the ring and the lamp, and through the wealth and power he acquires is transformed from a poor and prankish urchin to an honorable and wise man seeking the daughter of the highest symbol of authority on earth. In his insistence to ally himself with nobility and live the high life made possible by the magical powers he controls, Aladdin, unlike many other fantastic characters, does not go back to where he started. As in most fantasies, however, the road to wisdom, wealth, and love in *Aladdin* is fraught with danger and risk, represented mainly by the Moorish sorcerer whose sole goal was the acquisition of the lamp for its extraordinary powers. Aladdin also triumphs over the wiles of the scheming Vizier who has resolved to marry Morgiana to his son.

As an Oriental film, *Aladdin* partook of the reservoir of images and perceptions the West has developed for hundreds of years about the Orient. The mostly negative, rarely positive, portrayal of the Arab and his Oriental setting in the European translations of the *Arabian Nights* (and it should be added that there is no definitive original *Arabian Nights*, but only oral versions and incomplete rescensions) suited the already established view of the Orient as a land of danger and fantastic promise. The movies exploited this fantastic Orient, exaggerating its evil characters and thinning out its positive individuals beyond recognition. It may be risky to always read willful misrepresentation of the Orient in what by definition are playful film fantasies. Yet, a number of considerations point to a continuation of the traditional and negative view regarding the Orient. First, advancing the action in *Aladdin* are usually evil Oriental types, such as the treacherous and obsequious vizier and the evil sorcerer the likes of whom only the Orient could beget. Secondly, the casting of children in *Aladdin* may have been intended to secure a more global audience, as kids do bring their parents to the movie theaters to the delight of the industry; yet, an Orient peopled mostly by children may also connote and reinforce the idea of the infantilism of the East. The Orient's immaturity has long been adduced by Orientalists and colonialists alike as reasonably sufficient grounds for its takeover. Additionally, by relegating the Orient from a geographical entity to a mythical expanse, *Aladdin* followed an Orientalist practice aiming to dissociate the land from its people, no doubt as a first step to control it.

The Thief of Baghdad (1924)

In his published memoirs, *Each Man in His Time*, director Raoul Walsh recalls a conversation with actor Douglas Fairbanks during the preparation for *The Thief of Baghdad*. "We'll need Oriental types," remarked Fairbanks. "I know a few Syrians," replied Walsh, "but we'll need a couple of thousand extras.... Where do we get them?" A short moment later, Walsh broke in with the solution: "In Mexican town," referring to the south-central portion of Los Angeles, "a dark-haired Mexican with a head rag hiding everything except his eyes and nose and mouth will pass for an Arab any time." Walsh scorned himself for not receiving; this epiphany sooner, particularly as he knew that "many Mexicans had Indian blood, and were not those same Indians reputed to have come across the Bering Strait from Asia?" (Raoul Walsh 164). Even if it grazes some ethnic sensibilities, the exchange is indeed vintage Hollywood myopia. Only four years earlier, upon the release of another Oriental film, *An Arabian Knight*, a film trade magazine was urging theater owners to "play up" Japanese actor, Sessue Hayakawa, as an Arab to draw more patrons.

The Thief of Baghdad exploited the Orient as no few films have done before or since, and this is most evident in the film narrative itself as well as in the discourse surrounding the film's consumption. The film recounts the extraordinary change in fortune in the life of the Thief (played by Douglas Fairbanks), from a "wretched outcast" to hero and winner of the Princess's heart. When the Thief first sees the Princess he is instantly smitten by her beauty, and in his playful manner, he presents himself to her as "Ahmed, Prince of the Isles of the Seas, and of the Seven Palaces." Although she knows he is no prince, the Sultan's daughter gives him her ring. Ahmed has to ennoble himself to be worthy of her high station; and to this end, he goes to seek advice in a mosque, where he is told: "Allah hath made thy soul to yearn for happiness, but thou must earn it." Ahmed embarks thereafter on a long and perilous journey in search of the rare treasure demanded by the Princess as a condition for marriage. By the end of the journey, which takes him through "The Valley of Fire," "The Valley of the Monsters," "The Cavern of the Enchanted Trees," "The Old Man of the Midnight Sea," and "The Abode of the Winged Horse," he assembles rare treasures. The prizes, which include the Prince of the Indies' magical crystal (plucked from the eye of a forgotten idol near Kandahar), the Persian Prince's magic carpet, the Mongol Prince's magic apple from "the Island of Wak," are not only rare and precious but, it would soon be proved, vital in the rescue of the Princess, who has been poisoned by a female agent in the service of an evil Mongolian Prince. This evil prince plans to marry the daughter of the Caliph in order to take control of the city of Baghdad. When the plan fails, he decides to take the city with an army of twenty thousand men. Ahmed arrives at the right time and saves the beleaguered city and the Princess. He was helped to this victory by a hundred thousand soldiers whom he has conjured up through the sowing of the magical seeds of power at the gate of Baghdad.

Ahmed's arduous journey gives the film an episodic structure, where every phase is filled with fantastic occurrences excellently served by trick photography and special effects. From the rope that stiffened so that Ahmed could escape from his pursuers, through the famous underwater scenes as Ahmed is fighting the sea monsters, to the flying magic carpet, the film's effects were executed masterfully; no cost or effort spared. For the flying carpet scene, director Raoul Walsh used a crane and pulley to strengthen the illusion of flying. As he remembered it: "I made low-angle shots, added cut-ins of the people staring up from the streets —obtained by perching cameramen and myself on a platform at the top boom and shouting down— then resumed the slow pan showing the travelers on their way" (Raoul Walsh 168). In their effort to reproduce the supernatural enchantments and the magical atmosphere of the Orient, the filmmakers sought the services of an army of carpenters, builders, and glass blowers (responsible for the wonderful underwater glass city).

Although most critics believed *The Thief of Baghdad* a well-made fantasy, there was no agreement as to why Fairbanks undertook to make the film and what particular elements accounted for its success. For the first question, Alistair Cooke advanced that Fairbanks wanted to "better the example of the German historical costume film." Nevertheless, Cooke added, the film succeeded only in suffocating "the old beloved sprite in a mess of décor" (qtd. in Schickel, 1973: 82). The view that the athletic star became trapped in the sets and decor instead of being served by them was shared by critic Alexander Walker, who believed that "the armies of period historians, costume designers, special-effects men, and art decorators…do not support their leader so much as swamp him" (qtd. in Schickel, 1973: 82). Richard Schickel, however, thought highly of Fairbanks' film, finding it highly infused with "the basic values of the American film –action and humor and a certain light, self-mocking irony" (84). It is this quality which has led Benjamin Hampton to consider the *Thief of Baghdad* (along with *Ben Hur* and *King of Kings*) as "noteworthy achievements of the American civilization which inspired them." For Robert Sherwood, the interaction between the star and the magical opportunities offered by fantasyland explains the popular success of *The Thief of Baghdad*: "Fairbanks has gone far beyond the mere bounds of possibility; he has performed the superhuman feat of making his magic seem probable." (Qtd. in Schickel, 1973: 85)

Vachel Lindsay, in The Art of the Moving Picture, offered a fresh and most original reading of the film in the light of his esthetic of "architecture in motion". He remarked: "You can spend one whole evening just watching stairways and see how they leap like race horses from scene to scene …" becoming therefore "actors in the grand manner" (qtd. in Schickel, 1973: 86). In an argument that goes against Cooke's unease with the overpowering decor, Lindsay applauded the fact that the dynamic decor and setting help offset the typecasting of stars and the loss of vitality in other characters. Lindsay stressed: "It is a quality, not a defect, of the photoplays that while the actors tend to become types and hieroglyphics and dolls, on the other hand, dolls and hieroglyphics and mechanisms tend to become human. By an extension of this principle, non-human tones, textures, lines, and spaces take on a vitality almost like that of flesh and blood." (Qtd. in Tibbetts and Welsh 143-144)

Despite the pertinence of the views cited above, the Oriental factor in the construction and consumption of this famous fantasy was universally overlooked. This factor is all the more important as *The Thief of Baghdad* was released at a time when the Oriental genre was in high demand and movie audiences were flocking to see *The Sheik*, *The Arab*, *Under Two Flags* and other Oriental "photoplays". In fact, for many in the twenties, Fairbanks' film represented but another "Oriental subject," and no doubt its makers were fully conscious of the popular craze for things Arabian and Oriental. Thus, in addition to being a fantasy and a Fairbanks' vehicle, as Douglas Fairbanks was a hugely popular star in his own right, *The Thief of*

Baghdad owes its success and enduring appeal to the use of the various generic and cultural properties of the Oriental genre.

Pointing to this relationship, *The New York Times* opened its presentation of *The Thief of Baghdad* as follows: 'Imagine a clever satire on the *Arabian Nights* with marvelous photography and you have an inkling of Douglas Fairbanks's new picture" (19 March 1924). Indeed, the film credits the *Arabian Nights* as a source, situating itself within its overall network of themes and concerns. Thus, the film opens with a long title from the *Arabian Nights*; more exactly, the first few lines of the famous Burton translation: "Verily, the works of those gone before us have become instances and examples to men of our modern day, that folk may view what admonishing chances befell other folk and may therefore take warning." The Oriental setting and mood is thereupon instantly defined; yet, knowing Fairbanks' penchant for irony, the title's solemnity is somewhat humorous. What serious lessons would one learn from this fantasy? Perhaps a few time-honored formulas, such as the triumph of good over evil, the exhilarating feelings generated by power and wealth (the rags-to-riches motif), the value of dreams, and the merit of hard work.

Perhaps the greatest indication that *The Thief of Baghdad* was undertaken and meant to be enjoyed as an Oriental film for an audience enchanted with Oriental fare may be found in the thorough (over)exploitation of the Orient at hundreds of exhibition outlets throughout the United States. Exhibitors went to great lengths to give their movie theaters a thoroughly Oriental atmosphere. For a colorful example, the owner of Liberty Theatre introduced the film with "drums, ululating vocal offerings, odiferous incense, perfume from Baghdad, magic carpets and ushers in Arabian attire, who during the intermission made a brave effort to bear cups of Turkish coffee to the women in the audience" (*The New York Times* 19 March 1924).

Likewise, at the Stillman Theatre in Cleveland, the premiere of *The Thief* used a formidable media mix. In addition to an intense newspaper publicity campaign and merchants' tie-ups, the Theater's interior lobby was completely overhauled for the occasion, "draped in Oriental stuffs and rugs from a big Euclid avenue establishment, which also played up a Baghdad window display." The lobby also featured a presentation of a magic carpet, complete with Ahmed and the Princess on top of it, and a huge life-size mechanical elephant suggesting the atmosphere of the East. To finish the effect, especially designed art panels and Eastern vases were also displayed. Cooperation with this Theater for the occasion was provided by, among other institutions in the community, the Cleveland Public Library and a score of its branches in the form of displays of stills, literature, and plates bearing upon Baghdad and the art of the East. Most elaborate was the ambitious two-part stage presentation preceding the film showing in the form of a special overture by the Stillman orchestra under conductor Maurice Spitalny. As the music played in any such performance, curtains opened and the Caliph's necromancer began foretelling weird events over a caldron smoking with blue flames and clouds of incense. After this prologue, another set of curtains opened on a scene in the clouds with the Enchanted Rug seeming to move through space, carrying the characters of Ahmed and the Princess. Ahmed and the Princess, played by Fred J. true, a Cleveland baritone, and Ruth Leigh, soprano (from a Broadway Musical show), sang a love ballad, "Lovely Lady," composed by Carl Rupp (the words were adapted to be directly appropriate to the subject matter of *The Thief*). At the conclusion of the song the curtain closed and the picture started (*The Moving Picture World* 25 Jan. 1924).

Elaborate advertisement campaigns like these were by no means unique, at least with regards to special releases. What is significant here, as with other Oriental films of the period, is that the press and exhibition discourse centered almost exclusively on the Oriental setting, characters, and atmosphere. As a result, the exploitation was more generic than film-specific. For example, the burning of Oriental incense and the offering of Turkish coffee by male usherers in Arabian dress during the presentation of *The Thief*, hearken back more to the Sheik films –undoubtedly seeking the support of the flappers– than to any specific event in the film's story line.

The Thief of Baghdad furthermore shares a long list of characters, motifs, themes and images with the films belonging to the Oriental genre, from conniving and scheming Oriental potentates to beggars and thieves in the market place. Even though the plot line of *The Thief* carries Ahmed to places that are not part of the traditional Oriental imagery (such as the undersea locations and the Far-Eastern settings), the quintessential Oriental city of Baghdad remains the central arena of action, the origin and end of the hero's journey. The colorful scenes in the streets of Baghdad, although comic and centering on the antics of *The Thief*, represent an Orient very close to the one traditionally imaged by Western artists. The mosque, the harem, the palace and the seething bazaar are all part of the Oriental mosaic. Magic and its instruments, such as the carpet, the rope, and the tools that allow the hero to see the ailing Princess from great distances, or those that cause him to become invisible in times of danger (director Walsh claimed Ahmed's temporary invisibility was his idea), all help advance the action as well as reinforce the magical and mythical nature of the Orient.

Finally, since a chief concern of this study is to inquire about the nature of the Arab's portrayal in cinema, one may wonder if there is ground to believe that the Arab and the Orient in *The Thief of Baghdad* have been used negatively. Albeit the film is an acknowledged fantasy (not intended to vehicle a message of great social significance), and also exclusively animated by Oriental characters (excluding therefore the idea of victimization of Arabs by Westerners), it is safe to say that the Arabs in the film do not manage to transcend the unsympathetic roles allotted to them by the Orientalist tradition. It may be objected that the main character, the energetic and positive Ahmed/Fairbanks, is an Oriental; therefore his likeability should guarantee at least a balanced view of the East. Not enough in our view; for, although the hero bears the Oriental name 'Ahmed,' no great effort was made in the film to make him look or act specifically Oriental. Rendering identification even more difficult is the fact that, by the time *The Thief of Baghdad* was released, Fairbanks had already undergone a considerable degree of typecasting as a master swashbuckler and an all-American hero. Indeed, by 1924 Fairbanks was a too popular and loved by the audience as 'Doug' to be considered as anything else. Instead of suppressing Fairbanks in favor of the Arab persona, opposite strategies were adopted, such as a self-mocking style and a decision to portray him throughout the film as a half-naked character; notwithstanding the huge and bizarre earring.

Kismet (1920), and *The Lady of the Harem* (1926)

Robertson-Cole's 1920 screen version, *Kismet*, was based on Edward Knoblock's most successful and best-known play. It was directed by Louis Gasnier, with Otis Skinner playing the role of Hajj, the beggar and street poet. Hajj would be Otis Skinner's most famous role, on stage or in screen (Skinner also starred in a First National's talking version of *Kismet* in 1930). *Kismet* (meaning "fate") had been produced by Oscar Asche in 1911, playing in London's Garrick Theatre for more than two years. The huge success of the London performance attracted both American theater managers and the film studios to this Oriental play. According to the New York born playwright, "at once, all the managers in New York who had refused the play before were tumbling over each other to secure the rights" (Knoblock 10). When Robertson-Cole bought the screen rights in the United States, the play had already been made into a film in 1914 by England's Zenith Films, with Oscar Asche re-creating his stage role of Hajj. The play would become one of the most enduring stories of American cinema, stage, and television.

Although not based on any specific tale from the *Arabian Nights*, *Kismet* borrows extensively from this collection, even imitating its opening section. The long opening title proclaims, in the manner of a devout Arab fabulator who denies engaging in narration for pleasure but for the moral lesson to be garnered from the extraordinary story of Hajj: "Verily the works and words of those gone before us have become examples and admonitions to the men of our later day. And of such a kind is the story of Hajj, the beggar, who lived his life in this our peaceful city of Baghdad, one thousand years and one year ago…. Do ye take heed therein of the lesson taught by Fate, which the poets call *"Kismet"*. And mark well the chances and changes of time foredoomed to mortal man: lifting him now high, now sinking him low, even as the bucket in the well" (Knoblock 23).

The film covers Hajj's rise to the highest fortune in the land, and the fall from grace, in the space of one day; between dawn and sunset, precisely. During this time lapse, Hajj, a beggar at a Baghdad mosque, is arrested for stealing, put in jail, promised freedom by a scheming vizier if he kills the good Caliph, fails in the regicide attempt, is jailed anew, escapes, sees his beautiful daughter betrothed to the Caliph he had tried to kill, and is finally banished by the same Caliph (now his son in law) to his original begging station on the steps of the mosque, undisturbed by the events of the day that were after all only *"Kismet"* (fate or fortune). Scolding another beggar who took advantage of his absence and occupied his position by the Mosque, the defiant but now wiser and happier Hajj sums up the event of the day and reflects philosophically on his position in the overall scheme of things: "To the Caliph I may be dirt; but to dirt I am the Caliph.... I have lived today. Mine enemies dead... Mecca tomorrow. My say is said. So glory be to the One, the Eternal! He who begetteth not, nor is begot; the Ruler of Tide and Time"

Throughout the film, Hajj poses, steals, sings, reads poetry, and philosophizes; in short, uses his wits to serve his ends. He does not know fear because he is a fatalist. He is moved by everything but hardly affected by anything; not even by his raised fortunes as his daughter escapes a terrible fate on the hands of the wicked vizier and ends up marrying the Caliph.

On its release, *Kismet* was met by high praise from contemporary reviewers, who credited the source play and the performance of Otis Skinner in particular. One review stressed the importance of the film's fantastic character: "*Kismet* has value. Its story is different; its story is pleasantly fantastic, in spite of its murders; and it is a relief from the regular run of un-reality parading itself as true to life" (*The New York Times* 15 Nov. 1920). Lawrence Reid of the Moving Picture News called it "a truly artistic production and one which is a credit to motion pictures" (6 Nov. 1920). In addition to the film's Oriental color, Reid singled out as remarkable such events as "the great court reception before the divan of the commander of the Faithful, and that last agony of Mansur as he sinks to his death in the waters of his pool with Hajj leaning over and smiling down at him."

That this reviewer was so struck by the graphic agony resulting from Hajj's stylized revenge on the wicked vizier, is particularly fascinating. The violent scene chimes indeed with the notion of the East as a land of wanton and cruel acts. It is true that violence as well as extreme cruelty have been a staple of fantasies, introduced generally to highlight the relative peacefulness of the audience's real world. However, the Orient in *Kismet*, unlike Alice's Wonderland or other fantastic settings, is far from being a fictitious place; rather it is an enduring geographical, cultural, and ethnic reality. It is interesting to note that while characters from *The Wizard of Oz*, for example, are not said to possess "Ozian" qualities or vices, *Kismet*, for at least one reviewer, "offers a complicated story of Oriental cunning and intrigue" (*The Moving Picture World* 6 Nov. 1920). Oriental cunning is only part of the stock characterization of the East, which in this film includes a host of themes and images such as fatalism, revenge, harems, wicked viziers, slaves, and half-naked women reclining nonchalantly around rippling Oriental baths.

Finally, it is perhaps useful to ask if the character of Hajj in *Kismet* emerges as a positive one, at least as viewed within the overall evolution of the Oriental genre. While Hajj has been recognized as a picturesque philosopher, a fatalist, a humorist and playboy, no inductive leap was made to extend these mildly positive attributes to the Arab type, as has been done with regard to Hajj's cunning; deemed intrinsic to the Oriental region. *Kismet* demonstrates that an Arab character may attain qualified approval only through wit, guile and charm –all acquired qualities– and not through his inner nature. At best, one may conclude, the complex and fantastic persona of Hajj, like the Valentinian Sheik it antedated, has managed to telescope and absorb some of the best and worst attributes of the Arab type and the Oriental environment.

The suggestively titled *The Lady of the Harem* (Raoul Walsh, 1926) share with *The Thief of Baghdad* two main contributors: director Raoul Walsh, and Siamese-Born actor, So-Jin, who played the Mongol Prince in the second and assumed the role of the sinister Caliph in the first. However, it is with *Kismet* that *The Lady of the Harem* should be paired and compared, in view of its theatrical origin, its Arabian feel and style, and the labyrinthine politics of early Islamic Caliphates.

The Lady of the Harem is based on James Flecker's best known play, *Hassan: The Story of Hassan of Baghdad and How He Came to Make the Golden Journey to Samarkand* (London, 1922). A. L. Erlanger imported the play to New York, as he had done before with *Kismet* after this Oriental play had enjoyed some success in England. This time, however, the play failed on the American stage, resulting in its picture rights being sold to Hollywood.

Written in poetic prose, Hassan grew out Flecker's love for the literature of the Orient. Its origins go back to 1909 when Flecker wrote *The War Song of the Saracens*. On sick-leave in the Mediterranean in 1911, he read a small farcical play in Turkish, entitled "The Adventures of One Hassan, a Simple and Credulous Man whose Friends Amused Themselves by Playing Practical Jokes on Him with the Aid of a Hebrew Magician" (Redwood 15). Influenced by Mardrus' French translation of the *Arabian Nights*, Flecker decided to change the setting of the farce from Turkey to Baghdad. He liked to call the finished sketch his "New *Arabian Nights* play," adding,

125

somewhat prophetically, that "it will be more marvelously unsalable and unstageable than anything ever written" (qtd. in Redwood 15).

The film closely followed the plot line of the play, except that it opted for a conventional happy ending and increased the accent on nudity and sex. The story of the film traces some events during the reign of the fictitious Caliph of Kornassah, a man noted for his love for women and gold. When his soldiers steal a beautiful maid for him, her lover, Rafi, becomes extremely angry. The wronged lover, together with others equally oppressed by the Caliph's tyranny, plans a revolt against the potentate. When the Caliph is apprised of the plan, he becomes so terrorized that he started to go out into the streets, disguised as a merchant, hoping to find those plotting against him. On one such outing, the Caliph is imprisoned by the rebels, who do not recognize his true identity, but nevertheless think he is a traitor. The Caliph manages to escape with the help of Hassan, an ignorant candy-maker, who has also been wrongly imprisoned by the rebels. For helping the Caliph to escape, Hassan is generously rewarded with a high position in the court. When afterwards the Caliph crushes the revolt and begins torturing Rafi before the eyes of his beloved Pervanah, Hassan is so shocked by the cruelty and sadism of his benefactor that he resolves to go against him. He leaves the palace, joins the rebels, and becomes their leader. During a successful revolt, Hassan kills the Caliph and takes over as ruler of the land. His first order of business was none other than celebrating the union of the two great lovers, Rafi and Pervanah.

The film was awash with cruelty, no doubt seeping from the play –itself seething with violence and sadism. The Caliph revels in his sadistic sexual fantasies as he offers Rafi the choice between freedom if Pervanah returns to his harem, or his death before her eyes. He is particularly thrilled to hold the torture scene in the Palace garden, in "honor" and "as a mark of favor" to Hassan. Cruelty also runs through the vein of other characters. The fickle girl, Yasmin, sadistically enjoys the scene where the lovers are being tortured, admitting that she "laughed to see them writhe."

Unlike the fun-filled and exhilarating journey of the Thief, Aladdin, Hajj, and other Oriental fantasies' heroes, Hassan descends into a practical nerve-shattering dystopia. From the beginning, the innocent Hassan finds himself either victim or an instrument of other peoples' wicked desires. Hassan is allowed reprieve in the end of the film only because of the need for a conventional happy ending. The dream factory of Hollywood saw to it that the celluloid Hassan metes out justice by stabbing the evil Caliph in the back, ridding the people from his injustices and the lovers from his lust. In contrast, the play's ending is far less sanguine: when the palace fountain runs red with the blood of torture, Hassan and the poet/seer, Ishak, decide to take "the Golden Road to Samarkand." The poet captures their common disillusionment, as they leave troubled civilization: "I am leaving this city of slaves, this Baghdad of fornication. I have broken my lute and will write no more quasidahs in praise of the generosity of kings. I will try the barren road, and listen for the voice of the emptiness of earth. And thou shalt walk beside me" (*Kismet*).

Hassan's utter disillusionment in the play derives in great measure from the relentless pessimism of the playwright himself, in particular during Flecker's worsening state of health while writing Hassan. The stalking death, in the form of acute consumption, was all the more daunting to Flecker who had never developed a taste for organized religion. The mysterious, labyrinthine and blighted Orient became therefore a metaphor of his diseased and dissatisfied being, as the depravity and wanton destructiveness traditionally associated with the Orient mirrored Flecker's troubled life and vice versa.

If the film's ending had to be re-written for the satisfaction of Hollywood "happy ending" requirement, the sexual and sadistic components were retained and even magnified. The over-emphasis on titillating sex was blamed directly on director Walsh: "the directorial accent on sex, sex, sex seemed silly. Walsh kept parading the girls in front of the camera as if there were so many show girls, dressed so sparsely to give the Winter Garden mob a thrill" (*Variety* 25 August 1925). If the studio (Famous Players) hoped to achieve great box office returns through emphasizing nudity, they were wrong: *Variety* was quick to note that Walsh's "undressed stuff proved a dud." Flecker's prediction that his Hassan would be "marvelously unsalable and unstageable" was proved right, at least with regard to the American stage and cinema.

The lack of grip by this film is in part the result of the highly personal and poetic nature of the source play, and to some extent the audiences' growing preference for more realistic and accessible Oriental themes and characters (the extremely successful *The Son of the Sheik* and *Beau Geste* were released at approximately the same time). Another reason may have been the beginning of the decline in popularity of Oriental films, particularly those that, like *The Lady of the Harem*, unimaginatively piled up Oriental imagery for no other purpose than joining the scramble for lucrative Oriental subjects.

Chapter Ten

CONCLUSION

The Development of the Arab Stereotype in American Cinema

The foregoing chapters have showcased and explored the modes and patterns of packaging the exotic and mostly negative Arab type to audiences that far from passively consumed what Hollywood threw at them; but, through their possession of the Orientalist repertoire and by leveraging their patronage and support, helped feed and fan interest in the Oriental films during the silent era to a degree of genuine fascination. At this point into the analysis of dozens of films in this study, we may be justified in claiming a legitimacy allowing us to put forward a general statement regarding the representation of the Arab type in the all-important, formative first three decades of American cinema. Thus, for the frequently asked questions: "How does the Arab type emerge from the Oriental films of the period?" and, "how may one characterize the cinema dealing with Arabs?" the brief but much deliberated answer to the first question is: violent, lusty, and irrational; to the second it is: colonial, racist, and fantastic. The two sets of epithets provided by the first and second answer are deliberately symmetrical and find their grounding in lengthy analyses of the films belonging to each of the three categories identified in this study. Accordingly, the first epithet from each answer; namely, "violent" and "colonial," may well provide the summary of the so-called Colonial-Realist films; the second pair, "lusty" and "racist," constitutes the burden of the Psychological-Orientalist films; while the last pair, "irrational" and

129

"fantastic" best characterizes the Fantastic category. The verdict above may appear condemning; yet, with the reported notable exceptions surrounding mostly the ambiguous Sheik persona; Hollywood films featuring Arabs provide ample support for the lackluster judgment.

Of the three categories of the Oriental genre here expounded, the first has been the most condemning of Arabs and their world. Its plots read and evolve like modern versions of the Western Medieval collective wish to settle old scores with the Oriental archenemy. It may be retorted that cinema lives and thrives on action, which wars and fast-paced pursuits and counter-attacks provide in good quantities. However, the extensive film analyses leave no doubt that determining the winner and loser in films about Arabs owes more to the age-old antagonism between the two cultures than to a consideration for narrative closure or Hollywood's imposed desire for a happy ending. Additionally, notwithstanding the meandering through exotic detail and the frequent romanticizing of the natives' life-style in the films of this category, the presence of European garrisons and men in military uniforms in these films speaks volumes about the arrogance and unbalanced reality of colonialism. The Foreign Legion films provide the quintessential demonstration.

Although the East/West tension equally strongly informs the films of the Orientalist-Psychological group, what is most remarkable about these films is that the Arab type emerges as somewhat complex and multidimensional. Characteristically, the Arab male here is a lover, faithless and false as the desert mirage it is true, but he is regularly allowed to embark on an intricate emotional relationship with a Western female. The narrative moments of significance bestowed on some Arab characters, albeit transient in character, do reflect the perennial fascination with the Orient, running as an uninterrupted undercurrent to the centuries-old antagonism between West and East. This study has revealed that the positive change in the image of the Arab in films such as Valentino's *The Sheik* was favored and to some degree brought about by the changing mood of American society during the Jazz Age. Of great significance here was the emergence of women as major consumers of film fare who intelligently and forcefully used their box office vote to express and strengthen their newly acquired liberties. In particular, the flapper element of this female audience used the subversive film medium as a conduit and a test for their norm-flaunting social status. The tumultuous cinematic Orient served the social and individual rights agenda of this demographic segment in a number of ways: as a mirror reflection of the undergoing chaotic transformations in American society; as a space to breathe and achieve vicarious liberation from the still-existing Victorian behavior codes, and as an underdog ally, with whom female audiences shared the indignities of white male oppression and the desire to break free from this lopsided relationship. Through an intricate system of super stardom, romantic male behavior, and the ever-fascinating Oriental space, the Sheik persona as structured by Rudolph Valentino appealed to women as no other star persona has managed to do before or since. However, the positive aura surrounding a few Arab characters during the 1920s could not offset the barrage of negative images attached to Arabs in general. Even the mildly positive Valentino Sheik starts out as a lustful desert outlaw (despite the Paris education), not wholly dissimilar to the bandits who later fought him for the same female prey. Lust and particularly the craving for white Western women were dramatized in *The Sheik* as well as other films, not only for the obvious reason of audience titillation, but also for the lessons about the serious threat and consequences of the taboo of miscegenation. Films on Arabs did heed the societal interdiction related to inter-racial sex, as demonstrated, albeit farcically, by the English Lady in *The Sheik* as she belatedly discovers that Sheik Ahmed is after all not an Arab but a European and a Christian. Had he remained an Arab all along, the film ending would not suggest the prospects of a romantic union between him and the English lady. The societal shared perception and perhaps the rule was: either the Arab is a false and fickle lover or not a real Arab at all.

Nearly all Oriental films of the silent period, not only those belonging to the so-called Fantastic category, qualify to be called fantastic, at least in the sense that none expressly aimed —or succeeded if it tried— to document the life and habits of Orientals. Oriental film fantasies, as featured in this study, are however most distinguishable by their use of the supernatural, the mythical, the grotesque, and their exclusively Oriental setting. Like the characters from the *Arabian Nights*, the source of most of these fantasies, the Arabs who animate the action represent a wide range of human expressions and occupations: they are philosophers and fatalists

(*Kismet*), cruel despots, murderers, poets, and candy makers (*The Lady of the Harem*), magicians and orphans (*Aladdin*), thieves and spies (*The Thief of Bagdad*), and so on. There is however a significant difference: while the Arabian tales balanced their characters, investing them with various shadows of evil and good to reflect life's complexity, mystery and unintelligibility, Oriental fantasies opted instead for the simple polarity of good and evil, with more evil and sinister characters than agreeable ones. The Orient as vehicled through these movies incorporated mostly negative traits, such as irrationality, intemperance, lawlessness, and absolutism. Hence, the Oriental space in these films became not only a rack on which to hang what the West is not, but also a reminder of what the latter should not be or become.

While there is near unanimity about the negativity dominating the Arab portrayal in American cinema from the birth of the medium up till now, this study took the additional necessary steps to go back and explore the mindsets and the general conditions of production and consumption of these films. Different from the prevailing activists' and critics' stance which is fundamentally dismissive of the denigrating treatment of reel Arabs, this study dared to point to and situate filmically and sociologically the real moments of pleasure experienced by the millions of consumers of this type of film fare. The reasons for the audience's gratification were multiple. First, the Orientalist ethos supplying the reservoir of negative types has never been wholly damning; in many of its manifestations it is at least ambiguous. Second, films about Arabs are not only polysemic; that is, allowing for multiple, even contradictory, readings; but they have been known to deliberately play up the social and psychological contradictions through the interplay of "sound" (yes, the films were silent, but the music accompanying the exhibition of the films significantly heightened the sense of the Orient and may therefore be considered an intra-diegetic element), visuals, icons, and codes in order to allow for some titillating textual negotiations. Then there is the issue of generic complicity. Film audiences are generally attracted to genre films for the pleasure they know they will derive from meeting their cherished formulas and waiting to discover if these will be confirmed, augmented or challenged; and from a sense of communal belonging to a group of like-minded social and cultural actors. Third, the myriad psychological and social anxieties of the teen and twenties have made it possible for the Orient and the Arab type in film to become appropriated as allies (the flapper using the rogue Arab as a symbol of agitation) or metaphors (the Orient teetering between rationality and moral and civil bankruptcy) by the audiences to help alleviate and negotiate the anxiety of transitioning from the nineteenth-century moral and social order to a completely modern one.

As duly noted throughout this study, the Arab type in silent cinema has been the beneficiary of a stream of positive images. In addition to the celebrated Arab-lover type immortalized by Valentino in the 1920s, a number of Arab characters were allotted some (fugitive) moments of excellence and brilliance. In *Kismet*, for example, Hajj is likable for his come-what-may philosophy, his courage, and his gift for rhyme; while the Caliph, against all the heavy typecasting, is a totally honorable man whom genuine love transforms into a Romeo-like figure. Most significant of all, a number of films made during the 1910s (see respective analyses in previous chapters) utilized the Orient not as an exotic and danger-filled setting but as simply a different locale for human experiences and emotion to unfold. In these films, neither numerous nor replicated after the silent era, universal feelings of love, courage, faithfulness, and altruism were dished out according to merit and narrative demands and not along ethnic, geographical or stereotypical considerations.

The multiple examples of the Arab's nobility and humanity are notable in at least two respects. First, for an activist or a proponent of change in the portrayal of the Arab in modern cinema and media in general, the bright spots registered in silent cinema should provide ground for hope. One might advance the argument that if it was possible to nuance the Arab type before, then why not now or at a foreseeable future time? Secondly, and pertinent to the discussion below, the American cinema of the post-silent era has transferred all the negative characterizations of the Arab (with some modernization of the props) but failed conspicuously to re-produce the positive elements which have distinguished and made memorable some of the celluloid Arabs of the 1910s and 1920s.

The Evolution of the Oriental Genre

Generic evolution is a process best described by film critic Leo Braudy in the following dialogue: "Genre films ask the audience, "Do you still want to believe this?" Popularity is the audience answering, "Yes". Change in genre occurs when the audience says, "that's too infantile a form of what we believe. Show us something more complicated (Braudy in Schatz 38)." Braudy's imaginary exchange elucidates the tacit terms of the contract binding the genre filmmakers to the audience they serve. Communication between a genre and its consumers is always ongoing, articulated by box office feedback as well as such intermediary agents as posters, reviews, criticism, and other forms of exhortation. Concerning the Oriental genre, this 1921 advertisement invokes the dialogue above: "Do you like stories about the Sahara, with its mystery and its fascination? See An Arabian Night! (*The Moving Picture World* 25 Sep. 1925)"

As the above exhortation implies, Oriental films of the silent period were perceived and consumed as part of an entity referred to as "Oriental subjects," "Oriental dramas," "desert stuff," "Arabian stuff," "Sheik pictures," etc.; suggesting a widely recognized class of films with a distinct style, theme, and visual properties. So much so that when a particular Oriental film did not deliver its anticipated value, reviewers and critics duly invoked the cheated expectations of the audience and usually, directly or otherwise, called for more complexity and sophistication in the generic formula.

In their praise or condemnation, early reviewers and critics did not view the Oriental genre as a phenomenon that needed nurturing in its inexorable passage from birth, growth, and decay, as modern critics would do. If a particular film was successful, the genre was praised as relevant, but if the film failed it was for them a sign that the Oriental "stuff" was no longer effective. As a result of such visceral reactions, during the entire decade of the 1920s, reviewers continually predicted the imminent demise of what they considered no more than an Oriental fad in filmmaking. Yet, with every successful film, such as *The Sheik*, *The Arab*, *Beau Geste* or *The Thief of Bagdad*, faith in the Oriental formula was rekindled.

Examples of the contradictory views of the role and fate of the Oriental genre during the silent era abound. In its review of *The Tents of Allah* (1923), *The Moving Picture World* hinted that the (Oriental) genre had been perhaps overdone, but added its assurance that the film was "so entertaining, and the atmosphere so intriguing that it should please even where there has been a reaction against this type of attraction (*The Moving Picture World* 7 April 1923)." The same film was introduced by *Variety* thus: "at this late date [1923] desert stuff has had its vogue and the features with the Arabian steeds and grains of sand no longer have the appeal (*Variety* 5 April 1923)." Repeated statements about the outmodedness or the failing relevance of the Oriental genre may be explained by the fact that early reviewers and critics did not comprehend how genre operates (obviously, film genre criticism is a subsequent extrapolation). Most detractors bemoaned the lack of novelty in the "Sahara pictures," not fully recognizing that genre films are mostly repetitions of successful and tried formulas, with few novel elements introduced with controlled measure.

The foregoing reactions by early reviewers compound the difficulty of tracing a clear evolutionary path in the development of the Oriental genre. The Oriental formula was said to have began to lose its appeal –being allegedly overdone– even before the making in 1921 of Valentino' *The Sheik*, the landmark film that many modern critics believe started the genre. Reviews then yield only scant insight on how and when these films evolved, reached their classic age, and finally slipped out of the audience's favor. But, holding the Oriental genre to some current models of genre evolution offers equally few answers. The evolutionary schema of growth, flowering, and decay has already been criticized as "highly mechanistic" and "teleological (Neale 58)." The Oriental genre does not support this organic metaphor either; since the genre's development was demonstrably far from linear and the narrative and technical advances less clearly incremental. To some extent, excepting the extremely short films of the pre-1912 period, the narrative structure, the iconographic repertoire, and the characterization in the Oriental films were often as well developed in the teens as they were in the mid-twenties. There was indeed a quantitative explosion of films about the Orient during the 1920s, a virtual flowering of the Oriental genre; yet, the films also displayed numerous symptoms associated with a genre's decay, such as excessive repetition, parody, reflexivity, and chronic creative aridity.

Thomas Schatz's evolutionary model also emphasizes linear progression, in his case from the genre's transparency to opacity or self-conscious formalism. The sequence, transparency (where the form is invisible) and opacity (where film form draws attention to itself) is not entirely borne out by the development of the Oriental genre. Even as early as the formative years of the mid-1910s, some

Oriental films were far from transparent. The film versions of some *Arabian Nights'* tales, such as Ali Baba and Aladdin, showed a great deal of "formal interference," as the popularity of the tales from children books and other media meant that the film versions would be enjoyed, to a large measure, for the filmic treatment and special effects they bring to the stories. The magical possibilities of film were perfectly suited to the extraordinary feats of the Arabian genies, as palaces sprang to existence in less than a second, carpets took to the sky, and ordinary glass sparkled like rare diamond.

Another model, the Russian Formalists', is useful to understand the development and weakening of the Oriental genre; in particular as it has "the virtue of embedding the history of individual genres within the history, not just of generic formations, but of wider cultural formations as well (Neale 61)." Generic evolution, according to this model, is to be understood in terms of "succession," in the sense of "struggle" (ibid). According to this model, genres gradually lose their power through continual reproduction. Genres "are forced to the periphery by new genres often arising from a "vulgar" stratum if they cannot be reanimated through a restructuring (be it through the playing up of previously suppressed themes or methods, or through the taking up of materials or the taking over of functions from other genres)" (ibid). For the Oriental genre, this is appropriate in at least two ways. First, one may use this model to explain how the nascent cinema –arising from the 'vulgar' stratum of various technological contraptions of the second half of the nineteenth-century– took over the subject of the Orient, pushing to the periphery other treatments of the Orient (theatrical, journalistic, poetic and novelistic). The Oriental film genre thereafter appropriated the themes and materials previously used by the mostly literary genres concerned with the Orient, themselves being steeped into the cultural system of Orientalism. Since this model allows for genres borrowing from other genres, styles, and techniques, it could be argued that the Fantastic category of the Oriental genre, for example, borrowed and amalgamated Oriental lore and imagery, the fantastic stories from the *Arabian Nights*, the fantastic genre in folklore and literature, and the technical advances registered in the field of cinematography, from improved film stock to art direction. In general, the Oriental genre took over elements from such diverse sources as narrative fiction, poetry, drama, painting, religious rhetoric, nationalism, colonialism, militarism, Egyptology, travel accounts, the adventure film, the war film, children cinema, comedy, the documentary, and the scenic features.

The second application of the formalist model concerns the Oriental genre's decline. Here, no specific factor or group of causes may be advanced as solely responsible for the Oriental genre's loss of appeal after 1930. It could be said that just as this genre borrowed styles from different media and momentarily pushed the literary genres dealing with the Orient to the periphery, other (new) genres, techniques, and styles began to rise on the very ground occupied by the Oriental genre. For one thing, the momentous advent of sound coincided with a noticeable decrease of interest in Oriental films. While sound made it possible for American audiences to rediscover, through the many successful musicals, the colorful rhythms of its vaudeville houses, it has also brought about the consolidation of production companies. Because of the expenses involved with the licensing and use of the sound technology, the small companies that thrived on imitating or lampooning proven generic successes (for example, the Sheik formula) were simply forced out of business.

Moreover, the great economic depression did sober Americans to the fact that tragedies are not a monopoly of foreign lands and races. For at least the first few years of the Depression, Americans were forced to look home for the source of evil. The criminal underworld nurtured by the harsh economic times spawned rogues and assassins besides whom scheming Sheiks and silhouetted saber-wielding Bedouins appeared as dilettante delinquents. The gangster film genre of the thirties thrust urban decay on the same audiences that marveled at distant exotic lands and was charmed by the sophistication and chicanery of foreign lovers; be they Sheiks, tango dancers, or decadent Europeans. The foreboding clouds of World War II further cast a literally dark shadow on film; and the resulting genre, film noir, ferreted out sinister foreign agents from obscure basements, discrediting thus the foreign lover type, perhaps forever.

The Arab in Modern Cinema and Television

Films about the Arab and the Arab environment continued to be made in the United States and elsewhere in the West after 1930 simply because the Orient continued to exercise its traditional fascination on the Western psyche. The immensely popular, mostly romantic, and seemingly apolitical *Casablanca* (1942) owes some of its spectacular success to the allure of the Oriental setting, the romantic knot, and to the reality of the American invasion of North Africa. The invasion had taken place only a couple of weeks before the film distribution, and Hollywood could not have drummed up better publicity, tying the film to the invasion and to the Roosevelt summit in *Casablanca*. Few months later, the hilarious and stereotype-filled, *The Road to Morocco*, was released, certainly also with the events in North Africa on every mind, and particularly *Casablanca* still on every screen.

Strategically, for the history of the cinematic portrayal of Arabs, the iconic *Casablanca* is symptomatic of the shift from the Orient as a romantic and mythical space to the Orient as a geographical entity, now re-baptized as "the Middle East" and thrown as a chip in the shifting alliances of international relations and the balance-of-power game. Post-war American interest in the region meant that Arabs and the Oriental setting would cease to be entirely ethereal and would acquire a lastingly nagging tangibility. The establishment of the state of Israel and the resulting ongoing Arab-Israeli conflict, followed by a series of violent American encounters with Arabs and Muslims in the Middle East, created novel ominous perceptions of the Orient which soon filtered into American popular culture; already familiar with the traditional Arab type as a threatening other. All modern film critics are unanimous in their conclusion that the Hollywood's portrayal of the Arab went from bad to worse and then to worst. This study concurs only with the middle and final characterizations, as it believes that the initial stage of Arab representation was at least ambiguous— neither irredeemably negative nor clearly positive— allowing the Arab type to momentarily transcend its swarthiness to become a positive trope, enjoyed for its own sake but also used in the local tug-of-war between opposing social forces in the fast-changing America of the twenties.

Clearly, there has been a tightening of the screw, or a dumbing down process, with regard to the portrayal of Arabs in American cinema after the second war. To the clearly negative Orientalist legacy, a series of events have added their depressing imprint on the filmic existence of Arabs and Muslims. I would mention as formative influences the following phases, or historical events and happenings: 1) the establishment of Israel and the ensuing legend of the civilizing

Israelis versus the violent and nature-destroying Palestinians; as spun repeatedly by the Golan Globus film production company and PR machine; 2) the Iran fiasco, the Beirut Barracks bombing, and the Palestinian struggle; a triumvirate of events pitting for the first time American law enforcers and avengers against Arab "terrorists"; 3) the 1973 Oil Crisis and the eruption onto the world capitals of the rich and greedy Arab; 4) the Gulf War and the neo-conservatives' legitimization of islamophobia, especially following Samuel Huntington's clash-of-civilization war cry in 1993; and 5) the 9/11 cataclysm and its debilitating effect on the perception of Arabs and Muslims in America and beyond.

Thus, the 1960s witnessed the beginning of what may be considered an Oriental sub-genre, centering on the Arab-Israeli conflict. *Exodus* (Otto Preminger, 1961) began a series of films in which the Jewish settlers in Palestine are portrayed in a struggle for survival in inhospitable desert conditions compounded by what is presented as the inexplicable hate of the Arabs. Based on Leon Uris' novel, which was intended to popularize Israel with the American public, *Exodus* was a deliberate attempt to denigrate and even dehumanize the Arabs. Films in the vein of *Exodus* multiplied, thanks partly to the efforts and operations of Golan-Globus, the film production company with unmistakable pro-Israel sympathies.

Starting in 1970s and 1980s, scores of films were made featuring a new brand of American hero machine-gunning his way into and out of booby-trapped dungeons in Beirut, Baghdad or Teheran to win freedom for American hostages. The Western civilization hater and suicide bomber, the Afghanistan-trained and radicalized terrorist, and the suave Western-educated student highjacker are some refinements of the violent Arab type already present in Western imagination. The plots and action of these films strongly bring to mind the many silent movies featuring young Legionnaires bravely fending off from their garrison turrets the repeated attacks of Arab assailants. In the films of both periods, the outcome is the same: the triumph of the Western camp and the flight or destruction of the Bedouins or Arab terrorists.

There is however a notable difference between silent and modern films on Arabs, and that is the complete absence in recent films of any positive value attached to the Arab individual, his cause, his life, or his milieu. Even in the most condemning silent film, the exotic Oriental setting is usually separated from its inhabitants, allowing the lyricism of the setting to be expressed by images of dancing palm trees, glimmering sand dunes, spiraling minarets, and the choreography of movement in the markets and public places. None of this exotic beauty dwells in the post-war movies; certainly also, none of the resourcefulness, appeal, and charm of a Valentino Sheik (in the Sheik films) or a Skinner Hajj (in *Kismet*).

Instead, terrorism (a cognate of the violence traditionally associated with the Arab), white slavery (a corollary of the lustful Arab), and immeasurable petro-dollar wealth (chiming with the fabulous riches of the East), characterize the Arab type in modern cinema. Dozens of film titles demonstrate the tendency to rob the Arab of any human complexity and cast him in the demeaning colors of terror, lust, and greed. Sometimes, the denigrating treatment is unabashedly open; as in the television drama, *Under Siege* (NBC, 1986), where the FBI director tells an employer: "Those people – Arabs– are different from us. It's a whole different ball game. I mean the East and the Middle East. These people have their own mentality. They have their own notion of what's right and what's wrong. What's worth living for and dying for. But we insist on dealing with them as if they're the same as us. We'd better wake up (qtd. in Shaheen 1986: 11)".

While this kind of stereotype-filled discourse is always assured of an audience, many voices have risen to protest against it as blatant misrepresentation. Organized Arab-American intellectuals, from such groups as the National Association of Arab Americans, the Arab-American University Graduates, the American-Arab Anti-Discrimination Committee, and the Arab American Institute, are the most outspoken, often taking the protest to the media itself, occasionally achieving some limited success. During the filming in Washington D. C. of Protocol (1984), the American Arab Anti-Discrimination Committee learned that the script contained many stereotypes of Arabs. The Committee's director wrote complaining to the producer: "We do not suggest that Arabs should not be used, nor that they cannot be funny, only that you do not perpetuate the negative and hurtful images employed in depicting our community" (qtd. in Michalek 1986: 9). The producer promised that "*Protocol* will be a film that you will not be ashamed to take your children to (ibid)." The final product, commented Laurence Michalek, "while not overtly racist and malicious," relied on "stereotypes and dubious humor. The fictitious country was named 'El-Ohtar' ('rat hole' spelled backwards), and the Arabs generally come off as rich, blonde-crazy, and politically backward" (ibid). This was the first time an Arab-American group protested and received media attention. Years later, upon the protest of Arab-Americans, Disney Studio agreed to replace part of a song's lyrics in *Aladdin* (1992) containing the unfavorable reference to the Orient as a place where "they cut off your ear". Even non-Arabs and some professional groups agree that there is enormous slant and unfairness in the media toward the Arabs. In a letter to the Writers' Guild and Screen Actors Guild, writer-producer Ted Flicker wrote: "I think that honor requires that we, the makers of our nation's myths, consider the plight of these people [the Arabs] ... and help get rid of the Arab stereotypes" (qtd. in Shaheen 1986: 12).

Actions taken by Disney and others might suggest that the misrepresentation of the Arab is on the downside or is being countered and corrected as soon as it takes place. The fact is that, more often than not, the Arabs are still maligned and caricatured in modern American cinema and television. Unfortunately, there is no satisfying explanation as to why the Arab and his world are thus maligned in modern cinema and television. The attempts to provide an answer range from the partial to the naive. According to Michalek, the main reason Hollywood misrepresents the Arabs is that they "are the one large group of people of whom Americans know little about. The United States has very visible ethnic groups of Asian, Latin American, and African origin, as well as others from every other country in Europe, but there are few Arabs (8)." Like many, Michalek also subscribes to a popular explanation invoking the Jewish connection; pointing especially to the Jewish domination of Hollywood, and specifically to the filmic output of the studio, Cannon-Group/Golan-Globus. A different view, shared by many non-Arabs, was advanced by actor Omar Shariff in an interview published in Cineaste. Shariff concedes that the Arabs are not well represented; but, referring to the terrorism charge, he agrees that some of the terrorism portrayed in media is of their own making; as to the Jewish connection, he believes that the Jews are entitled to their opinion in defending their cause. Speaking like the poker player that he is, Shariff concludes: "I'd say that the Arab image is bad because the money is against it. For the time being, the Arabs are the bad guys because they have committed acts of terrorism and all that. I think that image will change. If they make a peace settlement, which I hope they will, then suddenly you will see films where the Arabs are the good guys" (qtd. in Rosen 1986)

Although the scope of this study (focusing on the films made during the silent era) absolves it from passing a judgment on exactly who and what is to be blamed for the misrepresentation of the Arab in modern visual media, there is perhaps room for a clarification. The verdict a few pages ago that silent films on Arabs are colonial, racist, and fantastic, is not a flattering one. Nearly always, the Arab in these films is portrayed as violent, lustful, and irrational. Modern cinema about the Arab has retained all the negative characterizations, but added more negative wrinkles (gambling, for example), and updated and made more destructive some props (the machine gun for the sword, the bomb for the dagger, hijacking planes instead of kidnapping white maidens, for example). What this says is that as far as the Arab image is concerned there is an unmistakable continuity between the silent cinematic tradition and the more recent one. Therefore, a more useful question about the modern portrayal of the Arab should not be why the Arab is depicted negatively in modern cinema and television, but what caused the intensification of the negative image of the Arab in recent films? For an answer to this question, one could advance, among others, the views expressed above and the cause-and-effects fallouts from the five geopolitical factors enumerated above (from the establishment of Israel and the concomitant US involvement in Middle Easter realities to the aftermath of 9/11 and the punditry of CNN and Fox News). I am, however, more interested in what the question presupposes: that there has always been a bedrock, a system of beliefs, a shared reservoir of concepts and conclusions about the Arab and the Oriental affecting the multiple channels of cultural intercourse, including broadcast and visual communication. Referred to throughout as the system of Orientalism, this body of thought pre-figured the shape of the silent films about the Arab and the Orient, and arguably to a great degree that of modern films as well. For, despite what may be thought about the demise or the irrelevance of the system of Orientalism in a more open and multicultural world, there is every indication, garnered from films and other types of discourse geared toward the traditional Orient, that what took centuries to establish may take a long time to unravel.

Chapter Eleven

FILMOGRAPHY:
FILMS ON ARABS AND ARABIC THEMES (1894-1930)

Note on the Filmography

Before this study undertook to piece-by-piece erect a filmography of films on Arabs covering the period 1894-1930, there existed no such listing. Later, it was gratifying to discover that this effort served the research needs of film and art historians. The most well-known published book on the Hollywood Arab, Jack Shaheen's *Reel Bad Arabs: How Hollywood Vilified a People*, incorporated this listing, spanning the thirty years of Silent Cinema, in its comprehensive filmography covering one-hundred-plus years of cinema history.

Of the 250 films entries of the present filmography, about two-thirds are fiction films; while the remainder is composed of documentaries, scenics and travelogues. Most of the films range in length from three to eight and ten reels, and only a few of the fiction films are one- or two-reelers. The non-fiction titles, especially the scenic views and travelogues of the early period, are extremely short; ranging from less than a minute during the first years of cinema to five minutes and more as films developed in length and technique.

Compiling the present filmography was no easy task. I spent three years perusing and parsing various bits of data in the newspapers and trade papers of the period on microfilms and microfiches in a number of libraries. Unfortunately, the catalogues spanning the period 1894-1930 are not as complete or exhaustive in their details as a researcher might wish them to be. For example, the very important volumes of *The American Film Institute Catalog of Motion Pictures Produced in the United States: Feature Films* do not cover the formative period 1894-1910. Unfortunately also, they do not include films of less than three reels, an omission that not only affects a large number of very important fiction films but as well nearly all documentaries and travelogues. Moreover, even when they include listings by subject, some catalogues lack comprehensive generic groupings to designate films featuring Arabic types and themes. Furthermore, the compilers were not geographically and historically attuned; consequently, there was some confusion surrounding such labels as 'Arab,' 'Turk,' 'Mohammedan,' 'Moslem,' and 'Syrian,' often used and construed interchangeably at the time by audiences and critics; and significantly even by the overwhelmed US Immigration Services of the period.

The Filmography

1894-1909
~ *Sheik Hadj Tahar, Hadj Cherif*
Kinetoscope Company (Black Maria). 6 October 1894. Two of four Arab "numbers" presented on this day.

~ *Fatima*
International Film Company. 1897. The American Mutoscope and Biograph Co. also photographed the dancer, Fatima, at Coney Island in the same year.

~ *A Street Arab*
Edison. 21 April 1898.

~ *Arabian Gun Twirler*
Thomas Edison. 20 March 1898.

~ *Allahabad, the Arabian Wizard*
American Mutoscope & Biograph Co. 11 November 1902.

~ *Arab Act, Luna Park (Coney Island)*
American Mutoscope & Biograph Co., 1903.

~ *Arabian Jewish Dance*
Thomas Edison. 17 June 1903.

~ *Egyptian Boys in Swimming Race* (Documentary)
Thomas Edison. 10 June 1903. A short film (1 min) made by A. C. Abadie in Luxor, Egypt.

~ *Egyptian Fakir with Dancing Monkey* (Documentary)
Thomas Edison. A. C. Abadie. 8 June 1903. 1 1/2 min.

~ *Egyptian Market Scene* (Documentary)
Thomas Edison. June 1903. A. C. Abadie. 1/2 min.

~ *Excavating Scene at the Pyramids of Sakkaroh*
Thomas Edison. 1903

~ *Going to Market, Luxor, Egypt* (Travelogue)
Thomas Edison. 17 June 1903. A. C. Abadie. 49 sec.

~ *Herd of Sheep on the Way to Jerusalem* (Documentary)
Thomas Edison. 1903.

~ *Fording the Nile River on Donkeys* (Documentary)
Thomas Edison. June 1903. A. C. Abadie. 2 min.

~ *Jerusalem's Busiest Street, Showing Mount Zion*
(Travelogue/Documentary)
Edison. 17 June 1903.

~ *Market Scene in Old Cairo, Egypt* (Documentary)
Thomas Edison. 28 March 1903. A. C. Abadie. 1 min.

~ *Panoramic View of Beyrouth, Syria* (Documentary)
Thomas Edison. June 1903. A. C. Abadie. 1. 20 min.

~ *Panoramic View of an Egyptian Cattle Market*
(Travelogue/Documentary)
Thomas Edison. June 1903. A. C. Abadie. 2 min.

~ *Passengers Embarking from SS Augusta Victoria at Beyrouth* (Travelogue)
   Thomas Edison. 1903.

~ *Primitive Irrigation in Egypt* (Documentary)
   Thomas Edison. June 1903. A. C. Abadie. 1 min.

~ *Shearing a Donkey in Egypt* (Documentary)
   Thomas Edison. June 1903. A. C. Abadie. 1 min.

~ *Street Scene at Jaffa* (Travelogue/Documentary)
   Thomas Edison. June 1903. A. C. Abadie. 40 secs.

~ *Tourists Embarking at Jaffa* (Travelogue)
   Thomas Edison. 17 June 1903. A. C. Abadie. 1. 26 min.

~ *Tourist on Donkey for the Pyramid of Sakkarah* (Travelogue/Documentary)
   Thomas Edison. 1903.

~ *Tourist Returning on Donkey from Mispah* (Travelogue/Documentary)
   Thomas Edison. 1903.

~ *Tourist Taking Water from the River Jordan* (Travelogue)
   Thomas Edison. 1903.

~ *Kairowan, Algiers* (Documentary)
   Source unknown. C. 1905. Library of Congress Paper Print Collection. 5 min.

~ *Aladdin's Lamp*
   Pathé Frères. 1907.

~ *Ali Barboyou et Ali Bouf à l'huile*
   Méliès. 1907.

~ *Fatima's Dance*
International. 1907.

~ *From Cairo to Khartoum* (Documentary)
Eclipse. 10 August 1907.

~ *Arabian Dagger*
Pathé Frères. 6 June 1908. 459 ft.

~ *The Flight from the Seraglio*
Great Northern Film Co. 23 May, 1908. 625 ft.

~ *Making Arabian Pottery* (Documentary)
Pathé Frères. 3 October 1908. 475 ft.

~ *The Mohammedan at Home* (Documentary)
Producer unknown. 19 December 1908.

~ *Native Life in Sudan* (Travelogue/Documentary)
Pathé. 4 July, 1908. 459 ft.

~ *Off to Morocco*
Gaumont. Released by Kleine Optical Co., 1908. 794 ft.

~ *A Tale of a Harem: The Caliph and the Pirate*
Vitagraph. 12 September 1908. 456 ft.

~ *Yussuf the pirate*
Raleigh & Robert. Released by Kleine Optical Co., 1908. 774 ft.

~ *Arabian Cavalry* (Documentary)
Independent Films. 29 May 1909. 380 ft.

~ *Arabian Pilgrimage* (Documentary)
Pathé Frères. 7 August 1909.

~ *The Cobbler and the Caliph*
Vitagraph. 10 July 1909. 585 ft.

~ *Home of the Arabians* (Documentary)
Independent Films. 29 May 1909. 350 ft.

~ *In the Sultan's Power*
Selig Polyscope Co. 12 June 1909. 100 ft.

~ *The Oriental Mystic*
Vitagraph. 29 May 1909.

~ *A Visit to Biskra* (Travelogue/Documentary)
Pathé Frères. 11 September 1909. 443 ft.

~ *Won in the Desert*
Selig Polyscope Co. 17 July 1909.

~ *The Firemen of Cairo* (Documentary)
Eclair. 20 August 1910.

1910-1919
~ *Lost in the Sudan*
Selig Polyscope. 20 August 1910.

~ *Nomadic Tribes in El-Kantara Gorges, Algeria* (Documentary)
Pathé Frères. 1910? Hand-tinted. 1 reel.

~ *Roosevelt in Cairo* (Travelogue/Documentary)
Urban-Eclipse. Released By G. Kleine. 21 May 1910

~ *An African Village, North Africa* (Documentary)
Pathé Frères; released in the U.S. by George Kleine. 1911.

~ *Christian and Moor*
Edison. 1 August 1911.

~ *Jerusalem Delivered*
15 July 1911. 4 reels.

~ *Oasis in the Sahara Desert* (Documentary)
Gaumont. 1 July 1911.

~ *The Pasha's Daughter*
Thanhouser Company. July 1911.

~ *Tunis, Africa: The City of White* (Documentary)
Gaumont. 6 May 1911.

~ *A Turkish Cigarette*
Selig. 14 August 1911.

~ *Under the Palm Trees of Tunis* (Documentary)
Gaumont. 18 July 1911.

~ *A Walk in Tunis* (Travelogue/Documentary)
Lux. 13 May 1911.

~ *A Turkish Cigarette*
Selig. 14 August 1911.

~ *Aladdin-Up-To-Date*
Edison. 3 September 1912.

~ *The Ancient Port of Jaffa* (Documentary)
Kalem. 11 September 1912.

~ *The Arab's Bride*
Ambrosio. 28 September 1912.

~ *Arabian Customs* (Documentary)
Eclair. 13 May 1912.

~ *Arabian Infamy*
Ambrosio. 25 September 1912.

~ *Arabian Pottery* (Documentary)
Eclair. 3 February 1912.

~ *Arabian Sports* (Documentary)
Vitagraph. 9 November 1912.

~ *An Arabian Tragedy*
Kalem. 19 June, 1912.

~ *The Battle of Two Palms or Italian-Turkish War*
(Documentary)
Released in the United States by Crown Features Co. 25 June 1912. 2 reels. The pictures were taken for historical record for the Italian Government under the supervision of Cav. Luca Comerio, the official photographer of the king of Italy.

~ *Captured by the Bedouins*
Kalem. 26 June 1912.

~ *The City of Mosques* (Travelogue/Documentary)
Eclair. 25 February 1912.

~ *The City of Tripoli* (Travelogue/Documentary)
Cines. 19 March 1912.

~ *Egypt* (Travelogue/Documentary)
Kalem. 20 May 1912.

~ *Egypt, the Mysterious* (Travelogue/Documentary)
Kalem. 15 May 1912.

~ *Egyptian Sport* (Travelogue/Documentary)
Kalem. 19 July 1912.

~ *Farming in Tunis* (Travelogue/Documentary)
C. G. P. C. 30 January 1912.

~ *Fatima*
Cines. 31 May 1912.

~ *The Fighting Dervishes of the Desert*
Kalem. 27 May 1912.

~ *A Glimpse of Tripoli* (Travelogue/Documentary)
Eclipse. 28 February 1912.

~ *Into the Desert*
Thanhouser. 16 April 1912.

~ *Italian-Turkish Battle*
See The Battle of the Two Palms.

~ *A Little Journey in Tunis* (Travelogue/Documentary)
C. G. P. C. 10 September 1912.

~ *Luxor, Egypt* (Travelogue/Documentary)
Kalem. 25 May 1912.

~ *The Moorish Bride*
Cines. 9 May 1912.

~ *A Moslem Lady's Day* (Documentary)
Eclair. 25 August 1912.

~ *Mosques and Turkish Palaces* (Travelogue))
Cines. 29 October 1912.

~ *A Motor Trip to the Garden of Allah* (Travelogue)
Parker Read Productions. 8 June 1912.
Credits: Pres. & Dir. Parker Read

~ *The Potters of the Nile* (Documentary)
Kalem. 3 May 1912.

~ *Prisoner of the Harem*
Kalem. 19 July 1912.

~ *Pseudo-Sultan*
PathéPlay. 27 January 1912.

~ *Ramses, King of Egypt*
Cines. 12 August 1912.

~ *Sidi Hadji Moursouck*
Pathé. 19 December 1912.

~ *Tragedy of the Desert*
Kalem. 1 July 1912. 2 reels.
Cast: Jack Clark, Gautier, Robert Vignola, McGowan, Hollister.

~ *Turkish Police*
Eclair. 25 January 1912.

~ *Under Two Flags*
Gem Company. 9 July 1912. 2 reels.
Credits: Dir. Harry Nichols. Source: based on the novel *Under Two Flags*, by Ouida Bergère–pseudonym of Louise De La Ramée. (London, 1867).
Cast: Vivian Preston, Hershall Mayal.

~ *Cairo, Egypt and its Environs* (Documentary)
PathéPlay. 2 April 1913.

~ *The Conscience of Hassan Bey*
Biograph. 18 December 1913.
Credits: Dir. Christy Cabanne.

~ *The Fall of Constantinople*
Gaumont. 1 November 1913. 3 reels, hand-colored.

~ *The Greed of Osman Bey*
Edison. 28 July 1913.

Credits: Dir. M. M. Katterjohn. Cast: Gertrude McCoy, Barry O'Moore, Bigelow Cooper.

~ *The Guerrillas of Algiers (or The Mosque in the Desert)*
Eclair. Features Ideal Co. 6 December 1913. 3 reels.
Credits: based on the novel, *Jean de Poudre*, by De Brissays.

~ *Hannigan's Dream*
PathéPlay. 10 July 1913.

~ *Jaffa, the Seaport of Jerusalem* (Documentary)
Edison. 22 October 1913.

~ *Mosques and Towns of Caliphs and Mamelukes*
(Travelogue/Documentary)
Mutual. 8 May 1913.
Native Industries in Sudan, Egypt (Travelogue/Documentary)
C. G. P. C. 28 February 1913.

~ *Oasis of Gabes* (Travelogue/Documentary)
Pathé. 27 January 1914.

~ *Quaint Spots in Cairo* (Documentary)
Thomas A. Edison, Inc. 14 August 1913.

~ *A Princess Of Bagdad*
Helen Gardner Picture Players. Dist. State Rights; Charles Fuller Distribution Co. September, 1913. 6 reels.
Credits: Dir. & Scen. Charles L. Gaskill.
Cast: Hellen Gardener.

~ *Arab Troops* (Documentary)
Pathé. 31 August 1914.

~ *The Corsair*
Pathé Frères. Dist. Eclectic Film Co. August 1914. 4 reels.
Credits: Dir. Frank Powell; Scen. George Fitzmaurice. Source: inspired by the poem, "The Corsair," by Lord Byron, 1814.
Cast: Crane Wilbur, Anna Rose, Edward Jose, M. O. Penn,

George W. Page.

~ *The Dishonored Medal*

Reliance Motion Picture Corp. Dist. Mutual Film Corp. 3 May 1914. 4 reels.

Credits: Supv. D. W. Griffith; Dir. W. Christy Cabanne.

Cast: Miriam Cooper, George Gebhard, Raoul L. Walsh, Frank Bennett, Mabel Van Buren, Dark Cloud.

~ *Fire And Sword*

Kismet Feature Film Co. Dist. State Rights. February 1914. 6 reels.

Credits: Dir. T. Hayes Hunter. Cast: Isabel Rea, Tom McEvoy.

~ *Imar The Servitor*

Majestic Motion Picture, Co. Dist. Mutual Film Corp. Continental Feature Film Corp. April 1914. 4 reels. Credits: Dir. John B. O'Brien; Scen. Daniel Carson Goodman.

Cast: William Garwood.

~ *The Last Egyptian*

Oz Film Manufacturing Corp. Dist. Alliance Film Corp. L. Frank Baum. 1914.

Credits: Dir. L. Frank Baum. Source: based on the novel, The Last Egyptian, by L. Frank Baum (Philadelphia, 1908) Cast: J. Farrel McDonnald, Vivian Reed, Jefferson Osborne, Mai Wells, Jane Urban, J. Charles Haydon, Howard Davis.

~ *The Next in Command*

Pasquali American Co. Dist. Picture Playhouse Film Co. 14 August 1914. 4 reels.

Credits: Dir. J. Searle Dawley.

Cast: James Gordon, F. A. Turner, Bettie Harte, Frank Sidwell.

~ *A Princess of the Desert*

Edison. 18 April 1914.

~ *In the Shadow of the Mosque*
Eclair. 22 April 1914. 2 reels.

~ *The Span of Life*
Kinotophote Corp. Dist. State Rights. 7 December 1914. 4-5 reels.
Credits: Dir. Edward Mackay; Scen. Catherine Carr; Photog. George C. Coudert. Source: from the play, *The Span of Life*, by Sutton Vane (New York, 1893).
Cast: Lionel Barrymore, Gladys Wynne, Lysler Chambers, Ogdon Childe.

~ *The Arab*
Jesse L. Lasky Feature Play Co. Dist. Paramount Pictures Corp. 14 June 1915. 5 reels.
Credits:: Pres. Jesse L. Lasky; Dir. Cecil B. DeMille. Source: Edgar Selwyn's play, *The Arab* (New York, Sep 1915).
Cast: Edgar Selwyn, Horace Carpenter, Milton Brown, Billy Elmer, Sidey Deane, Gertrude Robinson, Park Jones, Theodore Roberts.

~ *The Arab's Vengeance*
Mutual Film Corp. 16 December 1915. 2 reels.
Cast: Roy Watson, John Oaker, Thomas Morissay, Margaret Gibson, B. Singh.

~ *Bella Donna*
Famous Players-Lasky Corp. in association with the Charles Froham Co. Dist. Paramount Pictures Corp. 15 November 1615. 5 reels.
Credits: Dir. Edwin S. Porter & Hugh Ford. Source: Robert Smythe Hichens' novel, *Bella Donna* (London, 1911), and the play of the same title by James Bernard Fagan (London, 9 December 1911)
Cast: Pauline Frederick, Thomas Holding, Julia L'Estrange, Eugene Ormonde, George Majeroni, Edmund Shalet, Helen Sinnott.

~ *The Black Box* (Installment. #11: A Desert Vengeance)
Universal Film Mfg. 10 May 1915. 2 reels.
Credits: Dir. & Story Otis Turner. Source: based on the novel by E. Phillips Oppenheimer.

~ *The Breath of Araby*
8 May 1915. 3 reels.

~ *The Carpet from Bagdad*
Selig Polyscope; Selig Red Seal Players. Dist. V.L.S.E, Inc. 3 May 1915. 5 reels.

Credits: Dir. Colin Campbell. Source: Harold MacGrath's novel, The Carpet From Bagdad (Indianapolis, 1911).

Cast: Cathlyn Williams, Wheeler Oakman, Guy Oliver, Eugene Besserer, Frank Clark, Charles Clary, Harry Lonsdale, Fred Huntley.

~ *The Man from Egypt*
Vitagraph. 14 July 1915.

Credits: Dir. Lawrence Semon. Story, Graham Baker and Lawrence Semon. Cast: Hughey Mack, Jowel Hunt.

~ *The Morals of Marcus*
Famous Players Film Co. Dist. Paramount Pictures Corp. 18 January 1915. 5 reels.

Credits: Pres. Charles Frohman; Dir. Edwin S. Porter and Hugh Ford. Source: based on the novel, *The Morals of Marcus Ordeyne*, by William John Locke (London, 1906).

Cast: Marie Doro, Eugene Ormonde, Ida Darling, Julia L'Estrange, Rassell Bassett, frank Andrews. Note: There would be two remakes of this film: Realart Pictures, *Morals* (1921), Directed by William Taylor, and *The Morals of Marcus* (1935), Directed by Miles Mander.

~ *The Rug Maker's Daughter*
Bosworth, Inc. in association with the Oliver Morosco Photoplay Co. 5 July 1915. 5 reels.

Credits: Dir. Oscar Apfel. Story, Julia Crawford Ivers.

Cast: Maud Allen, Forrest Stanley, Jane Darwell, Howard Davis, Herbert Standing, Laura Woods Gushing, Harrington Gibbs.

~ *Saved from the Harem*
Lubin Manufacturing Co.; Dist. General Film Co. 27 December 1915. 4 reels.

Credits: Dir. William Melville. Story, Julian Louis Lamothe and Wilbert Melville.

Cast: Melvyn Mayo, Adelaide Bronte, Violet McMillan, L. C. Shumway, George Routh, Jay Morley.

~ *A Sultana of the Desert*
Selig Polyscope. 5 October 1915. 2 reels. Cast: Kathlyn Williams, Thomas Santschi.

~ *Under the Crescent* (a six-part Series)
Gold Seal. Universal Co. May-June, 1915.
Credits: Prod & Dir. Burton King, Scen. Neil Shipman.

~ #1. *The Purple Iris* (25 May 1915. 2 reels)

~ #2. *The Cage of the Golden Bars* (2 June 1915. 2 reels)

~ #3. *In the Shadow of the Pyramids* (8 June 1915. 2 reels)

~ #4. *For the Honor of a Woman* (16 June 1915. 2 reels)

~ #5. *In the Name of the King* (29 June 1915. 2 reels)

~ #6. *The Crown of Death* (29 June 1915. 2 reels)

~ *Under Two Flags*
Biograph. June 1915. 3 reels.
Credits: Source: based on the novel *Under Two Flags*, by Ouida Bergère, (London, 1867).

Cast: Louise Vale, Franklin Richie, Herbert Barring, Jack Drumier, Helen Bray, Charles H. Mailes.

~ *The Unknown*
Jesse Lasky Feature Play Co. Dist. Paramount Pictures Corp. 9 December 1915. 5 reels.
Credits: Dir. George Melford; Ass. Dir. C. H. Mitchell; Scen. Margaret Turbull. Source: based on the novel, *The Red Mirage*, by Ida Alexa Ross Wylie (London, 1913).

Cast: Lou Tellegen, Theodore Roberts, Dorothy Davenport, Hal

Clements, Tom Forman, Raymond Hatton, Horace B. Carpenter.

~ *Algeria, Old and New* (Travelogue))
Pathé. 15 April 1916. The film shows aspects of modern life, introduced in Algeria by the French. Scenes of oases and the desert are also shown.

~ *A Daughter of the Gods*
Fox Film Corp. Dist. Fox Film Corp. 17 October 1916. 10 reels.

Credits: Pres. William Fox; Dir. Herbert Brenon; Story, Herbert Brenon; Scen. Herbert Brenon; Photog. J. Roy Hunt, Andre Barlatier; Ed. Hettie Gey baker; Art Dir. John D. Braddon; Tech Dir. George Fitch; Cost. Irene Lee; Props, Joseph Allen Turner; Musical Accomp. Robert Hood Bowers.

Cast: Annette Kellerman, William E. Shay, Hal De Forrest, Mademoiselle Marcelle, Edward Boring, Violet Horer, Jane Lee, Stuart Holmes.

~ *The Garden of Allah*
Selig Polyscope Co. Dist. State Rights. 25 December 1916. 10 reels.

Credits: Supv. W. N. Selig; Dir. Colin Campbell; Ass-Dir. Al Green; Scen. Gilson Willets; Art Dir. Gabriel Pollock. Source: Roberts Smithe Hichens' novel, *The Garden of Allah* (London, 1904).

Cast: Helen Ware, Thomas Santschi, Will Machin, Matt B. Snyder, Harry Lonsdale, Eugene Besserer, James Bradbury, Al W. Wilson, Cecil Holland.

~ *The Harem Scarem Deacon*
Joker. Universal Film Mfg. Co. 15 July 1916. 1 reel.

Credits: Dir. Allen Curtis; Story, Eugene Lewis.

Cast: Gale Henry, William Franey, Chass Conklin, Milburn Moranti.

~ *The Light That Failed*
Feature Film Corp. Dist. Pathé Exchange, Inc.; Gold Rooster Plays. 15 October 1916. 5 reels.

Credits: Prod Edward José, Dir. Edward José; Scen. George B. Seitz; Photog. Ben Struckman. Source: based on the novelette, *The*

Light That Failed, by Rudyard Kipling (place of publication undetermined, 1898). Cast: Robert Edeson, Jose Collins, Lillian Tucker, Calude Fleming.

~ *The Road to Love*

Oliver Morosco Photoplay Co. Dist. Paramount Pictures Corp. 7 December 1916. 5 reels.

Credits: Dir. Scott sidney; Scen. Gardner Hunting; Story, Blanche Dougan Cole; Photog. James C. Van Trees. Cast: Lenore Ulritch, Collin Chase, Lucille Ward, Estelle Allen, Alfred Osberg, Hershell Mayal, Joe Massey, Alfred Hollingworth.

~ *The Rummy Act of Omar K. M.*

Mutual Film Co. 16 July 1916.

Cast: Oral Humphrey, Leo Banks, Margaret Nichols, Joe Massey.

~ *The Towns of Tunis* (Travelogue/Documentary)

Pathé. 29 April 1916.

~ *Under Two Flags*

Fox Film Corp. Dist. Fox Film Corp. 31 July 1916. 6 reels.

Credits: Dir. J. Gordon Edwards; Scen. George Hall; Photog. Phillip E. Rosen. Source: based on the novel *Under Two Flags*, by Ouida Begère (London, 1867).

Cast: Theda Bara, Herbert Hayes, Stuart Holmes, Stanhope WheatCroft, Joseph Crehan, Charles Craig, Claire Whitney.

~ *Aladdin and the Wonderful Lamp*

Fox Film Corp. Dist. Fox Film Corp. 14 October 1917. 8 reels. A Fox Kiddies Feature.

Credits: Pres. W. Fox; Dir. C. M Franklin, S. A. Franklin; Scen. Bernard McConville; Photog. Harry Gerstad. Source: based on the story *"Aladdin ...,"* from the *Arabian Nights*.

Cast: Francis Carpenter, Fred Turner, Virginia Lee Gorbin, Alfred Paget, Violet Radcliffe, Buddy Messinger, Mary Messinger, Carmen De Rue, Raymond Lee.

~ *Aladdin from Broadway*

Vitagraph Co. of America; A Blue Ribbon Feature. Dist. Greater

Vitagraph V.L.S.E. 19 March 1917. 5 reels.

Credits: Dir. William Wolbert; Scen. Helmer Walton Bergman; Photog. Reginald Lyions. Source: Frederick Stewart Isham's novel, *Aladdin From Broadway*.

Cast: Edith Storey, Antonio Moreno, William Duncan, Otto Lederer.

~ *Ali Baba and the Forty Thieves*

Fox Film Corp. Dist. Fox Film Corp. 24 November 1917. 5 reels.

Credits: Pres. William Fox; Dir. S. A. Franklin and C. M. Franklin; Scen. Bernard McConville. Source: The *Arabian Nights*. Cast: George Stone, Gertrude Messinger, Lewis Seargent, Buddie Messinger, Raymond Nye, Raymond Lee, Charies Hincus, Marie Messinger.

~ *Barbary Sheep*

Artcraft Pictures Corp. Dist. Artcraft Pictures Corp. 10 September 1917. 5 reels.

Credits: Dir. Maurice Tourneur; Scen. Charles Maigne; Photog. John Van Den Broeck; Art Dir. Ben Carre. Source: based on the novel, *Barbary Sheep*, by Robert Hichens (London, 1907).

Cast: Elsie Ferguson, Lumsden Hare, Pedro De Cordoba, Macy Harlam, Alex Shannon, Maude Ford.

~ *Bound In Morocco*

Douglas Fairbanks Pictures Corp. Dist. Famous Players Lasky Corp. 5 August 1917. 5 reels.

Credits: Dir. & Scen. Allan Dwan; Photog. Hugh McLung.

Cast: Douglas Fairbanks, Pauline Curly, Edith Chapman, Tully Marshall, Frank Campeau, Jay Dwiggins, Fred Burns, Albert McQuarrie.

~ *The Lad and the Lion*

Selig Polyscope Co.; Red Seal Players. Dist. K. E. S. E. Service. 14 May 1917. 5 reels.

Credits: Dir. Alfred Green; Photog. Harry Neuman. Source: based on the short story, "The Lad and the Lion," by Edgar Rice Burroughs in *All-Story Weekly* (June 30-July 14, 1917).

Cast: Vivian Reed, Will Machin, Charles Le Moyne, Al F. Wilson, Lafayette McKee, Captain Ricardo, Cecil Holland.

~ *The Sixteenth Wife*
Vitagraph Co. of America; A Blue Ribbon Feature. Dist. Greater Vitagraph (V. L. S. E.). 14 May 1917. 5 reels.

Credits: Dir. Charles Brabin; Scen. Van Buren Powell; Photog. Clark R. Nickerson. Source: based on a story by Molly Elliot Seawell (pub. date undetermined).

Cast: Peggy Hyland, Marc McDermott, George J. Forth, Templer Saxe.

~ *Ali Baba and the 40 Thieves*
Fox. George E. Stone. Dir. Sidney Franklin. 1918.

~ *Eye for Eye*
Nazimova Productions, Inc. Dist. Metro Pictures Corp. November 1918. 7 reels.

Credits: Pres. Richard A. Rowland and Maxwell Karger; Dir. Albert Capellani; Supv Maxwell Karger; Photog. Eugene Gandio; Art Dir. Henri Menessier; Scen. June Mathis and Albert Kapellani; Art Titl. Anthony Tauzky. Source: based on the play, *L'Occident*, by Henry Kistemaeckers (Paris, 4 November 1913).

Cast: Alla Nazimova, Charles Bryant, Donnald Gallaher, Sally Crute, E. L. Fernandez, John Rinhard, Louis Stern, Charles Eldridge.

~ *The White Man's Law*
Famous Players-Lasky Corp. Dist. Paramount Pictures. 6 May 1918. 7 reels.

Credits: Pres. Jesse L. Lasky; Dir. James Young; Ass-Dir. John Browne; Scen. Marion Fairfax; Photog. Charles Rosher. Story, Marion Fairfax and John B. Browne.

Cast: Sessue Hayakawa, Florence Vidor, Jack Hott, Herbert Standing, Mayor Kelso, Forrest Seabury, Joseph Swickard, Ernst Joy, Charles West.

~ *Flame of the Desert*
Diva Pictures, Inc.; Goldwyn Pictures Corp. Dist. Goldwyn Distributing Corp. 9 November 1919. 5 reels.

Credits: Dir. Reginald Barker; Scen. Richard Schayer; Photog.

Percy Hilburn. Story, Charles E. Logue. Cast: Geraldine Farrar, Lou Tellegen, Alec B. Francis, Edythe Chapman, Cusson Ferguson, Macy Harlam, Syn De Cone, Milton Ross, Miles Dobson.

~ Her Purchase Price
Brunton B. Features, Inc. Dist. Robertson-Cole Corp. 1 September 1919. 5 reels.
Credits: Dir. Howard Hickman; Scen. Harvey Thew; Photog. Gus Ferguson.
Cast: Bessie Barriscale, Albert Roscoe, Joseph Dowling, Kathlyn Williams, Stanhope Wheatcroft, Irene Rich, Henry Kolker.

~ The Man Who Turned White
Jesse D. Hampton Productions. Dist. Robertson-Cole Co., through Exhibitors Mutual Distributing Corp. 1 June 1919. 5 reels.
Credits: Dir. Frank Frame; Scen. George Elwood Jenks; Photog. William C. Foster. Source: based on the short story, *"The Man Who Turned White,"* by F. McGrew Willis (pub. date undetermined).
Cast: H. B. Warner, Barbara Cast:lton, Wedgewood Nowell, Carmen Phillips, Manuel Ojeda, Jay Dwiggins, Walter Perry.

~ With Allenby in Palestine and Lawrence of Arabia
(Documentary)
Lowell Thomas. 1919. 10 reels.
Credits: Lowell Thomas; Photog. Harry Chase.
Cast: Lieut. Col. Thomas Edward Lawrence (Lawrence of Arabia), Field Marshall Edmund Allenby.

1920-1930
~ An Arabian Knight
Haworth Pictures Corp. Dist. Robertson-Cole Dist. Corp. 22 August 1920. 5 reels.
Credits: Dir. Charles Swickard; Scen. Richard Schayer; Story, Gene Wright; Photog. Frank D. Williams; Art Dir. Robert J. Ellis; Art Titles, Lilian Drain.
Cast: Sessue Hayakawa, Lillian Hall, Jean Acker, Marie Pavis.

~ Kismet
Waldorf Film Corp. Dist. Robertson-Cole Distributing Corp. 14

November 1920. 5 reels.

Credits: Dir. Louis J. Gasnier; Scen. Charles E. Whittacker, Tony Goudio, Glen McWilliams and Joseph Du Bray; Art Dir. Frank D. Ormstrom, Frederick Earl McMurtrie. Source: Edward Knoblock, *Kismet: An Arabian Night' in Three Acts* (New York, 1911).

Cast: Otis Skinner, Rosemary Theby, Elinor Fair, Mathilda Comont, Nicholas Dunaev, Herschel Mayall, Fred Lancaster, Leon Bary, Sidney Smith, Hamilton Reselle.

~ *Moon Madness*

Haworth Studios. Dist. Robertson-Cole Distributing Corp. July 1920. 6 reels.

Credits: Dir. Colin Campbell; Scen. J. Grub Alexander; Story, J. Grub Alexander; Photog. Fred Schoedsack. Cast: Edith Storey, Sam De Grasse, Joseph Swickard, Wallace MacDonald, Irene Hunt, William Courtleigh, Frankie Lee, Frederick Starr.

~ *A Trip through Cairo* (Travelogue/Documentary)

Producer unknown. Circa 1920.

The film examines Egyptian agriculture, irrigation methods, fishing, palaces, tombs, mosques, bazaars, and the scenery along the Nile river.

~ *The Virgin of Stamboul*

Universal Film Manufacturing Co. Dist. Universal Film Manufacturing Co. 29 March 1920. 7 reels.

Credits: Pres. Carl Laemmle; Dir. Tod Browning and William Parker; Story, H. H. Van Loan; Photog. William Fildew; Mus Accomp., arranged by M. Winkler.

Cast: Priscilla Dean, Eugene Forde, Wheeler Oakman, Wallace Beery, E. A. Warren, Edward Burns, Nigel De Brulier, Ethel Richie, Clyde Benson, Yvette Mitchell.

~ *Cheated Hearts*

Universal Film Manufacturing Co. 12 December 1921. 5 reels.

Credits: Pres. Carl Laemmle; Dir. Hobart Henley; Scen. Wallace Clifton; Photog. Virgil Miller. Source: William Farquhar Payson, *Barry Gordon* (New York, 1908).

Cast: Herbert Rawlinson, Warner Baxter, Marjorie Daw, Dorris

Pawn.

~ *The Man of Stone*
Selznick Pictures. Dist. Select Pictures. 10 November 1921. 5 reels.

Credits: Pres. Lewis J. Selznick; Dir. George Archainbaud; Scen. Lewis Allen Browne; Story, John Lynch, Edmund Goulding; Photog. Jules Gronjager.

Cast: Conway Tearle, Betty Howe, Martha Mansfield, Collin Campbell, Warren Cook.

~ *The Sheik*
Famous Players-Lasky. Dist. Paramount Pictures. 30 October 1921. 7 reels.

Credits: Pres. Jesse L. Lasky; Dir. George Melford; Scen. Monte Katterjohn; Photog. william Marshall. Source: Edith Maude Hull's novel, *The Sheik* (London, 1919).

Cast:; Rudolph Valentino, Agnes Ayres, Adolph Menjou, Walter Long.

~ *The Syrian Immigrant* (Documentary)
Eastern Star Film Co. September 1921. 8 reels. Cast: Nicholas S. Haber, Estella MacKintosh. An educational film, showing the historical points of Syria, Palestine, and Egypt, as well as the story of the Syrian progress in the United States. Note: Film's country of origin not determined.

~ *Always the Woman*
Betty Compson Prod. Dist. Goldwyn Distributing Corp. 11 July 1922. 6 reels.

Credits: Dir. Arthur Rosson. Story, Perley Poore Sheehan; Photog. Ernest G. Palmer. Cast: Betty Compson, Emery Johnson, Doris Pawn, Gerald Pring, Richard Rosson, Arthur Delmore, Macey Harlam.

~ *Anna Ascends*
Famous Players-Lasky. Dist. Paramount Pictures. 19 November 1922. 6 reels.

Credits: Pres. Adolph Zukor; Dir. Victor Flemming; Scen.

Margaret Turbull; Photog. Gilbert Warrenton. Source: Harry Chapman Ford, *Anna Ascends* (New York opening, 22 September 1920).

Cast: Alice Brady, Robert Ellis, David Powell, Nita Naldi, Charles Gerard, Edward Durand.

~ *Arabia*

William Fox. Fox Film Corp. 5 November 1922. 5 reels.

Credits: Pres. William Fox; Dir. & Scen. Lynn Reynolds; Ed. & Titles, Hettie Grey Baker; Photog. Don Clark. Story, Lynn Reynolds, Tom Mix.

Cast: Tom Mix, Barbara Bedford, George Hernandez, Norman Selb, Edward Piel.

~ *Arabian Love*

William Fox. Fox Film Corp. 9 April 1922. 5 reels.

Credits: Dir. Jerome Storm; Story & Scen. Jules Furthham; Photog. Joe August.

Cast: John Gilbert, Barbara Bedford, Barberra La Marr, Herschel Mayall, Robert Kortman, William Orlamond.

~ *Burning Sand*

Famous Players-Lasky. Dist. Paramount Pictures. 3 September 1922. 7 reels.

Credits: Pres. J. L. Lasky; Dir. George Melford; Adapt. Olga Printzlau, Walderman Young; Photog. Bert Glennon. Source: *Burning Sands*, by Arthur Weigall (New York, 1921). Cast: Wanda Hawley, Milton Sills, Louise Dresser, Jacqueline Logan.

~ *Omar the Tentmaker*

Richard Walton Tully Prod. Dist. Associated First National Pictures. December 1922. 8 reels.

Credits: Dir. James Young; Adapt. R. W. Tully; Photog. George Benoit; Art Dir. Wilfred Buckland. Source: Richard Walton Tully, *Omar the Tentmaker* (New York opening, 13 January 1914).

Cast: Guy Bates Post, Virginia Brown Faire, Nigel De Brulier, Noah Beery, Rose Dione, Patsy Ruth Miller, Will Jim Hatton, Boris Karloff.

~ *The Sheik of Araby*

Dist. R. C. Pictures. May 1922. 5 reels.

Note: This film is a revival of *The Man Who Turned White* (Robertson-Cole, 1919), advertised as re-edited and re-titled, but is essentially the same in length and story line.

~ *The Sheik's Wife*

Vitagraph. 5 reels. 1 March 1922.

Credits: Pres. Albert E. Smith; Dir. & Scen. Henry Roussel.

Cast: Emmy Lynn, Marcel Vibert, Albert Bras, Gustav Bogart, Frank Medor, Thomas Thornton, Allice Fille, Carl Fisher.

~ *A Trip Through Syria*

Faris and Debs. 12 February 1922 [New York State]. 5 reels. A documentary? No information on this film has been found. The Country of origin is not determined.

~ *Under Two Flags*

Universal-Jewel Film. 23 September 1922. 8 reels.

Credits: Pres. Carl Laemmle; Dir. Tod Browning; Scen. E. T. Lowe, Elliott Clawson; Photog. William Fildew. Source: based on the novel, *Under Two Flags*, by Ouida–pseudonym of Louise De La Ramée–(London, 1867).

Cast: Priscilla Dean, James Kirkwood, John Davidson, Stuart Holmes, Ethel Gray Terry, Robert Mack, Burton Law, Albert Pollet. Note. This film is the fourth remake of the Ouida story. The first was made by Gem Company in 1912, the second by Biograph in 1915, and the third by Fox in 1916. See respective entries in this filmography.

~ *When the Desert Calls*

Pyramid Pictures. Dist. American Releasing Corp. 8 October 1922. 6 reels.

Credits: Dir. Ray C. Smaltwood; Adapt. Peter Milne, George Duchesne; Photog. Michael Joyce; Art Dir. Ben Carre; Ed. & Asst Dir. George McGuire. Source: Donald McGibney, "When the Desert Calls," in *Ladies Home Journal*.

~ *Aladdin: The Story of the Wonderful Lamp*
Credits: Dir. Joe Rock and Norman Taurog. 1923.

~ *Arabia's Last Alarm*
William Fox. 2 November 1923. 2 reels.
Credits: Dir. Tom Buckingham.

~ *Bella Donna*
Famous Players-Lasky. Dist. Paramount Pictures Corp. 1 April 1923. 8 reels.
Credits: Pres. Adolph Zukor; Dir. George Fitzmaurice; Scen. Ouida Bergere; Photog. Arthur Miller; Tech-Dir. Dudley Stuart Corlett. Source: Robert Smythe Hichens' novel, *Bella Dona*, (London, 1911).
Cast: Pola Negri, Conway Tearle, Conrad Nagel, Adolph Menjou, Claude King, lois Wilson, Macy Harlam, Robert Schable.

~ *The Dancer from the Nile*
William P. S. Production. 1923 Cast: Carmel Myers, Malcom McGregor, June Eldridge.

~ *Dark Secrets*
Famous Players-Lasky. Dist. Paramount Pictures. 21 January 1923. 6 reels.
Credits: Pres. Adolph Zukor; Dir. Victor Flemming, Story & Scen. Edmund Goulding, Photog. Hal Rosson.
Cast: Dorothy Dalton, Robert Ellis, José Ruben, Ellen Cassidy, Pat Hartigan, Warren Cook, Julia Swayne Gordon.

~ *The Exiles*
Fox Film Corp. 14 October 1923. 5 reels.
Credits: Pres. William Fox; Dir. Edmund Mortimer; Scen. Fred Jackson; Adapt. John Russel. Source: Richard Harding Davis, *The Exiles, and Other Stories* (New York, 1894).
Cast: John Gilbert, Betty Bouton, John Webb Dillon, Margaret Fielding, Fred Warren.

~ *One Stolen Night*
Vitagraph Co. of America. 29 January 1923. 5 reels.

Credits: Dir. Robert Ensminger; Scen. Bradley J. Smollen; Photog. Steve Smith, Jr. Source: D. D. Calhoun, *"The Arab"* (pub. date undetermined).

Cast: Alice Calhoun, Herbert Hayes, Otto Hoffman, Adele Farrington, Russ Powell, Oliver Hardy. Note: Remade in 1929 by Warner Bros.

~ *The Shriek of Araby*

Mack Sennet Production. Dist. Allied Producers and Distributors. 5 March 1923. 5 reels.

Credits: Pres. Mack Sennet; Dir. F. Richard Jones; Author Mack Sennet; Photog. Homer Scott, Robert Walters; Ed. Allen McNeil. Cast: Ben Turpin, Katheryn McGuire, George Cooper, Charles Stevenson, Rey Grey, Louis Fronde, Dick Sutherland.

~ *A Son of the Desert*

American Releasing Corp. March, 1923. 3 reels.

Credits: Dir. & Scen. William Merrill. Cast: William MCCorick, Marin Sais, Robert Burns, Faith Hope, James Welsh.

~ *The Song of Love*

Norma Talmadge Prod. Dist. Associated First National Pictures. 24 December 1923. 8 reels.

Credits: Pres. Joseph M. Schenck; Dir. Chester Franklin, Francis Marion; Adapt. Francis Marion; Photog. Antonio Gaudio. Source: Margaret Peterson, *Dust of Desire* (New York, 1922).

Cast: Norma Talmadge, Joseph Schildkraut, Arthur Edmund Carew, Lawrence Wheat, Maude Wayne, Earle Schenk, Hector V. Sarno, Alberto Prisco, Mario Crillo.

~ *The Tents of Allah*

Encore Pictures. Dist. Associated Exhibitors. 4 March 1923. 7 reels.

Credits: Pres. Edward McManus; Dir. & Story Charles A. Logue; Photog. Abe Fried, Eugene O'Donnell.

Cast: Monte Blue, Mary Alden, Frank Currier, Mary Thurman.

~ *The Thrill Chaser*

Universal Pictures. 26 November 1923. 6 reels.

Credits: Dir. Edward Sedgwick; Scen. Richard Schayer; Story, E. Sedgwick, Raymond L. Schrock; Photog. Virgil Miller.

Cast: Hoot Gibson, James Neill, Billie Dove, W. E. Lawrence.

~ *The Arab*

Metro-Goldwyn Distributing Corp. 16 July 1924. 7 reels.

Credits: Dir. & Writ. Rex Ingram; Photog. John F. Seitz. Source: Edgar Selwyn's play, *The Arab* (New York, 1911).

Cast: Ramon Navarro, Alice Terry, Maxudian, Jean De Limur, Paul Vermoyal, Adelqui Millar, Alexandresco.

~ *A Cafe in Cairo*

Hunt Stromberg Prod. Dist. Producers Distributing Corp. 7 December 1924. 6 reels.

Credits: Pres. Hunt Stromberg; Dir. Chet Withey; Adapt. & Scen. Harvey Gates; Photog. Sol Polito; Art Dir. Edward Withers; Ed Harry L. Decker. Source: Izola Forrester, "A Cafe in Cairo," in *Ainslee's Magazine*.

Cast: Priscilla Dean, Rosert Ellis, Carl Stockade, Evelyn Selbie, Harry woods, John Steppling, Marie Crisp, Carmen Phillips.

~ *Desert Blues*

Educational Films Corporation of America. 13 October 1924. 1 reel.

Credits: Dir. Albert Ray. Credits: Virginia Vance, Cliff Bowes.

~ *The Desert Sheik*

Truart Film Corp. Dist. Film Booking Offices of America. 26 July 1924. 6 reels.

Credits: Prod. A. C. Bromhead; Dir. Tom Terris; Scen. Alice Ramsey; Titl. & Ed. Arthur Hoerl; Photog. A. St. A. Brown, H. W. Bishop. Source: Arthur Conan Doyle, *A Desert Drama, Being the Tragedy of the Korosko* (London, 1898).

Cast: Wanda Hawley, Pedro De Cordoba, Edith Craig, Arthur Cullen, Stewart Rome, Douglas Munzo, Hamed El Gabrey. Note: Filmed on location, in Egypt.

~ *The 40th Door*

Pathé Exchange. 17 August 1924. 6 reels.

Credits: Prod C. W. Patton; Dir. George B. Seitz; Scen. Frank Leon Smith; Photog. Vernon Walker. Source: Mary Hasting Bradley, *The Fortieth Door* (New York, 1920).

Cast: Allene Ray, Bruce Gordon, David Dunbar, Anna May Wong, Frances Mann, Frank Lockteen, Lillian gale, Bernard Siegel, White Horse, Omar Whitehead.

~ *The Lost Empire* (Travelogue/Documentary)

Edward A. Salisbury. Dist. Frederick J. Burgard. 25 March 1924. 6 reels.

Credits: Pres. Edward A. Salisbury; Titl. & Ed. Merian Cooper; Photog. Ernest B. Schoedsack.

~ *Sahara Blues*

Century. 15 October 1924. 2 reels.

Cast: Al Hart, Hilliard Karr, Jack Earle, Bartine Burkett, The Century Folly Girls.

~ *The Sea Hawk*

Frank Lloyd Prod. Dist. Ass. First Natinal Pictures. 2 June 1924. 12 reels.

Credits: Dir. Frank Lloyd ; Scen. J. G. Hawks; Titl. Walter Anthony; Photog. Norbert Brodin; Art Dir. Stephen Goosson; Ed Edward M. Roskam; Cost. Walter Israel. Source: *The Sea Hawk*, by Rafael Sabatini (London, 1915).

Cast: Milton Sills, Enid Bennett, Lloyd Hughes, Wallace McDonnald.

~ *The Shadow of the East*

Fox Film Corp. 27 January 1924. 6 reels.

Credits: Pres. William Fox; Dir. George Archainbaud; Scen. Frederic Hatton; Photog. Jules Cronjager. Source: Edith Maude Hall, *The Shadow of the East* (Boston, 1921).

Cast: Frank Mayo, Mildred Harris, Norman Kerry, Bertarm Grassby, Evelyn Brent, Edithe Chapman, Joseph Swickard Note: Revived as Shadow of the Desert.

~ *A Son of the Sahara*

Edwin Carewe Production. Dist. First National Pictures. 13 April

1924. 8 reels.

Credits: Dir. Edwin Carewe, René Plaisetty; Scen. Adelaide Heilbron; Photog. Robert Kurrle; Art Dir. John D. Schulze; Ed Robert De Lacy; Ass-Dir. Wallace Fox. Source: Louis Gerard, *A Son of the Sahara* (New York, 1922).

Cast: Claire Windsor, Bert Lytell, Walter McGrail, Rosemary Theby, Montague Love, Paul Panzer. Note: Filmed on location, in Algeria.

~ *The Thief of Bagdad*

Douglas Fairbanks Pictures. Dist. United Artists. 18 March 1924. 14 reels. [Release Length 12 reels].

Credits: Dir. Raoul Walsh; Scen. Lotta Woods; Story, Elton Thomas; Photog. Arthur Edeson; Art Dir. William Cameron Menzies; Tech Dir. Robert Fairbanks; Ed. William Nolan; Mus Comp. Mortimer Wilson, Ass-Dir. James T. O' Donnohue; Cost Dir. Mitchel Leisen.

Cast: Douglas Fairbanks, Snitz Edwards, Charles Belcher, Julanne Johnston, Anna May Wong, Winter Blossom, Tote Du Crowe, So-jin, Nambu, Sadakichi Hartman, Noble Johnson.

~ *Grief in Bagdad*

Fox Film Corp. 4 January 1925. 2 reels.
Credits: Dir. Benjamin Stoloff.

~ *Grief in Bagdad*

Hal Roach. Pathé Exchange. 10 April 1925. 1 reel.
Cast: Earle Mohan, Billy Engle, Dolores Johnston.

~ *The Lady Who Lied*

First National Pictures. 12 July 1925. 8 reels.

Credits: Pres. Edwin Carewe; Dir. Edwin Carewe; Scen. Lois Zellner, Madge Tyrone; Adapt. lois Leeson; Photog. Al M. green; Art Dir. John D, Schulze; Ed. LeRoy Etone.

Cast: Louis Stone, Virginia Valli, Louis Payne, Nita Naldi, Edward Earle, Leo White, Purnell Pratt, Sam Appel, Zalk Zarana, George Lewis.

~ *Maid in Morocco*

Lupino Lane Comedies. Educational Film Exchanges. 11 December 1925. 2 reels.

Credits: Supv. Jack White.

Cast: Lupino Lane, Helen Foster, Wallace Lupino.

~ *Peggy of the Secret Service*

Davis Distributing Division, Dist. 16 November 1925. 5 reels.

Credits: Prod Mrs. S. Cole; Dir. V. P. McGowan; Scen. William Lester; Story, Finis Fox; Photog. Bob Cline.

Cast: Peggy O'Day, Eddie Phillips, W. H. Ryno, Clarence L. Sherwood, Dan Peterson, Richard Neill, V. L. Barnes.

~ *The Winding Stair*

Fox Film Corp. 25 October 1925. 6 reels.

Credits: Dir. John Griffith Wray; Scen. Julian Lamotte; Photog. Karl Struss. Source: Alfred Edward Woodley Mason, *The Winding Stair* (New York, 1923).

Cast: Alma Rubens, Edmund Lowe, Warner Oland, Mahlon Hamilton, Emily Fitzroy, Chester Conklin, Frank Leigh.

~ *Beau Geste*

Famous Players-Lasky. Dist. Paramount Pictures. 25 August 1926. 10-11 reels.

Credits: Pres. Adolph Zukor, Jesse L. Lasky; Dir. Herbert Brenon; Photog. Roy Hunt; Art Dir. Julian Boone Flemming; Mus Score Hugo Riesenfeld; Ass Dir. Ray Lissner. Source: Percival Christopher Wren, *Beau Geste* (New York, 1925).

Cast: Ronald Colman, Neil Hamilton, Ralph Forbes, Alyce Joyce, Mary Brian, Noah Beery, Norman Trevor, William Powell.

~ *Felix Shatters the Sheik (a cartoon)*

Educational Films Exchange. 1 reel. 19 November 1926. Credits: Pat Sullivan, author.

~ *The Lady of the Harem*

Famous Players-Lasky. Dist. Paramount Pictures. 1 November, 1926. 6 reels.

Credits: Pres. Adolph Zukor, J. L. Lasky; Dir. Raoul Walsh; Scr-

Play James T. O'Donnohoe; Photog. Victor Milne. Source: James Flecker's play, *Hassan: the Story of Hassan of Bagdad and How He Came to Make the Golden Journey to Samarkand* (London, 1922)

Cast: Ernest Torrence, W. Collier, Greta Nissen, Louise Fazenda, Andre De Beranger, So Jin, Frank Leigh.

~ *Made for Love*

Cinema Corp of America. Dist. Producers Distributing Corp. 9 January 1926. 7 reels.

Credits: Pres. Cecil B. De Mille; Dir. Paule Sloane; Prod-Ed Elmer Harris; Story-adapt Garrett Fort; Photog. Arthur Miller; Art Dir. Max Parker; Ass-Dir. William J. Scully.

Cast: Leatrice Joy, Edmund Burns, Ethel Wales, Bertram Grassby, Brandon Hurst, Frank Butler, Lincoln Stedman.

~ *Old Loves and New*

Sam E. Rork Productions. Dist. First National Pictures. 11 April 1926. 8 reels.

Credits: Pres. Marion Fairfax; Dir. Maurice Tourneur; Ed Patricia Rooney; Ass-Dir. Ben Silve; Scen. Marion Fairfax. Source: Edithe Maude Hull, *The Desert Healer* (Boston, 1923)

Cast: Lewis Stone, Barbera Bedford, Walter Pigeon, Catherine MacDonnald, Tully Marshall, Anne Rork, Arthur Rankin.

~ *The Silent Lover*

First National Pictures. 21 November 1926. 7 reels.

Credits: Dir. George Archainbaud; Scen. Carey Wilson. Source: Lajos Bíró's play, Der Legionër (1920).

Cast: Milton Sills, Natalie Kingston, William Humphrey, Arthur Edmund Carewe, William V, Moug, Viola Diana, Claude king, Charlie Murray, Arthur Stone, Alma Bennet, Montagu Love.

~ *The Son of the Sheik*

Feature Production. Dist. United Artists. 9 July 1926. 7 reels.

Credits: Prod John Considine, Jr.; Dir. George Fitzmaurice; Titl. George Marion, Jr.; Adapt. Frances Marion, Fred de Gresac; Photog. George Barnes; Art Dir. W. Cameron Menzies. Source: Edith Maude Hull, *The Sons of the Sheik* (Boston,1925).

Cast: Rudolph Valentino, Vilma Banky, George Fawcett,

Montague Love, Karl Dane.

~ *The White Black Sheep*

Inspiration Pictures. Dist. First National Pictures. 12 December 1926. 7 reels.

Credits: Dir. Sidney Olcott; Adapt. Jerome N. Wilson, Agnes Pat McKenna; Story, Violet E. Powell; Photog. David W. Gobbett.

Cast: Richard Barthelemes, Patsy Kuhn Miller, Constance Howard, Erville Anderson, W. H. Tooker, Gino Corrado, Albert Prisco.

~ *All Aboard*

B & H Enterprises. Dist. First National Pictures. 1 May 1927. 7 reels.

Credits: Pres. C. C. Burr; Dir. Charles Hines; Story, Matt Taylor; Photog. George Peters. Cast: Johnny Hines, Edna Murphy, Dot Farley, Henry Barrows, Frank Hagney.

~ *Fighting Love*

De Mille Pictures. Dist. Producers Distributing Corp. 14 February 1927. 7 reels.

Credits: Supv Bertrand Mullhauser; Dir. Nils Olaf Chrisander; Adapt. Beulah Marie Dix; Photog. Henry Gronjager. Source: Rosita Forbes, *If the Gods Laugh* (London, 1925).

Cast: Jetta Goudal, Victor Varconi, Henry B. Walthall, Louis Natheaux, Josephine Crowell.

~ *The Forbidden Woman*

De Mille Pictures. Dist. Pathé Exchange. 29 October 1927. 7 reels.

Credits: Supv. William C. De Mille; Dir. Paul L. Stein; Adapt.. Clara Berager; Photog. David Abel; Art Dir. Michell Leisen, Wilfred Buckland; Ass-Dir. Curt Rehfeld; Cost. Adrian. Source: Elmer Harris, "Brothers," (pub. date undetermined).

Cast: Jetta Goudal, Ivan Lebedeff, Leonid Snegoff, Josephine Norman, Victor Varconi, Joseph Schildkraut.

~ *The Garden of Allah*

Rex Ingram. Dist. M-G-M Distribution Corp. 2 September 1927. 9 reels.

Credits: Supv-Dir. Rex Ingram; Titl. Martin Brown; Adapt. Willis Goldbeck; Photog. Lee Garmes, Monroe Bennett, Marcel Lucien; Ed Arthur Ellis. Source: Robert Smythe Hichens, *The Garden of Allah* (London, 1904).

Cast: Alice Terry, Ivan Petrovich, Boris Androvsky, Marcel Vibert, H. H. Wright, Ben Sadour, Rebha Ben Salah. Note: Filmed in North-African locations, including Biskra, Algeria.

~ She's a Sheik

Paramount Famous Players-Lasky Corp. 12 November 1927. 6 reels.

Credits: Pres. Adolpf Zukor, Jesse L. Lasky; Dir. Clarence Badger; Scr-Play, Lloyd Corrigan, Grover Jones; Titl. George Marion, Jr.; Photog. Roy hunt. Story, John McDermott.

Cast: Bebe Daniels, Richard Arlen, William Powell, Josephine Dunn.

~ Soft Cushions

Paramount Famous Lasky Corp. 27 August 1927. 7 reels.

Credits: Pres. Adolph Zukor, J. L. Lasky; Dir. Edward F. Cline; Scr-Play,Wade Boteler, Frederick Chapin; Story, George Radolph Chester; Photog. Jack MacKenzie; Sets, Ben Carre.

Cast: Douglas McLean, Sue Carol, Richard Karle, Russel Powell, Frank Brulier, Albert Prisco, Boris Karloff, Albert Gran.

~ Turkish Delight

De Mille Pictures. Dist. Pathé Exchange. 11 November 1927. 6 reels.

Credits: Supv. C. Gardner Sullivan; Dir. Paule Sloane; Scen. Tay Garnett; Titl. John Grafft; Adapt. Albert Selby Le Vino; Story, Irvin S. Cobb; Photog. Jacob E. Badaracco; Art Dir. Max Barker; Ed. Margaret Darrell; Ass-Dir. William J. Scully.

Cast: Julia Faye, Rudlph Schildkraut, Kenneth Thompson, Louis Natheaux, May Robson, Harry Allen, Toby Claude.

~ Two Arabian Knights

Caddo Co. Dist. United Artists. 22 October 1927. 9 reels.

Credits: Pres. Howard Hughes, John W. Considine, Jr. Supv J. W. Considine, Jr; Prod Mgr Walter Mayo, Leeds Baster; Dir. Lewis

Milestone; Scr-Play James T. O'Donnohoe, Wallace Smith; Titl. George Marion, Jr.; Photog. Antonio Gaudio, Joseph August; Art Dir. William Cameron Menzies; Tech Dir. Ned Mann; Ass-Dir. Nate Watt; Source: Donald McGibbey, "Two Arabian Knights," in *McLure's Magazine*.

Cast: William Boyd, Mary Astor, Louis Wolheim, Michael Vavitch, Ian Keith, De Witt Jennings.

~ *Arabia* (Travelogue/Documentary)
Pathé Exchange, Inc. 1928. Silent.

~ *Beau Sabreur*
Paramount Famous Players-Lasky Corp. 7 January 1928. 7 reels. Silent.

Credits: Pres. Adolph Zukor, Jesse L. Lasky.; Dir. John Waters; Titl. Julian Johnson; Adapt. Tom J. Geraghty; Photog. C. Edgar Schoenbaum; Ed. Rose Lowenger. Source: Percival Christopher Wren, Beau Sabreur.

Cast: Gary Cooper, Evelyn Brent, Noah Beery, W. Powell, Roscoe Karns.

~ *Date Culture in Iraq* (Documentary)
Dept. of Agriculture. Circa 1928. 3 reels. Silent.
Credits: Photog. Roy W. Nixon.

~ *Desert, Baghdad* (Travelogue/Documentary)
Source unknown. Circa 1928. Located in the Library of Congress.

~ *The Desert Bride*
Columbia Pictures. 26 March 1928. 6 reels.
Credits: Prod. Harry Cohn; Dir. Walter Lang; Scen. Elmer Harris; Adapt. Anthony Coldeway; Photog. Ray June; Art Dir. Robert E Lee; Ed. Arthur Roberts; Ass-Dir. Max Cohn. Source: Ewart Adamson, "The Adventuress," (pub. date undetermined).

Cast: Betty Compson, Allan Forest, Edward Martindel, Otto Mattiesson, Roscoe Karns.

~ *The Desert Song*
Warner Bros. Pictures. 8 April 1928. 13 reels. Sound.

Credits: Dir. Roy Del Ruth; Scen-Dial Harvey Gates; Photog. Bernard McGill; Ed. Ralph Dawson. Cost. Earl Luick. Songs: "Riff Song," "French Military Marching Song," etc., Oscar Hammerstein, II. Source: Otto Harbach, Frank Mandel, Oscar Hammerstein, II, *The Desert Song: A Musical Play in Two Acts* (New York, 1932).

~ *An Egyptian Adventure* (Travelogue))
Four Stars Films. 1928. 2 reels. Silent.
Credits: Prod L. C. de Rochemont, Jack Glen.

~ *Fazil*
Fox Film. 4 June 1928. Mus Score & sd effects, Movietone. 7 reels. Silent.
Credits: Pres. William Fox; Dir. Howard Hawks; Scen. Seton J. Miller; Adapt. Phillip Klein; Photog. L. William O'Connell; Ass-Dir. James Tinling; Ed Ralph Dixon. Source: Pierre Frondaie, "L'Insoumise," in *La Petite Illustrations Library of Plays*, no 80 (Paris, 1922).
Cast: Charles Farrell, Geta Nissen, Mae Bush, Vadim Uraneff, Tyler Brooke, Eddie Sturgis, Josephine Borio, John Boles.

~ *Fleetwing*
Fox Film Corp. 24 June 1928. 5 reels.
Credits: Pres. W. Fox; Dir. Lambert Hillyer; Scen. Elizabeth Picket; Photog. Frank Good; Ed Alexander Troffey; Asst-Dir. Virgil Hart.
Cast: Barry Norton, Dorothy Janis, Ben Bard, Robert Kortman, Erville Anderson.

~ *King Cowboy*
FBO Pictures. 26 November 1928. 7 reels. Silent.
Credits: Dir. Robert De Lacy; Scr. Frank Howard Clark; Titl. Hellen Gregg, Randolph Bartlett; Story, S. E. V. Taylor; Photog. Norman Devol; Ed Henry Weher, Todd Cheesman; Ass-Dir. James Dugan.
Cast: Tom Mix, Sally Blane, Lew Meehan, Barney Furey, Frank Leigh, Wynn Mace, Robert Flemming.

~ *One Stolen Night*

Warner Bros. Pictures. 16 March 1928. 6 reels.

Credits: Dir. Edward T. Lowe; Photog. Frank Kesson. Source: D. D. Calhoun, "*The Arab*".

Cast: Betty Browson, William Collier, Jr., Mitchell Lewis, Harry Todd, Charles Hill Mailes. Note: A remake of the 1923 film.

~ *Plastered in Paris*

Fox Film Corp. 23 September 1928. Sd Eff. Movietone. 6 reels.

Credits: Pres. William Fox: Dir. Benjamin Stoloff; Scen. Harry Brand, Andrew Rice; Dial Edwin Burke; Titl. Malcolm Stuart Boylan; Story, Harry Sweet, Lov Breslow; Photog. Charles Clark.

Cast: Sammy Cohen, Jack Pennick, Lola Salvi, Ivan Linow, Hugh Allan, Marion Byron, Albert Conti.

~ *The Four Feathers*

Paramount Famous Lasky Corp. 12 January 1929. Sd Eff. Movietone. 8 reels. Silent.

Credits: Prod David Selznick; Dir. Merian C. Cooper, Ernest B. Schoedsack, Lothar Mendes; Screenplay Howard Estabrook; Titl. Julian Johnson, John Farrow; Adapt. Hope Loring; Photog. Robert Kurrle, Merian C. Cooper, Ernest B. Schoedsack; Ed E. B. Shoedsack; Mus Score William Frederick Peters; Ass-Dir. Ivan Thomas. Source: Alfred Edward Woodley Mason, *The Four Feathers* (London, 1902).

Cast: Richard Arlen, Fay Wray, Clive Brook, William Powell, Theodore Von Eltz, Noah Beery, Zack Williams, Noble Johnson, Philippe De Lacy.

~ *Love in the Desert*

FBO Pictures. 17 March 1929. Talking Sequences. Sd Eff. Photophane. 7 reels. Silent.

Credits: Dir. George Melford, Scr & Dial Harvey Thew, Paul Percy; Titl Randolph Bartlett; Story, Louis Sarecky, Harvey Thew; Photog. Paul Perry; Ed Mildred Richter. Cost. Walter Pulunkett.

Cast: Olive Borden, Hugh Trevor, Noah Beery, Frank Leigh, Pearl Varvell, W. H. Tooker, Ida Darling, Allan Roscoe.

~ *With Car and Camera around the World* (Travelogue)

Aloha Wanderwell. 11 November 1929. 6 reels.

Credits: Photog. Walter Wanderwell.

Note: Motion Picture News (21 December, 1929) quotes the following for the credits: "Author God, for He Created the earth and its people. Scenario by all Peoples."

~ *Kismet*

First National Pictures. 30 October 1930. 10 reels. Sound.

Credits: Prod Robert North; Dir. John Francis Dillon; Scen. Howard Estabrook; Photog. John Seitz; Ed Al Hall, Sound, Joseph Kane. Source: Edward Knoblock, *Kismet: An "Arabian Night" in Three Acts* (New York, 1911).

Cast: Ottis Skinner, Loretta Young, David Manners, Sidney Blackmer, Mary Duncan, Montagu Love, Theodore Von Eltz, John St. Polis.

~ *The Cohens and the Kellys in Africa*

Universal Pictures. 19 December 1930. 8 reels. Sound.

Credits: Dir. Vin Moore; Scen. W. K. Wells; Dialogue, W. K. Wells, Edmund Luddy; Photog. Hal Mohr.

Cast: George Sidney, Charles Murray, Vera Gordon, Kate Price, Frank Davis, Lloyd Whitlock.

~ *Egypt, Land of the Pyramids* (Documentary)

Metro-Goldwyn-Mayer. James A. FitzPatrick's Traveltaks Series. Circa 1930. 2 reels.

Credits: Photog. Hubert S. Dawley.

~ *Morocco*

Paramount-Publix Corp. 14 November 1930. 12 reels. Sound.

Credits: Dir. Joseph Von Sternberg; Scen. & Dial. Jules Furtham; Photog. Lee Garmes; Adpt. Lucien Ballard; Art Dir. Hans Dreier; Ed. Sam Winston. Songs: "Give Me the Man Who Does Things," "What Am I Bid for My Apples?" Leo Robin, Karl Hajos.

Cast: Gary Cooper, Marlene Dietrich, Adolph Menjou, Juliette Compton, Francis MacDonald, Albert Conti, Eve Southern.

WORKS CITED

Allen, Robert C. and Douglas Gomery. *Film History: Theory and Practice*. New York: Alfred A. Knopf, 1985.

Anderegg, Michael A. *David Lean*. Boston: Twayne Publishers, 1984.

Arnold, Alan. *Valentino*. New York: Library Publishers, 1954.

Berg, Charles M. *An Investigation of the Motives for and Realization of Music to Accompany the American Silent Film, 1994-1927*. New York: Arno Press, 1976.

Berg, Scott. *Goldwyn*. New York: Ballantine Books, 1989.

Berstein, Mathew and Gaylyn Studlar. *Visions of the East: Orientalism in Film*. Rutgers Univ. Press. 1997.

Bidwell, Robin. *Morocco under Colonial Rule*. London: Frank Cass, 1973.

Blond, Georges. *Histoire de la Légion Etrangère, 1831-1981*. Paris: Plon, 1981.

Bogdanovich, Peter. *Alan Dwan: The Last Pioneer*. New York: Praeger, 1971.

Bogle, Donald. *Toms, Coons, Mulattos, Mammies and Bucks: An interpretive History of Blacks in American Film*. New York: Viking, 1973.

Boulanger, Pierre. *Le Cinéma colonial*. Paris: Edition Seghers, 1975.

Jaques Bousquet. *Les thèmes des rêves dans la littérature Romantique*. Paris, 1964.

Bronlow, Kevin. *The Parade Gone By*. New York: Alfred A. Knopf, 1968.

Brown, Gene, ed. *The Moving Picture World Encyclopedia of Film: 1896-1928*. New York: New York Times Books, 1984.

Burch, Noël. *Life to Those Shadows*. Translated by Ben Brewster. Berkeley: The Univ. of California Press, 1990.

Burton, Richard, trans. *The Book of the Thousand Nights a Night*. London: H. S. Nichols, 1897.

Buscombe, Edward. In *Film Genre Reader*. Ed. Barry Keith Grant. Austin: University of Texas Press, 1986.

Caldwell, Genoa. The *Man Who Photographed the World*: Burton Holmes, Travelogues, 1886-1938. New York: Harry N. Abrams, 1977.

Caracciolo, Peter, ed. *The Arabian Nights in English Literature*. London: MacMillan, 1988.

Catalog of Copyright Entries: Motion Pictures 1912-1639. Washington: The Library of Congress, 1951.

Cawelti, John. *Adventure, Mystery and Romance*. Chicago: Univ. of California Press, 1976.

Chew, S. C. *The Crescent and the Rose: Islam and England during the Renaissance*. New York, 1937.

Coyle, William, ed. *Aspects of the Fantastic: Selected Essays from the Second International Conference on the Fantastic in Literature and Film*. London: Greenwood Press, 1981.

Cooke, Alistair. *Douglas Fairbanks: The Making of a Screen Character*. New York: Museum of Modern Art, 1940.

Cripps, Thomas. *Black Film as Genre*. Bloomington, Indiana Univ. Press, 1979.

_____ . *Slow Fade to Black: The Negro in American Film 1900-1942*. London: Oxford Univ. Press, 1977.

Daniel, Norman. *Islam and the West: The Making of an Image*. Edinburgh, 1960.

DeNovo John A. *American Interests in the Middle East 1900-1939*. Minneapolis: Univ. of Minnesota Press, 1963.

Erens, Patricia. *The Jews in American Cinema*. Bloomington: Indiana Univ. press, 1984.

Fielding, Raymond. *The American Newsreel, 1911-67*. Norman: Univ. of Oklahoma Press, 1972.

Frazer, John. *The Hollywood History of the World*. New York: Fawcett Columbine, 1988.

Friedman, Lester D. *Hollywood's Image of the Jew*. New York: Ungar Publishing, 1982.

Gehring, Wes D., ed. *Handbook of American Film Genres*. New York: Greenwood Press, 1988.

Gledhill, Christine. "A Contemporary Film Noir and Feminist

Criticism." *Women in Film Noir.* Ed. E. Ann Kaplan. London: British Film Institute, 1978, 6-21.

Griffith, Richard. *The Movie Stars.* New York: Doubleday, 1970.

Grossir, Claudel. *L'Islam des romantiques: 1811-1840.* Paris: Editions Maisonneuve et Larose, 1984.

Hampton, Benjamin. *History of the American Film Industry.* New York: Covici, Friede, 1931.

Hansen, Miriam. "Pleasure, Ambivalence, Identification: Valentino and Female Spectatorship." *Cinema Journal* 25, No. 4, Summer 1986.

Hanson, Partricia K, ed. *The American Film Institute Catalog of Motion Pictures Produced in The United States: Feature Films 1911-1920.* Berkeley: Univ. of California Press, 1988.

Harpole, Charles (General Editor). *History of the American Cinema.* New York: Charles Scribner's Sons, 1990.

Haskell, Molly. *From Reverence to Rape: The Treatment of Women in the Movies.* New York: Holt, Rinehart, 1973.

Hendricks, Gordon. *The Edison Motion Picture Myth.* Berkeley: Univ. of California Press, 1961.

Heggoy, Andrew, et al. Ed. *Through Foreign Eyes: Western Attitudes toward North Africa.* University Press of America, 1982.

Higashi, Sumiko. *Virgins, Vamps and Flappers: The American Silent Movie Heroine.* Montreal: Eden Press, 1978.

Hogg, James, ed. *The Leysin Version of James Elroy Flecker's Hassan.* Austria, Salzburg: Universität Salzburg, 1976.

Hofmann, Charles. *Sounds for Silents.* New York: Drama Book Specialists Publications, 1970.

Horwitz, Rita. *An Index to Volume 1 of "The Moving Picture World and View Photographer."* American Film Institute, 1974.

Hugo, Victor. *Odes et Ballades, et les Orientales.* Paris: 1940.

Hussain, Asaf, Robert Olson and Jamil Qureshi, eds. *Orientalism, Islam, and Islamists.* Brattleboro, Ut.: Aman Books, 1984.

Jacobs, Lewis. *The Rise of the American Film: A Critical History.* New York: Teachers College Press, 1939.

Jarvie, Ian. *Movies and Society.* New York: Basic Books, 1970.

Jones, E. Othello's *Countrymen: The African in English Renaissance Drama.* London: 1965.

Kabbani, Rana. *Europe's Myths of Orient. Bloomington:* Indiana Univ. Press, 1986.

Kaminsky, Stuart M. *American Film Genre: Approaches to a Critical Theory of Popular Film*. Dayton, Ohio: Pflaumm, 1974.

Koszarski, Richard. *An Evening Entertainment: The Age of the Silent Feature Picture, 1915-1928*. New York: Charles Scribner's Sons, 1990.

_____ , ed. *Hollywood Directors, 1914-1940*. new York: Oxford Univ. Press, 1983.

Knoblock, Edward. *Kismet and Other Plays*. London: Chapman & Hall, 1957.

Kracauer, Siegfried. *From Galagari to Hitler*. Princeton, N.J.: Princeton Univ. Press, 1948.

_____ . "National Types as Hollywood Presents Them." *Public Opinion Quarterly*, 13 (1949): 53-72.

Lalande, Jean-Pierre. "Artaud's Theatre of Cruelty and the Fantastic," in *Aspects of the Fantastic: Selected Essays from the Second International Conference on the Fantastic in Literature and Film*. London: Greenwood Press, 1981.

Lahue, Kalton C. *Motion Picture Pioneer: The Selig Polyscope Company*. South Brunswick, N.J.: A. S. Barnes, 1973.

Leab, Daniel. *From Sambo to Superstar: The Black Experience in Motion Pictures*. Boston: Houghton Mifflin, 1975.

Levin, Martin, ed. *Hollywood and the Great Fan Magazines*. New York: Arbor House, 1970.

Lewis, Windham. *Journey into Barbary*. Santa Barbara: Black Sparrow Press, 1983.

Lindsay, Vachel. *The Art of the Moving Picture*. New York: Liveright Publishing, 1970.

Lippman, Walter. *Public Opinion*. New York: Harcourt, 1922.

Mackenzie, Norman A. *The Magic of Rudolph Valentino*. London: The Research Publishing Co., 1974.

Magill, Frank N., ed. *Magill's Survey of Cinema: Silent Films*. New Jersey, Englewood Cliffs: Salem Press, 1982.

McLean, Albert F., Jr. *American Vaudeville as Ritual*. Lexington: Univ. of Kentucky Press, 1965.

Mercer, Charles. *The Foreign Legion: The Vivid History of a Unique Military Tradition*. London: Arthur Barker, 1964.

Mesguish, Félix. *Tours de manivelle: souvenirs d'un chasseur d'images*. Paris: Bernard Grassett, 1933.

Metlitzki, Dorothee. *The Matter of Araby in Medieval England*. New

Haven, 1977.

Miller, Randall M., ed. *Ethnic Images in the American Film and Television*. Philadelphia: The Beach Institute, 1978.

Mitry, Jean. *Dictionnaire du cinema*. Paris. Larousse, 1963.

_____ , ed. *The Kaleidoscopic Lens: How Hollywood Views Ethnic Groups*. Englewood, N.J.: Ozer, 1980.

Motion Pictures 1894-1912. Washington: the Library of Congress, 1953.

Munden, Kenneth W., ed. *The American Film Institute Catalog of Motion Pictures Produced in The United States: Feature Films 1921-1930*. New York: Bowker, 1971.

Neale, Stephen. *Genre*. London: British Film Institute, 1980.

_____ . "Questions of Genre," *Screen* 31: 1 (Spring 1990): 45-66.

Negri, Pola. *Memoirs of a Star*. Garden City, N. Y.: Doubleday, 1970.

The New York Times Film Reviews: 1913-1968. Vol. 1, 2, 3, 4 (1907-1933). New York: Times Books, 1990.

Niver, Kemp R. *The First Twenty Years: A Segment of Film History*. Ed. Bebe Bergsten. Los Angeles: Locale Research Group, 1968.

_____ . *Motion Pictures from the Library of Congress Paper Print Collection 1894-1912*. Ed. Bebe Bergsten. Berkeley: Univ. of California Press, 1967.

O'Leary, Liam. *The Silent Cinema*. New York: E. P. Dutton, 1965.

_____ . *Rex Ingram, Master of the Silent Cinema*. Dublin: Academy Press, 1980.

Powell, Michael. *A Life in the Movies*. London: Faber and Faber, 1980.

Pratt, George C., ed. *Spellbound in Darkness: Readings in the History and Criticism of the Silent Film*. Rochester: The Univ. of Rochester, 1966.

Ramsey, Terry. *A Million and One Nights: A History of the Motion Pictures*. London: Frank Cass, 1926.

Redwood, Dawn. *Flecker and Delius. The Making of "Hassan"*. London: Thames Publishing, 1978.

Rosen, Marjorie. *Popcorn Venus: Women, Movies and the American Dream*. New York: Coward, McCann, 1973.

Sadoul, Georges. *Histoire générale du cinéma. Vol. 1, L'invention du cinéma, 1832-1897*. Vol. 2, *Les pionniers du cinéma: De Méliès à Pathé, 1897-1909*. Paris: Denoël, 1947-48.

Said, Edward. *Orientalism*. New York: Pantheon, 1978.

_____ . *Covering Islam: How the Media and the Experts Determine How We See the Rest of the World*. New York: Pantheon, 1981.

Schatz, Thomas. *Hollywood Genres: Formulas, Filmmaking, and the Studio*

System. Philadelphia: Temple Univ. Press, 1981.

Schickel, Richard. *The Stars.* New York: The Dial Press, 1962.

_____ . *His Picture in the Papers: A Speculation on Celebrity in America Based on the Life of Douglas Fairbanks.* New York: Charterhouse, 1973.

Schwab, Raymond. *The Oriental Renaissance.* Trans. Gene Patterson-Black. New York: Columbia University Press, 1984.

Shaar, Stuart. "Orientalism at the Service of Imperialism," *Race and Class* XVI: 1 (1979) 69.

Shaheen, Jack. *Reel Bad Arabs: How Hollywood Vilifies a People.* New York: Olive Branch Press, 2001.

_____ "The Hollywood Arab: 1984-1986." *Journal of Popular Film and Television* 14: 4 (Winter 1987).

Sheehan, Perley Poore. *Hollywood as a World Center.* Hollywood, CA: Hollywood Citizen Press, 1924.

Shohat, Ella and Robert Stam. *Unthinking Eurocentrism: Multiculturalism and the Media.* London: Routledge, 1994.

Shulman, Irving. *Valentino.* New York: Trident Press, 1967.

Slide, Anthony. *Aspects of American Film Prior to 1920.* Metuchen, N.J.: The Scarecrow Press, 1978.

_____ *The Griffith Actresses.* New York: A. S. Barnes, 1973.

_____ , ed. *Selected Film Criticism: 1896-1911.* Metuchen.: The Scarecrow Press, 1982.

_____ , ed. *Selected Film Criticism: 1912-1920.* Metuchen: The Scarecrow Press, 1982.

_____ , ed. *Selected Film Criticism: 1921-1930.* Metuchen: The Scarecrow Press, 1982.

Southern, R. W. *Western Views of Islam in the Middle Ages.* Cambridge: Harvard Univ. Press, 1980.

Stookey, Robert W. *America and the Arab World.* New York: John Wiley & Sons, 1975.

Studlar, Gaylyn. *This Mad Masquerade: Stardom and Masculinity in the Jazz Age.* Columbia Univ. Press, 1996.

Studlar, Gaylyn and Mathew Bernstein. *Visions of the East: Orientalism in Film.* London: I B Tauris, 1997.

There is a New Star in Heaven...Valentino. Internationale Filmtespiele Berlin, Stiftung Deutsche Kinemathek Retrospektive. Berlin: Verlag Volker Spiess, 1979.

Tibbetts, John C., and James M. Welsh. *His Majesty the American: The*

Cinema of Douglas Fairbanks, Sr. New York: A. S. Barnes, 1977.

Todorov, Tzvetan. *The Fantastic: A Structural Approach to a Literary Genre.* Ithaca: Cornell Univ. Press, 1975.

Truffaut, Francois. "A Kind Word for Critics," in *Harpers* (October 1972)

Turner, Bryan S. "Orientalism and the Problem of Civil Society in Islam." In *Orientalism, Islam, and Islamists.* Editors A. Hussain, R. Olson, and J. Qureshi, 23–42. Brattleboro, VT: London: Routledge & Kegan Paul, 1974.

Variety Film Reviews. Vols. 1, 2 & 3. New York: R. R. Bowker, 1983.

_____ . *Stars of the Silents.* Metuchen, N.J.: Scarecrow Press, 1987.

Walsh, Raoul. *Each Man in His Time.* New York: Farrar, Straus and Giroux, 1974.

Williams, Allan. "Is a Radical Genre Criticism Possible?" *Quarterly Review of Film Studies.* Vol. 9, no. 2. Spring, 1984

Zingg, Paul. "Sand, Camels, and the USA: American Perceptions of North Africa." *Through Foreign Eyes: Western Attitudes Toward North Africa.* Ed. Alf Andrew Heggoy. Lanham: University Press of America, 1982.

ABOUT THE AUTHOR

Abdelmajid Hajji obtained a PhD in Film from the University of Kansas in 1993. He served as Dean of the School of Humanities and as Vice President of Moulay Ismail University in Meknes, Morocco. He is now full professor of Media, Film, and International Communication at Moulay Ismail University in Meknes, and Al Alakhawayn University in Ifrane, Morocco. Two terms spent at the University of Texas at Austin in 1998 and 1999, as a Fulbright Post-Doctoral Researcher and then as a Visiting Research Fellow, allowed him to continue work on this book. Mr. Hajji is also the President of the Moroccan Fulbright Alumni Association, MFAA.